COMPETING FOR CLIENTS

COMPETING FOR CLIENTS

BRUCE W. MARCUS

PROBUS PUBLISHING COMPANY
Chicago, Illinois

This publication is designed to provide accurate and authoritative information in regard to the subject matter covered. It is sold with the understanding that the publisher is not engaged in rendering legal, accounting or other professional service. If legal advice or other expert assistance is required, the services of a competent professional person should be sought.

FROM A DECLARATION OF PRINCIPLES JOINTLY ADOPTED BY A COMMITTEE OF THE AMERICAN BAR ASSOCIATION AND A COMMITTEE OF PUBLISHERS

Library of Congress Cataloging-in-Publication Data

Marcus, Bruce W., 1925-   Competing for clients.

    Includes index.
    1. Professions–Marketing.   I. Title.
HD8038.A1M37   1986| 658.8   85-27109
ISBN 0-917253-26-4

Library of Congress Catalog Card No. 85-27109

Printed in the United States of America

    3   4   5   6   7   8   9   0

To
Mana
and
David, Rachael, Michael, Michelle, Jonathan, Shirley, Joe, Lucy
and
Robert

Preface

Let me tell you a story.

Some time ago, I was responsible for advertising for a Big Eight accounting firm. We had decided that the way to advertise was not nationally, but office by office, with the thrust of each campaign focused on the distinctive capabilities of each office and the nature of the business community it served.

After considerable research in the city that was to be our laboratory, the advertising agency, one of the creative giants, came up with a campaign that was simply all wrong. It was a good campaign for a bank or a brokerage firm, singing the praises of our services and what we can and will do for you. But there was no way that it was going to do anything for an accounting firm.

The battle in the conference room was bombastic, with blood flowing liberally from wounded egos on all sides. "But we *know* what you do," they cried, "we spent days down there living with your people."

"Never mind what we *do*," I kept saying. "What do the clients *want* and how do we supply it?"

We were getting nowhere. Finally, I said, "Look, let's take a break and get some fresh coffee."

As the client, I was served first. The account supervisor, an attractive young woman, was served next. She sat down across the corner of the table, as everybody else stood at the coffee urn at the other end of the conference room.

In a voice both intimate and loud enough to be heard at the other end of the room, I said, "Mary, I'd like you to have dinner with me tonight." It startled her. Ears perked up at the coffee urn.

"I have a beautiful penthouse apartment with a magnificent view of the city," I said, "and the sight at dusk is breathtaking." She got increasingly nervous. A client was coming on to her.

"A friend will let me borrow his French chef, and we can have a lovely, intimate candlelight dinner, just the two of us." She didn't know whether to laugh or cry. Small talk stopped at the urn.

"Oh, there's just one more thing," I said. "There's a snow storm expected, and you might want to bring a nightgown, just in case you get snowed in." She turned white. I thought she was going to hit me.

When the electricity in the room approached an explosion point, I leaned forward to her, and said, "Now Mary, that may be what I'm selling—but it isn't necessarily what you're willing to buy, is it?" It took only a fraction of a moment for everybody to get the point.

And that's how this very creative agency created one of the most successful ad campaigns done for a professional service to that time.

The point of this story is that in the new world of marketing professional services, even the best creative minds in marketing have had to learn new approaches and new ways to use old techniques. And that's what this book is about.

There are more stories. When I was head of the Eastern Division of what was then one of the country's largest public relations firm, I used to go out on new business calls with the firm's managing partner and founder. He would sell by listing the services we performed and how they would benefit the prospect. I would sell by showing the client how well I understood his business. In a sense, we were both doing the same thing—dealing with the prospect's needs and how we could meet them, but our approaches were distinctly different. And we both brought in a lot of new clients.

The point is that in marketing, there is more than one path. I hope that comes clear in the following pages.

In the early days of marketing professional services, at the time I joined Arthur Young, public relations for accounting firms was random and seemed unfocused. Two or three outside practitioners were doing good jobs for their clients (notably, Jim Donley for Peat,

Marwick, Mellissa Krantz of Kekst & Co. for Price Waterhouse and Harold Wolfson for Ernst & Whinney), but they were severely limited by being outsiders, and by their clients' general reticence to appear to be too "promotional".

By organizing an internal department to function as a house agency, with each public relations staff person serving his "accounts" (the tax department, auditing, the consulting practice, etc.), and with each responsible for total immersion in his or her accounts' activities, we stormed the press. In competitive clipping counts, we were getting more than twice as many clippings as our nearest competitor, and they were stories of substance in major publications.

When I left, the clipping count diminished to a trickle, and other firms' counts increased. I then joined another firm, did the same things again, only better, and once again, became king of the clippings. A great feeling.

But what it meant was simply that there is a distinctive difference in the way public relations—indeed, all of marketing—is done for professional services and the way it's done for products or nonprofessional services (banks, airlines, etc.). The success, in both cases, resided not in any personal magic of mine, but in the techniques. And that's another reason for this book.

There is more. At one firm, we learned enough about the differences in marketing to develop direct mail techniques distinctly for professional services that changed the picture from abject discouragement about direct mail, and dismal, expensive failure, to programs that produced returns of 50 percent (yes, *50 percent.*)

Yes, things have changed. The ad campaigns and marketing programs being done today by people like Ken Wright of Arthur Young, perhaps the most knowledgeable marketing professional in the accounting profession, are producing extraordinary results. He is part of a new breed of specialists in marketing professional services—people who come not from the academic world, but from the battle front, where we've all learned the hard way.

Marketing professional services is indeed a new discipline, with its own forms and techniques, and a growing body of experience. Much of it, and much that's in this book, we've learned by trying and failing, and by rethinking old skills and inventing new ones. The pioneering contributions of marketing giants like Henry Schachte, the retired head of J. Walter Thompson, were astonishing, and will be appreciated for generations to come. We've had to endure false starts, and skepticism, and head-on battles with professionals who would rather have shed their skins than their hide-bound traditions. And there have been, as well, marvelous moments of success and enlightenment and support from top-notch professionals who learned to move into the new world.

The purpose of this book, which attempts to cover the ground from theory to detailed techniques, is primarily to educate—to make the professional a better consumer of marketing services.

There is no great expectation that an accountant or a lawyer or a consultant will read the chapter on copywriting and become an award-winning writer, or read about media buying or production and become expert in those fields. But if reading about these techniques breeds understanding, then better marketing will be done, and professionals will be better marketers.

There is a fond hope, as well, that this book contributes a modicum of innovation to the world of marketing, and to the thinking of marketing professionals who must develop programs in the field.

And there is a large hope that the small practitioner, who must do much of his marketing for himself, will learn enough from this book to do an effective job of it.

Helping in this way is, I know, a tall order, but that's why there's so much detail in this book. There had to be, if these three audiences are to be properly served.

Every writer I know wants to write the definitive and last word on his subject. I'm no different. But I know that in this subject, there is no last and definitive word. This book is, at best, a beginning.

And as I used to say in my memo writing days, if you have any questions, call me.

Bruce W. Marcus

Acknowledgments

I get by, as the song goes, with a little help from my friends.

This book was not much more than a formless collection of facts and notions—really just the beginnings of a book—when I asked a few friends who know more than somewhat about this subject to look at it. Smartest thing I ever did.

Henry Schachte, retired president of J. Walter Thompson and certainly one of the all-time greats of advertising and marketing, read it carefully, and sent me a three-page letter. What he said in that letter resulted in shaping this book; in giving it context and direction.

Ken Wright, who was with me for many of the wars fought in the name of marketing professional services, and is now National Director of Marketing Development for Arthur Young & Co., kept my nose to the grindstone in many a place in these pages. I would no more think of putting this book on the presses without Ken's having seen it first than I would walk off the end of a cliff. Ken is, after all, one of the most knowledgeable and experienced marketers in this field, and certainly one of the sagest.

Elias "Buck" Buchwald, vice chairman of Burson-Marsteller, put his finger on so many sore spots in the early draft that his observations were a blueprint to revision. Burson-Marsteller is the world's largest public relations firm. Buck is even larger—in heart, spirit and intellect.

Mik Chwalek, who turned research into an art form at Coopers & Lybrand, not only unbent the chapter on research, but showed even greater insight in her exceptionally helpful comments on the rest of the book.

Shirley Potter, who probably knows more about the psychology of communication than anybody, looked at the subject from a very different point of view, and then guided me through some extraordinary landmines and pitfalls.

My good friend Frank Dellacorte, a very senior executive at the great international public relations firm, Hill and Knowlton, very meticulously reviewed the manuscript, and then very imaginatively made crucial and invaluable suggestions.

Rob Hilliard, an exceptional performer in public relations for accounting firms and others, and Mike Dunleavy, the bright and skillful marketer at Main Hurdman KMG, both contributed valuable ideas. Jerry Schwartz, who built the public relations firm of G.S. Schwartz into one of the best in the business, was helpful in more ways than I can recount. Carol Stangby, perhaps the most talented promotion writer at *Business Week,* contributed substantially. My accountant, Norman Berg, and my attorney, Stephen Silberfein, each read the manuscript as ultimate consumers, and made shrewd and cogent observations that found their way into the final version.

My son Jonathan, who knows more about computers and how to make them do extraordinary things than almost anybody, not only taught me most of what I know about how to use one, but wrote the program that reduced the time to write the Index from one month to *51 seconds.* That, plus other things that Jon taught me, make it possible to produce this book six months sooner.

Bernice Pietracatella keyed much of the manuscript on her word processor, which cut about six months off the production time. She was especially adept at it, combining intelligence and skill. This book, by the way, is a product of word processing, and was even set from my own disks. Technology omnia vincit.

Every family must, I suppose, be patient with its breadwinner from time to time, no matter what his occupation. But I can't imagine an occupation that demands more patience of its distaff side, and progeny, than does writing. Producing a book is done with the same slavish and compulsive attention as is digging your way out of Alcatraz with a purloined spoon. Can you imagine what life is like with one such digger? And particularly one on deadlines? My special gratitude and love to my good crew, and thanks for their patience and understanding.

It's nice, too, to reach this point and still have gratitude for one's publisher. This is my fifth book, but the first in which I arrived at this point in the process with my publisher still held in high regard. Thanks, Probus. You do nice work.

My thanks to the sources of ads and other borrowed material that appears in this book, for their kind permission to reproduce it all. And especially thanks to the generosity of The Realtors' National Marketing Institute for permission to use material from the book I wrote for them entitled *Marketing Professional Services in Real Estate.*

All these people, and more than I can list in these few paragraphs, have made it possible for me to produce this. They range from Harvey, my friend and mailman, who saved me many a trip to the post office to mail the chapters to Chicago, to the many good people along the way who helped me learn the craft delineated in these pages. And they include the several partners and others in accounting and law firms who tried hard to understand this strange new craft, and ultimately did to the point of bringing wisdom to it all. While there are several, those who particularly stand out are Don Aronson, John Dyment and Mike Garrett.

Writing, they say, is a solitary task. And so say I. But I get by with a little help from my friends. Thank you all.

Bruce W. Marcus

Contents

Introduction

In 1978, the United States Supreme Court, in an astonishing and far-reaching decision, overturned those aspects of the canons of ethics of professional societies that, until then, had effectively precluded frank marketing.

Until then, and for many years before that, lawyers, doctors, dentists, accountants and others in certificated, client-serving professions could not advertise, could not promote, could not solicit clients uninvited. So long had these restrictions prevailed, in fact, that they had become ingrained in the professional demean of practicioners. Self-promotion, or anything that might be construed as self-promotion, was not only prohibited by fiat, but was frowned upon by other professionals, and frequently by clients as well. The prohibition became more than a function of ethical codes; it became a tenet, a way of life. To behave otherwise was clearly (horrors forfend) "unprofessional".

Which doesn't mean that there wasn't some form of "practice development" in common use. Clearly, something was being done that propelled some law firms and accounting firms to international size and stature, even as their fellows remained small. Some doctors thrived well beyond the success of their colleagues, and giant consulting firms emerged from small partnerships and solo practices. Even among non-certificated professionals, such as public relations firms and advertising agencies, some thrived while others stagnated or lan-

1

guished, and not always as a measure of either superior performance our astute management.

What was done, in the way of practice development, could hardly be called marketing, as we commonly think of the word. One simply made one's presence more obvious and ubiquitous. One joined the right clubs—those with prospective clients or patients as members. One gave speeches before learned groups of fellow business people, in which skill and expertise were exposed. An occasional seminar for business people imparted helpful information, perhaps about the new tax law, or the advantages of one kind of corporate structure over another. Brochures and newsletters on crucial subjects for clients were common, and if they found their way into the hands of non-clients, that was not inappropriate, if it was done "ethically" and professionally.

But flagrant promotion was a taboo. Advertising was strictly prohibited by all professional societies and governing bodies. And perhaps the strictest prohibition of all—of the most unthinkable and heinous of crimes—was soliciting another professional's clients. Frank marketing was simply unthought of . . . out of the question . . . unprofessional.

And then came the Supreme Court decision. The prohibitions against frank marketing were struck down.

For generations, concepts of probity had pervaded the professions. Accountants were not to be merely independent, but well beyond the fray of public quarrel or exposure. Lawyers, even in their advocacy, were to be beyond the pale of commerce. The privacy of the medical profession, with its freedom from the demands of the marketplace, was sacrosanct. Even so amorphous a profession as public relations had a code of ethics that prohibited soliciting other firms' clients. And now comes marketing, the crux of which is visibility and commercial interchange.

Realistically, only two things were changed by the Supreme Court ruling. First, professionals were suddenly allowed to advertise. This opened a number of possibilities, all of which, thus far, have for the most part been explored only tentatively or (with notable exceptions) primatively.

The second and infinitely more important change was the new ability to directly solicit clients—even the clients of other professionals.

This was more than a change in law—it was a change in tradition, and it fell upon professionals like a hail storm on a clear July day. It began a chain of events that continues to barrel along at breakneck speed, altering forever the texture of professional practice.

Most significantly, as doctors, dentists, lawyers, accountants, consultants and other professionals began to explore ways to function under the new rules, competitiveness acquired a new demean. Timidly, tentatively at first—you can legislate a change in the rules much more easily than you can legislate a change in decades of ingrained tradition—the professionals explored marketing. And then, suddenly, they began to realize that they no longer competed with one another with skills and reputation alone. They competed in marketing as well. Today, in the professions, the firms that succeed best will be not just those that perform best, but those that market best.

And realizing this, there was a sudden surge in marketing activities. Marketing consultants were brought in and specialists in the several disciplines of marketing were hired. There was a scramble for advertising agencies and public relations firms. Within two years, for example, at least four of the Big Eight accounting firms were competing for the top two national public relations firms. Law firms, slightly more gun shy, took a little longer, but then began having discreet "discussions and explorations" with public relations firms and advertising agencies.

Several Big Eight accounting firms, attempting to be first to market, started advertising almost immediately. Arthur Young was the first in print with several full page ads in Fortune, Business Week and the like, followed by Deloitte, Haskins & Sells.

In law, medicine and dentistry, on the other hand, it was the smaller practitioner who moved quickly to advertising. The legal clinic serving the small client sprang into existence, virtually an invention of advertising. Dental clinics opened in shopping malls, aided by advertising and direct mail. It was the first example, in professional services, of market feedback, in which serving the perceived needs of a market created a new service vehicle. In fact, the new legal, medical and dental clinics institutionalized their performance of the professions, turning personalized service into something that could be sold like a loaf of bread. Like bank services, this uniform professional service became a commodity that could be sold under the old rules of marketing.

The classic professional, however, discovered something fascinating. The old rules of marketing—the techniques that so readily sold products and such non-professional services as banks and airlines—just didn't seem to work. Other professionals, such as architects and engineers, had the same revelation.

No sudden flocking of new clients, nor burst of public name recognition, nor ripples of excitement in the firmament.

It was more than just a matter of advertising that didn't work, or of press releases not appearing in the papers. It was, rather, the sudden realization that there was a lack of rationale for what was being done. And without a rationale, the target was missed by the marketing shots being fired.

An ad for a product is a relatively simple thing. If you advertise lollipops for sale, you know how effective your ad is because you know how many lollipops you sell. If you have a heavy campaign for soap, and your share of market increases, you know how well your campaign worked.

But the professional services consumer, unlike the lollipops consumer, may not be ready to retain those services just at the moment the ad appears. Is the advertising wasted? How do you know if it works? How do you know what, if anything, works?

With introspection and experience, some significant differences began to emerge. For example, can you advertise that you do a better audit, or a better tax return, or that your firm wins more cases in court than any other, or that you do neater appendectomies? Of course not.

All professionals perform essentially the same services. How do you persuade somebody—particularly on a large-scale marketing basis—that you perform those services better, or that you're smarter than your competitor?

You can, of course, advertise that you understand the issues of the day, and that you are the "business man's" accountant or lawyer; this is what the first Big Eight accounting firm ads tried to do. That comes under the heading of institutional advertising. If you spend many millions of dollars doing it, you may ultimately impress some people sufficiently for them to turn to you when they need a lawyer or an accountant. But considering the kind of budget you'd need for it to work, you'd be bankrupt by the time the first prospect responded to the campaign.

And while the ingredients and process of a product may be quality controlled, how do you do that in a service, in which every individual, and every business, has a different and perhaps unique need?

That's what began to dawn on professionals first—that frank marketing requires a new way for the professional to reach out to prospects. It requires a different kind of advertising and public relations, and even selling.

What, then, *is* marketing? And why didn't traditional marketing techniques work for professional services?

There are as many definitions of marketing, I suppose, as there are marketing people. Ultimately, it's a discipline and a process that moves products or services to market effectively, and therefore profitably. It can be broken down into four very basic elements:

- Define your market
- Define your product (or service)
- Define your marketing tools
- Manage your marketing tools

Every marketing professional knows that—it's basic marketing.

But when the service you offer is a professional service, tailored to the needs of myriad individual clients, and is as multifarious as it is in any professional practice, then you don't fathom your market the way you do for a product. The body of knowledge about why women buy soap is vast. Every airline marketer knows why people choose one airline over another, and every bank marketer knows a great deal about how to get a customer to switch his account from one bank to another, or to buy another bank service. Who knows, though, how to get an audit committee to switch from one accounting firm to another, or what really motivates an individual or a corporate executive to choose one law firm over another?

It's not that this information isn't discernible. It's that nobody ever had to get it before. Beyond knowing the basic needs that people have for professional services, professionals simply never had to find out what the markets for their services really are, and what those markets really want, or even who the decision makers in the marketplace really are, and so they didn't know how to do find out.

In traditional marketing, when you know what your market wants, you adjust your product—or the way you position or present it—to meet the needs of the marketplace. The classic story, of course, is the one about Henry Ford, who said you can have any color car you want so long as you want black. He lost out to General Motors, which realized that people wanted their cars in different colors.

If the professional service you have to offer is so varied, so individualized, then obviously you can't package or position it in the same way you would a cake of soap or even an investment vehicle—products or services cherished for their consistency and uniformity. It becomes infinitely more complex than anything the marketing professionals have ever had to face before. And because it had never been done before, thoughtful marketing professionals were perplexed; others marched blindly forward, enthusiastically repeating expensive mistakes. Nothing from the past seemed to fit just right.

As for the tools—advertising, public relations, direct mail, and even straight selling—these new disciplines bedazzled the professionals. Not only did they scarcely understand them, but the tools themselves had to be used in a new and unfamiliar way. Moreover, these tools work best only in a total marketing context, and not as abstracts. If you don't clearly understand the marketing context, then how do you devise an ad campaign that makes sense, or judge one devised by an ad agency? How do you develop a public relations program that isn't more than wasted energy? When you can't rely on professional salesmen, and must depend upon the professional who performs the service to do the selling, what do we draw from traditional selling skills to close the sale and bring in the client?

In managing the tools, from where is the expertise to come? Internally, from a partner who is a lawyer or an accountant? Externally, from a marketing professional who doesn't understand law or accounting or medical practice?

As if these factors alone didn't add enough confusion, there is the problem of the nature of the firms that perform professional services. They are, for the most part, partnerships. Even in professional corporations, every member is a professional, and therefore the equivalent of a partner.

In a classic corporation, there are the marketing professionals and there is the chief executive officer or the board of directors. When the powers of a corporation approve a marketing program, then the rest of the people get out of the way and let the professionals work. In a partnership, however, where the marketing expense comes out of every partner's profits, then every partner is a participant in the program, and will have his say.

And even in the broad context of all professions, there are strategies that are unique to each profession.

Accounting firms, perhaps because of the broad range of services they offer and the stronger competition they face, have been more aggressive in marketing than any of the other professions. The larger firms, with offices in many cities throughout the country and the world, have been more aggressive in their national marketing efforts, although they are learning that professional marketing techniques function best on a local level.

Law firms tend not to be national in the sense that accounting firms are, although that's changing. Still, a major accounting firm may have eighty or a hundred offices; few law firms have more than two or three. And while many large law firms draw their clients nationally, there has been virtually no national advertising. In fact, except for the legal clinics and the smaller practitioners, lawyers have been somewhat more reluctant than other professionals to move into advertising and frank marketing.

Medicine and dentistry face a somewhat different problem. Obviously, their practices are local and usually limited to a single geographic area. And except for the clinics, certain medical and dental disciplines are more promotional than others. Ads for plastic surgeons abound; ads for brain surgeons do not. And then, of course, there is the significant difference that these professions seek patients—individuals who come to the practitioner's site—rather than clients, who usually function within the realm of their own business (personal or otherwise).

Architects, consultants and others are somewhat freer in their marketing efforts in that they can be more imaginative and expansive in projecting their capabilities.

The distinctions among the professions that make one profession more or less aggressive in marketing than the others are rapidly breaking down as the competition for clients becomes more acute.

Still, functioning within the prescribed boundaries of professional ethics requires more skill and imagination, and this competition is bringing these qualities to the fore.

With all of the traditions of professionalism that impede marketing breaking down and eroding, and as some firms within each profession succeed more substantively than others, the whole area for marketing professional services becomes more active.

The techniques for competing for clients are clearly present and available. What is yet to be developed is experience, skill and the imagination to use these techniques in ways that bring successful competition in the professional marketplace.

What is emerging are clear and overriding factors that define the distinction between marketing a professional service and marketing a product or a non-professional service, and that dictate developing new marketing techniques.

There may be a thousand people behind a product—those who finance it and design it and manufacture it and distribute it. But the interface between all of those people and the consumer is the product itself. It's all the consumer ever sees or knows about the company.

The interface between the consumer of the professional service and the professional firm that supplies that service, on the other hand, is the professional who performs the service. An entire firm can rise or fall on the performance of its individuals.

When the consumer buys a box of soap, he or she does so without a second thought that the quality and characteristics of that box might in any way differ from that of the last box she bought. The quality and characteristics of the service performed by each professional is a function of the next job he or she performs, and not the last.

Virtually all non-professional services—banking and other financial services, airlines, even dry cleaning—are discrete and limited, and are virtually commodities. They they are uniform and consistent, and may be described in a finite way, even as can be a product. Certainly, this is not so of a professional service, where the performance fits the unique needs of the individual client, and where, therefore, the range of services is practically infinite. You can warehouse soap; there is no way to inventory professional services.

How, in the face of all of this, does one market a distinction from one's competitors? How does one credibly and ethically project quality and expertise?

Even if traditional ethical practices allowed such distinctions to be made in public utterances, how can they be proven—particularly where professional services are offered by individuals, and not by quality-controlled machines? And particularly where all professions offer the same service (although the quality of delivery may differ). There is an answer, of course, to both this and other questions raised thus far—else why this book? But the answer doesn't come from the traditional practices of marketing.

And therein hangs the tale. Marketing professional services is very different from marketing anything else. It is new and pioneering territory, with only a few years of practical experience.

But it is a growing body of knowledge. More and more professionals are doing it, and learning how to do it well. They are learning by trial and error, and they are learning by recognizing the distinctions between the old and the new, and using old skills imaginatively to make new rules. The thinking is different, and comes from a different point of view. And thinking there is, which is beginning to show good results.

The following pages are devoted to exploring the techniques of marketing professional services, in the context of the new experience and the new thinking. It is, to an extent, old wine in new bottles. But it is, as well, a new brew of the old wine.

A word about how this book is organized.

It really consists of two parts—a discussion of how and why marketing professional services differs from other aspects of marketing, as a basis for planning a marketing strategy, and a breakdown of the techniques of the various disciplines of marketing. A handbook and a kind of a "how-to", if you will. This last is necessary, I feel, because many of the basic techniques take on a different cast when applied to professional services. Good copywriting is good copywriting, but in a world in which you can't say "we do better audits", good copywriting is an idea of a different color.

In detailing these techniques, there is no overt attempt to try to turn accountants and doctors and lawyers and consultants into advertising or public relations technicians. Presumably, you'll hire professionals in those fields. But if you understand the processes, you'll be better able to participate in your own marketing planning, and to instruct, guide and judge the performances of those who must function for you. In other words, the attempt here is to make you a better consumer of marketing services.

For the marketing professional, it is fondly hoped that this book will serve to help you rethink your skills in terms of the unique needs of the professional for whom you must function.

I recognize, also, that while this book is organized in the order of a textbook, and is structured as a handbook, life—and especially professional life—is not a textbook case history. Most of you are now active in your own practices, and as much concerned, perhaps, with keeping the clients you have as with getting new ones. Keeping clients, of course, is as much an objective of marketing as is practice development. And many of you have well-established practice development structures. You may find, then, that this book will serve you best as both an overview and as a source of ideas.

That's fine. It's purpose is to serve—to be useful in any context. It is assumed, in fact, that a mark of a professional is that he or she doesn't abdicate intelligence in the face of expertise from another discipline. Marketing is as much an art form, given the basic skills, as it is a set of rules, and both the professional marketer and the consumer of marketing services must bring a large dollop of imagination to the table.

In fact, a singular purpose of this book is to function not as a final word on the subject, but rather as a beginning—a foundation to a new and important structure that will grow, develop and change with experience and the infusion of wisdom beyond these pages and this time.

When, in 1978, the United States Supreme Court, in an astonishing and far-reaching decision, overturned those aspects of the canons of ethics of professional societies that, until then, had effectively precluded frank marketing, they created an opportunity that has a great distance to go to reach its outer limits.

PART I

The Plan

CHAPTER 1

Practice Development Strategy

In the massive detail of marketing technology delineated in the following pages, it should never be forgotten that the aim of the exercise is to get new clients and to keep the ones you now have—to develop the practice.

There are, in each profession, legendary practitioners about whom it's said that they can go into a phone booth alone and walk out arm-in-arm with a new client.

Perhaps such instinctive marketing giants do exist, but they are rare, genuinely legendary, and one can hardly build or expand a practice in an orderly manner with just a few legends. Absent these paragons then, the need for active and aggressive marketing, and marketing strategy, becomes increasingly acute.

At least two factors dictate this urgency.

The first is markedly accelerating competition. Even before the change in the canons of ethics, the growing number of professionals produced by universities in virtually all disciplines increased competition. With the change in the canons of ethics, and the advent of marketing, the competition for clients becomes even more active. And where once it was fought solely on serendipitous reputation, or reputation for performance, or even random socializing, it is now fought with marketing skills. To an increasingly large degree, the professional firm with the better marketing program is the one that seems most likely to emerge as the most successful.

THE CHANGING MARKETPLACE

A second need for marketing professionalism is the changing nature of the marketplace itself.

There have been periods in our economic history when building a professional practice was infinitely simpler. The competition was not among professionals for clients, but rather for competent help to serve clients. The growth of the economy immediately following World War II created a shortage in every profession, and marketing consisted solely of being available.

That situation no longer exists. The economy is now very much larger and extremely complex, and specialization abounds in every profession. With very rare exceptions, there is no such thing today as a plain lawyer, or a doctor, or an accountant—there are negligence lawyers and corporate lawyers and litigators and divorce lawyers. There are internists and dermatologists and surgeons. There are auditors, and tax experts and computer specialists. This further complicates competition, and dictates the need for not only increased marketing efforts, but for better strategy in marketing.

There is also the interesting effect that marketing itself has on the marketplace, in which marketing strategies change the texture and dynamic of the market.

Marketing activities generate new attitudes toward a profession and its professionals in the minds of the prospective clientele, and new ideas for using that professional service. Good marketing educates consumers. When law firms market their ability to deal with estate problems, it makes the marketplace aware of estate problems they didn't know they had. When doctors publicly discuss techniques of self-examination for certain kinds of cancer, it changes the public attitudes toward dealing with cancer and health.

The market is constantly changing of its own volition, assaulted as it is by random forces; constantly shifting; constantly reweaving itself in pattern and texture. A change in legislation or the economy can cause substantial change in the market for accountants and lawyers. A new discovery in medicine, or a significant shift in demographics that increases the size of the geriatric population, changes the nature of medical practice. Increased internationalization, new financial instruments, the breakdown of barriers between financial institutions—the list of events that affect professional practice is long.

Industries mature, and technology forces change. What's the impact on the accounting profession of a decline in the rate at which the number of public corporations come into being, and of mergers, and how does that affect the audit as a source of new business? What's happening in the dental profession as fluoridation and other technology eliminates dental caries? Consider the effects on the legal profession, and on the medical profession as well, of changing attitudes towards negligence suits and malpractice suits. Consider the effects on the marketplace of the growing use and sophistication in computers. What do new concepts in financing and in taxation do to resegment the market's needs for new skills from a professional in any of the financial disciplines?

The point to consider is that if competition is increasing, and the market is changing, then classic practice development techniques are no longer sufficient. New techniques must be brought into play, and new strategies must be devised. Otherwise, professional firms that once thrived will languish and be eclipsed. Opportunities for young talent will be foreclosed and they will look to your competitors for their futures. Your ability to compete will be sharply curtailed.

MEETING CLIENT NEEDS

Given an understanding of the needs of the market, what can a professional service do to meet those needs? A lawyer is, after all, a lawyer and an accountant is an accountant and a dentist is a dentist.

The answer lies in the very nature of the professional service. Even within the realm of specialization, service and service concepts can be adjusted to meet the needs of the market. There is the piano player who will play anything you want to hear, so long as you want to hear *Melancholy Baby*. There is the piano player who sizes up his audience and plays classics for one group and show tunes for another. Both are piano players, but what a difference in the same thing.

So it is with professionals. A lawyer who specializes in divorces may be limited by a small, stable, conservative community. Or he may perceive that inherent in pursuing his divorce practice are negotiating skills that can serve clients in other ways. Heaven help the accountant, whatever his specialty, who doesn't realize the need for computer expertise by virtually all his clients.

Moreover, the nature of professional services is such that there is vast flexibility, even within a specialization and professional and ethical strictures, to adjust the nature of service to the needs of the client. The operating factor is not the limit of the specialization, but the concept of imaginatively expanding the professional capability to serve the dynamic of the client's business. Or to put it more simply, doing what the client needs from you professionally—not what you want to do just because it's what you do best.

That many professionals instinctively understand this can be seen readily by comparing the professional firm of today with those of a decade or so ago. The catalog of accounting firm services today is vast, compared with the limited scope of the accountant's activities in the past. And this is true of small firms as well as large. One need only look at the dental or medical clinics and group practices that exist today, some even in department stores, to realize that a great deal has changed in the concept of service. They represent the ideal of understanding the market; understanding the needs for ever-expanding professional services, and adjusting the services to meet those needs.

THE TRADITIONAL PRACTICE DEVELOPMENT TOOLS

In the old days, before the change in the canons of ethics, practice development meant anything you did to get clients that wasn't "unethical". Clearly proscribed were advertising, public relations that was self-promotional, and most significantly, soliciting other people's clients. Theoretically, the only way to build a practice was to sit quietly behind your desk, do good work, and wait for the clients or patients to come through the door. Referrals from other practitioners or clients were allright, and you could certainly remind your friends and relatives that you were in practice. But to promote your services beyond that was unethical and unprofessional.

And yet, within those lofty but stringent parameters, some mighty practices were built. How did it happen?

Practice development. Not advertising, nor public relations, nor direct selling or soliciting clients, but rather, a systematic process of exposure to potential clients.

Some of the techniques are basic and obvious. They include simply broadening the base of social contacts by joining country clubs and associations of business people, performing visible public service, or going into politics.

Obviously, if someone is thinking of changing his accountant or lawyer, he is going to turn first to those he knows or knows about. More business is done, goes the old saw, on the golf course than in the board room. An accountant who volunteers his services as treasurer of an important civic organization is going to be known to a lot of important business people in the community, all of whom will have had the opportunity to see his skills at first hand within a public service context. The lawyer who is active in his local political organization, or runs for office—even against an incumbent running in a safe district—is legitimately exposing his talents and skills, and building a personal reputation.

Nor have there ever been prohibitions against making speeches or appearing on informative panels before business groups, if the subjects were enlightening and educational to the audience. For the more skillful, this has long been a prime means of practice development.

And what about the seminar for clients on the ramifications of a new tax law, sponsored by an accounting or law firm, or even jointly with a bank, in which the panelists were prominent local accountants or lawyers? Only clients could be invited, but if non-clients are invited by clients or friends, new friends could be made. Then there is the memo—or even the newsletter—to clients, on a new law or accounting regulation, that finds its way into the hands of non-clients.

The list of ethical devices for practice development is long and in many cases, ingenious. And obviously, for the ingenious it worked. That's how small practitioners grew to become the big international firms. And there were usually one or two partners who ultimately moved from working in the practice to full-time practice development.

That's how it was done in the old days. In most respects, it's not wrong for today.

The difference is that in the highly competitive arena that's been developed, these practices must be organized, focused, and supported in most cases by technical marketing skills.

Today, no professional can build a substantial practice—and certainly not an international practice—on the golf course. It would be like digging your way out of Alcatraz with a purloined spoon. And in this highly competitive climate, it's as true for the small practitioner as it is for the giant firm. Perhaps more so, since the giant firm usually has the weight and advantage of reputation predicated on its size and the nature of its clientele.

In this new era of marketing, the organization memberships, the speeches, the seminars, and so forth, all of which predate the change in the canon of ethics, take on an entirely different texture. They become part of the larger context of marketing, and so must serve a broader purpose.

Take the seminar, for example. Professionals have been giving seminars for years, and many professionals are skilled at putting them together for clients.

But now, new elements enter the picture. Non-clients may be invited. Other professionals in the same field are offering seminars on the same subjects. Seminars may be advertised. You can charge admission to seminars you once gave free (which, incidentally, puts you in an entirely different business—the business of selling seminars). Seminars may now be publicized in ways that were not possible before. And because seminars should be part of a total marketing effort, they must be planned differently, as part of a totality rather than as isolated events, if they are to serve a proper marketing function.

Even joining the country club must be seen in a different light. With so many options for marketing a professional service, is the time and effort and money best spent that way than some other way? Are the organizations to which you and your partners belong the best ones in which to be active to meet prospective clients? Are just a few of the partners involved in organizational activity, or is it spread throughout the firm in ways that best serve the firm?

A useful approach is to make a periodic audit of memberships and other activities to evaluate who in the firm is doing what, and whether the time is being most advantageously spent. As in any other marketing effort, community, club and political activities should be planned.

Professionals with a large number of clients in a particular industry have learned the unique industry practices, jargon and technical terms that allow them to move comfortably in the industry. This capability and competence has long served to develop a practice, and is now especially marketable because it affords the opportunity to make a contribution to a client in that industry that goes well beyond the expertise of the profession itself.

Another traditional method used in practice development is to broaden the base of business contacts—what is commonly known today as networking. This is simply a function of cultivating business people and others who are prospective clients or patients. Particular emphasis should be placed on the influentials—those members of the business or financial community who may not themselves be prospective clients, but who are in a position to recommend your services. This includes other professionals such as lawyers and accountants, bankers, journalists, political figures and business people who are prominent in their industry or in the local business community.

It's difficult to say what works best in cultivating business contacts. This is a highly individual activity. Certainly included is being active in those organizations in which influentials and other business contacts are themselves active, whether it be the local Kiwanis or Rotary Club or civic organizations. The business lunch—having lunch periodically with a business contact—is another way in which relationships are developed and maintained. Some people enjoy socializing and are in a position to do so. Networking in this way functions best if there is a sense of mutual interest rather than one-sided pursuit.

Being invited to speak before a number of organizations is very flattering, but are they the right organizations? Are all of those speeches the best use of your time? Or do you choose your targets, and your subjects, and support your speeches, both before and after, with publicity and reprints that turn the speech into a powerful practice development tool?

Publicity, for some companies, is designed to do nothing more than to make the company name known. But in professional services, merely making the firm name known is not sufficient. It must be known in the context of an expertise that distinguishes you from your competitors.

And so even the traditional tools of practice development take on a new cast in the competitive marketing arena. In many respects, modern marketing is simply an organized, institutionalized and focused version of classic practice development. It brings order to what successful practitioners have been doing for generations. And, by applying the now available techniques of advertising, public relations and other promotional activities, it's something more.

PLANNING THE CAMPAIGN

Where once the practice could be developed by simply joining the right clubs and giving an occasional speech, this alone no longer works.

Where once there was a clear division of the market between the big firms and the little firms, this too is no longer the case. Big accounting and law firms, with hundreds of partners, now structure themselves to compete against one and two-partner firms for the small or emerging business. The small practitioner must now market his services just to hold his own.

Today, in the competitive marketplace, the process that ends in closing the sale is increasingly elaborate and requires strategy and skill. It begins with the conscious decision to grow and compete, departing substantially from serendipity. It moves to developing a marketing plan and a strategy, and then to executing that plan. It includes learning and practicing new skills, and how to manage new skills performed by others.

Even the successful practitioner, well along in marketing efforts, does well to periodically examine strategy and marketing efforts. If marketing activity changes the texture of the market, then successful marketing requires the professional to be even more alert and responsive to those changes.

Planning the marketing campaign begins, invariably, with defining the market. One wouldn't go to market with a product for which there is no demand, or a demand so limited that supplying the product isn't cost-effective. True, demand for products and services can sometimes be created, but only within limits. And only if it can be done on such a large scale as to make the effort worth the price.

In each profession the market is defined by both demographic factors —who, what, where and how many—and its changing needs. For the established practitioner, this may mean redefining the market.

Because the needs of the market for professional services are so multifaceted, the professional must understand exactly how those needs are structured, how they vary from one client to another, and how they change. It's very easy to understand that every public corporation needs an auditor or a corporate counsel, but that's rarely sufficient. For example, what about the possible ways in which an audit can be used? Is it a commodity, or can it be developed (without losing the independence of the auditor) into a management tool? Is that, in fact, what the client really wants?

Is it sufficient for the attorney to be merely reactive to his client's needs, or should he become more active in his client's business, and contribute to it with new legal services?

Nor is the medical or dental practice exempt from the need to understand its market. Does the community served want general practice or specialization? Is the future in high-priced service or in clinics?

What about the small firm and the small client? Is the client happy with just routine accounting services, or is he really longing for help with such aspects of his business as cash management, or computers? What are the needs for sophisticated consulting or legal services that integrate business and personal structures

The point is that no practice can be developed in today's competitive climate if there isn't a clear picture of the needs—the changing and varied needs—of the market place. This is recognized by most of the Big Eight accounting firms, which were built in recent years by serving giant companies, but now turn their attention to the smaller companies—those that are privately held or not yet emerging into larger companies. They perceived a need in the marketplace, and found a way to serve them.

And look at the several giant law firms that have grown as takeover or merger specialists.

An intelligently structured campaign should, like legs, be just long enough to reach the ground. It should be structured to meet the needs and desires of your firm and your clients—not his or her firm or clients. It is as particular and specific and unique to your firm as are the services you perform for your own clients.

If you are by choice a small practitioner, and merely want to maintain a moderate growth, then obviously a campaign for you will encompass deep immersion in very few of the techniques delineated in these pages.

If, on the other hand, you mean to grow and to compete actively, then your campaign must be carefully planned.

The techniques presented throughout this book are, essentially, tools. When they are used properly and skillfully, and in conjunction with one another, they can do some powerful building. How each one works, and how they are used in the marketing mix, is described in that chapter.

In all likelihood, most of the skills will be applied by professionals in each discipline. But the plan—the blueprint—must be done with your hand at the helm, no matter how many advertising or public relations or other marketing specialists you bring in.

Planning the campaign, then, includes familiarizing yourself with how the tools of marketing work, and what each contributes to the total marketing campaign.

It requires a great deal of introspection, in which you ask yourself about your own aims and objectives. Merely to want a very large firm, or one that differs substantially from what you have now, is not enough. You have to understand what's involved in developing that kind of practice. You have to accurately assess your own skills and preferences, and those of your partners, and how your skills and practice relate to the precise needs of your chosen market.

Budget must be understood, not just in terms of what things cost, and how much you're prepared to spend, but on the crucial factors of return on investment of your marketing dollar.

The Planning Matrix

While there are no planning patterns so universal as to be cast in stone, nor that can serve every business, there are some basic considerations for all firms.

Planning should begin with some thoughts on at lest the following:

- What kind of firm do I have now, and do I want to change its character, size, structure, services, market area? And if I want to change any of these elements, why?
- What are the real skills we have to offer?
- Do I really understand my market and its needs, or should I plan some formal explorations?

- How well do our skills fit what we perceive our market to want? If new skills are to be added or developed, are we capable of managing them?
- Should the emphasis be solely on maintaining and strengthening the current practice, or do we really want to grow? And if so, how big?
- How much commitment—measured in willingness to participate and in dollars—is available within the firm for marketing efforts?
- Is the commitment sufficiently large to warrant bringing in outside marketing help, or should we limit the effort to what we can do ourselves? And in either event, who's going to take the responsibility for managing the effort?
- If the market warrants it, are we prepared to either add staff, or train people, to better serve market needs?
- In view of the firm's size, markets, overhead, and the desires of the partners, are we prepared to rethink pricing?

Given the answer to questions such as these, a marketing plan can be developed, incorporating the following elements:

- Market—size and structure
- Budget
- Objectives—both firm and marketing
- Choice and mix of tools to achieve objectives, and in the framework of the budget.
- Expectations and time frame
- Who is to manage and who is to perform
- Structures for monitoring program, and for adjusting firm practices in response to marketing results

In marketing planning, there should be a clear distinction between wishes and reality. It's one thing to wish your firm were considerably larger; it's another thing to be prepared to do what's necessary to make it so.

These are, of course, standard planning elements, and developing a marketing campaign is very much a part of planning. The difference is that here, you're dealing with new and probably unfamiliar elements, including the fact that in most cases you're probably going to have to depend upon the skills of other people—the marketing professionals.

NEW SERVICES

There are times when this exploration of the marketplace results in identifying a need for a new service within the context of a profession. New opportunities frequently arise for new configurations of old skills to be put together as "products", and offered to a market as an existing service.

For example, consultants very quickly saw the need for computer training for small businesses. Accountants, particularly in the larger accounting firms saw the need for more sophisticated services to be offered to small and emerging businesses. The change in the economy and the expansion of the middle class dictated a market need for personal financial planning and management. The need for inexpensive routine legal services for the middle class has bred the highly successful legal clinic.

Developing a new service requires, in many cases, parallel marketing strategy to the overall strategy serving the firm. The approach to introducing a new service must be organized—much the same as the strategy used by manufacturers to introduce a new product:

- The need for the new service once identified, must be defined as clearly as possible. Where the need is just emerging, the need and the potential market must be defined and carefully assessed.
- The firm's inventory of skills must be surveyed to determine what skills must be brought to bear, who has them, and what additional training may be necessary.
- A dedicated leader to develop a program and staff must be designated, supported, and given the incentives to succeed.
- The service must be developed as a marketable package. It must be clearly defined in terms of the need it's to meet, how it's to be performed and delivered, who is to do it, how much will be charged for it, how it is to be sold, how much of it is to be sold by what date, and so forth
- A full-scale marketing program, including budget and test markets, must be developed.

Test marketing a new service requires that in addition to the marketing program, there must be some mechanism for reporting market reaction, such as surveys and market research. The pitfall in test marketing is that if too little time, money and effort are devoted to the test market the results will be skewed and distorted, leading to the possibility of either losing a major opportunity or investing poorly in an exaggerated opportunity.

When there is a clear picture of the nature of the market for a new service, and of how that service is to be performed, delivered and marketed, then it can be integrated into the overall marketing program.

MANAGING THE MARKETING EFFORT

The entire effort must be managed, because in marketing, as in your profession, nothing happens without somebody doing it; nothing happens effectively without somebody paying attention.

In a corporation, managing the marketing effort is relatively simple. There's usually a senior executive responsible for marketing. He or she runs the operation without disturbing very many other people in the organization.

This is possible, of course, where a product is produced. But in marketing professional services, even a staff marketing director requires the full cooperation and participation of every member of the firm who performs the service. This becomes exceedingly difficult in a partnership. The nature of a partnership affords each partner equal access to management, and certainly to marketing. At the same time, very few firms are large enough to have their own full time marketing staffs. And those that do have marketing staffs usually don't make partners of the marketing directors.

The result is that the marketing effort is frequently directed by a nonpartner who has the skills but no authority, or a nonprofessional marketer who does have authority but not the skills. If there has been any single problem that's impeded the growth of marketing in professional services, it's this peculiar paradox.

And yet the partnership structure is the one in which marketing must function. There is indeed a great deal of professionalism required for successful marketing. Marketing, as this book should demonstrate, has a clearly defined body of skills and techniques. Marketing professionals must bring to bear experience, imagination and judgment in exercising their skills.

Marketing, to lawyers, accountants and other professionals, is an alien discipline. Moreover, since frank marketing is new to the professions, there is little experience to help understand the marketer, or more significantly, what to expect from marketing.

All this will change, of course, as the body of experience in marketing professional services builds, and as professionals begin to relate results to efforts. But it has a long way to go. And in the meantime, many professional firms still, unfortunately, approach marketing as a committee of the entire partnership.

However the problem is resolved, managing the marketing effort can and must consume a great deal of time and attention. If the firm can't sustain a staff marketing professional then it must rely upon outside services or attempt to function without professional help. In either case, reason dictates that the responsibility for marketing, then, be given to one individual who has the time, the authority and the inclination to manage the effort. It must be coordinated. The program must be developed and the number of people involved in its execution must be supervised and sometimes driven. Outside agencies must be dealt with, and internal staffs must be managed. Unfortunately, the best devised marketing program will falter miserably if it is not properly managed.

BUDGETING

Budgeting a marketing program is a function of many elements, some of which are intangible.

The elements to be budgeted are outlined in the appendix. The question as to how much to allocate to a marketing budget is a different matter. It's a function of judgment in several areas:

- How large is the potential growth, measured in terms of dollar volume on an annual (or budget year) basis?
- How professionally run is the program to be?
- What percentage of current income shall be used to allocate a marketing budget?
- Will it be necessary, or even desirable, to alter pricing structure to accommodate marketing costs?
- What percentage of a future income shall be designated for marketing?

- How much money is actually available to invest in marketing, regardless of ratios to current or projected sales?
- How seriously and carefully will the effort be managed?
- What are the local cost factors (e.g. advertising and public relations costs, etc.)?
- How should these expenses be allocated back to various profit centers?
- What relationship is to be established between expectations and time frame?

Because marketing professional services is relatively new, there is too little absolute experience for any individual firm to know exactly how to budget and to gauge what it can expect for its money. However, each year experience will contribute to sharpening the ability to budget more precisely. Marketing, particularly for a company that's new to it, requires nurturing and time. Expectations of return on investment, at least at the beginning, must be reasonable, else there will be early disappointment and premature judgment (and possibly abortion) of a campaign that might, with patience, be successful.

MEASURING THE EFFORT

That marketing is an effort that functions well only as a totality is yet another reality we know from experience. No ad will so bestir a reader that he responds by retaining a professional on the basis of it. A knowledgeable article in a respectable journal may engender new respect for the expertise of its author, and that respect may well result in further discussion between the author and the reader, but ultimately the author of that article will have to personally convince that reader to retain him.

A profoundly successful marketing program may educate, persuade, enhance reputation and perception, and build unique and extraordinary proclivities toward a firm, but an individual will ultimately have to make the sale. How much toothpaste would Colgate sell if each tube had to be sold by Colgate's president? How many mainframe computers would IBM sell if each one had to be sold by IBM's chairman?

A direct mail letter offering a bible bound in genuine leather for only $9.95 may result in five percent of the recipients' sending in checks and order forms, and be deemed a success. But how do you judge the success of a hundred letters sent to business people, offering assistance in improving cash management? And if ten of those recipients ultimately do become clients, how much of it was attributable to the letter, how much to a firm's reputation that might have been enhanced by having been quoted on the subject in *Inc Magazine*, and how much to the ability of the partner or partners who closed the sale?

There is the question, as well, of whether the same techniques that will work for the large firm, with its national reputation and vast resources, as for the small firm, with perhaps two or three partners.

For the small firm seeking to compete with the large firm for national business, the answer is negative, unless the small firm offers a distinctive expertise not readily available elsewhere. But for the small firm trying to expand its practice in its own geographic area, the answer is a resounding yes. Any magazine will publish an intelligent article by a lone practitioner as readily as if the article were written by the managing partner of the largest firm in its field in the country. A well-planned direct mail campaign will be as effective for the small firm as it is for the large one. The effort of a small firm to define its market is as important as it is for the large, and will pay off as well in kind.

That is, in fact, yet another unique characteristic of professional services marketing. Virtually every technique works as well for the small firm as for the large one. One reason, of course, is that in both small and large firms, a service is offered and performed by an individual, and so it is presumed that the service offered is deliverable by an individual. This is not the case for a manufacturer who works out of his garage, nor for a bank or an airline. There is indeed very little in professional services marketing, as you will see in following chapters, that is not as potentially effective for a small professional firm as for a large one.

SUMMARY

It should be remembered, no matter what the activities, that the aim of the exercise is to get new clients and to keep the ones you have.

The need for planned marketing becomes urgent, as a result of markedly accelerating competition and changing market configurations. Too, marketing activities generate new attitudes and change the market's structure. At the same time, the market is constantly changing on its own in ways that increase competition.

A market is defined not just by demographics, but more importantly, by the needs of clients and prospective clients.

The traditional practice development tools—joining organizations, networking, political activities, speeches, seminars, etc.—still work, but must now be organized, focused, and supported by technical marketing skills. The traditional tools take on a new cast in the competitive marketing arena.

Planning begins with the market defined in terms of objectives and capabilities, and by assessing the firm's skills relative to the market's needs. The firm's commitment to developing or attaining new skills must be examined.

Significant elements of planning are:

• Market—size and structure
• Budget
• Objectives—both firm and marketing
• Choice and mix of tools to achieve objectives, and in the framework of the budget.
• Expectations and time frame
• Who is to manage and who is to perform
• Structures for monitoring program, and for adjusting firm practices in response to marketing results

The marketing effort must be carefully managed, both internally and externally, and must be measured against pre-determined, reasonable expectations.

CHAPTER 2

Analyzing The Market

How much better can a professional understand his or her market? After all, the nature of professional services is such that the market seems self-defined. People need doctors because there is illness. People need lawyers because the body of law requires educated and skillful interpretation and advocacy. People need tax specialists because the tax laws are too complex for the untrained, they need accountants because accounting is a technical skill and they need auditors when the law and the capital markets require audits.

But in fact, these are only the broad strokes. In a society and business world as complex as ours, the market for a surgeon is not the psychiatric patient, nor is the corporation the market for the divorce lawyer. And even though the market for the auditor is primarily the 10,000 or so public corporations, or the private company that frequently seeks credit, one can hardly define the market for the small, two-partner auditing firm as the multinational corporation.

The market for any product or service is defined by needs or wants, and nobody sells anything that the market doesn't need—or can be persuaded that it needs.

But in defining the professional services market, one sees not just a need, but an urgency of need. Urgency of need is perhaps one definition of professional services, and perhaps a strong reason why the professions are so strongly regulated.

Within the broad need, however, is a spectrum and variety. The need for services is varied—more so, perhaps, than for most products, and differs from business to business and from individual to individual. More subtle, and perhaps more important to marketing, is that the way the market needs the service delivered or performed differs substantially from one prospective client to another.

To know how to market, it's urgent, then, to understand the service that's needed, and the way the market wants it personalized and tailored, and delivered. And it's important to know how the market's needs really relate to what it is that you can do.

Fathoming your market, in this context, is so inherent to any marketing effort that it must be done on one level or another, no matter how broad or narrow your marketing plans; no matter whether you are planning a major marketing program or just tuning up a practice you deem to be otherwise satisfactory at the moment.

DEFINING A MARKET

What, in fact, is a market?

One technical definition might be that a market is any single group of potential clients or purchasers of your service that can be reached by a common appeal. Mechanically, it can be defined by common factors, such as income, age, economic status, occupation, social status, and so forth. But for the professional, it goes much beyond that.

There must be the added ingredient of the group's common need for a specific service that the professional can perform. All corporations need lawyers and accountants. But is the multinational corporation a viable market for the two-partner law firm with an SEC practice, most of whose clients are small public companies with sales of under $50 million?

On the other hand, a small firm specializing in, say, immigration law can very well serve both large and small corporations, either directly or as an auxiliary to a corporation's primary law firm.

The professional has the flexibility to change the scope of his market by changing the scope of his services. An attorney specializing in corporate and SEC law, for example, may determine that there is a potential market in acquisitions, mergers and takeovers. The expertise may well be within the realm of his experience, or at least the scope of his experience, or he may broaden his expertise to expand his market.

A classic example of this exists in the current drive of Big Eight accounting firms to capture small and emerging businesses as clients. Until relatively recently, smaller firms were not considered cost-effective clients, for either the Big Eight accounting firms nor the smaller company. But market saturation in the Fortune 1200, and the reluctance of large companies to change auditors, dictated the need to expand market scope. Ways were found to train specialists and to establish operations, within the Big Eight firms, to serve the smaller company cost-effectively. Thus, a new market was opened—one that had not before been feasible or attractive.

Nor is there just one market for any professional, no matter how specialized. For the professional, a market may consist of many specific markets, or segments. But it must be remembered that each market segment must be addressed separately.

Moreover, it must be recognized that several segments may overlap, even though the appeal to each segment may be different. For example, the market segment for a firm's auditing services may consist of the same people that constitute the market segment for cash management services.

The problem of distribution is also distinctive. Among other things, a manufacturer must define his market in terms of his ability to distribute his product. A highly perishable product, for example, can be sold only where it can be delivered cost-effectively within a given time span. Profit margins and transportation costs further decide geographic distribution area.

The geographic boundaries of a professional's market, on the other hand, can be defined by his willingness to travel himself. The small or individual practitioner may have a nationwide practice because of his personal reputation or rare expertise, or he may choose to practice solely in his own home town. This is sometimes determined by the nature of the expertise. The one surgeon who is a pioneer in an exotic procedure may find himself lured anywhere in the world. The internationally renowned criminal defense attorney may spend half his life on airplanes, although attorneys are licensed by state bar associations and may practice only in those states in which they are licensed. The tax specialist with extraordinary experience in an esoteric field may be in universal demand.

MARKET FACTORS

How, then, is a market defined?

- *By geographic area.* This is defined by each professional in terms of the geographic area he is capable of serving (or willing to serve).
- *By business or industry.* This may be a vertical breakdown (manufacturing, corporations, etc.), or it may break down by industry. Professional practices differ industry by industry. For example, the accounting procedures for the motion picture industry are very different than for a computer company.
- *By size.* Potential clients of a particular size or economic structure.
- *By service need.* This is a function of both perceived need, relative to the professional's capability to perform, and a need that can be generated by marketing.
- *Configuration.* A market segment must be configured in a way that it is reachable, by any means of communication, cost-effectively. For example, all companies with pension funds have some common problems, and are reachable through pension publications.
- *Competition.* There must be a keen awareness of competition. A market in which one or several firms are deeply entrenched must be viewed differently than one in which no firm dominates. Is there a capability to penetrate it? Is it cost-effective to attack a market in which another firm is dominant?
- *Other Factors.* Depending upon the profession, there are myriad other factors that must be considered, including social. An architect who chooses to do public housing, for example, or an attorney specializing in pro bono work, must consider community relations and social factors as part of the market definition. Other factors include any distinctive element that defines your own practice.

Given an understanding of market segments and their parameters, some measure of investigation must be made to clearly define the market. No marketing program can work effectively, and certainly not cost-effectively, without clear definition. To do otherwise is to waste considerable time, effort and money to reach the wrong people with the wrong message.

SOURCES OF INFORMATION

If there is one word that obtains in market analysis that word is perspective.

At all times, perspective must be sustained in both defining market segments and, as well, in analyzing market data.

There is an important distinction to be made between the words *data* and *information*. Data are isolated raw facts. They mean nothing until integrated and correlated to demonstrate patterns of similarity or common and mutually supported purpose, and blessed with intuition—and then focused toward the specific end of telling you what you want to know.

Then—and then only—is it information.

This point is best illustrated by a statement made by Theodore Levitt, a professor of marketing at the Harvard Graduate School of Business Administration. In his book, *Marketing for Business Growth* (McGraw-Hill, New York, 1974), he says,

> Take the case of the Irish Tourist Board. For years it was enormously successful in building tourist business, congratulating itself for having constantly overfulfilled its objective of generating overseas trade revenue. But the facts were quite the reverse. The Board had targeted high-income, high-spending tourists. When they got to Ireland, they stayed in luxurious, foreign-owned urban hotels, drank imported Scotch whiskey, ate imported beef steak, and rented imported motor cars. Had the target been lower-income tourists, satisfied with staying in less luxurious, domestically-owned hotels, eating in native restaurants, taking trains and buses, and saving by buying picnic lunches of locally grown food at locally owned stores, less might have been spent by each tourist, but Ireland would have earned more.

The point he so aptly demonstrates is that merely accumulating data leads to information that is less productive. It is certainly more time-consuming. It's important to decide, beforehand, what you need to know for your own professional marketing needs, and not be overwhelmed with useless data simply because so much of it is available and it's so easy to assemble.

PRIMARY AND SECONDARY RESEARCH

In the parlance of market research, there are two categories of research—*primary* and *secondary*.

Primary data is material you gather yourself, at first hand. It may be through direct field research, through surveys, interviews or focus groups, or it may be information you ask your own clients.

Secondary data is material you glean from existing sources, such as published government census figures or research done by others for other purposes. Of this material there is a plethora, and useful though it may be, it can inundate you if you don't use it selectively and wisely. There is an astonishing amount of information available from government and industry sources, as well as from companies and even the advertising departments of publications. An outstanding source of information is your own professional society, as well as the professional journals in your field. It's useful, therefore, to begin any market research with secondary sources, using primary research to fill in the blanks.

It makes good economic sense to adopt a policy that precludes reinventing the wheel in research. What you should be after is to get your hands on the best, most responsible sources of information, and proceed from there.

Secondary Sources

By far the best secondary source of facts is the government—federal, state and local. Another major source is the computer-accessed data base system, such as *Dialog*, *Lexis/Nexis* and *Dow Jones*. A great deal of federal and industry data is available from these data bases, as well as from libraries or directly from the government.

Perhaps the three most useful sources of demographic information are published by the U.S. Department of Commerce. They are *The Statistical Abstract of the United States*, the *County and City Data Book*, and the *Survey of Current Business*.

The Statistical Abstract summarizes more than a thousand tables of information compiled by all branches of the U.S. government, including the Census Bureau, and includes a great deal of demographic information broken down by state. It has a footnoted bibliography that gives sources from which the information was derived, so that further delving becomes easily feasible.

The *County and City Data Book* is published every three years and gives even more detailed local information than does the *Abstract*. Its focus is on statistics for all counties of the United States, as well as for cities with a population of more than 25,000.

The *Survey of Current Business* is a monthly publication that contains a great variety of current data and general statistics on all aspects of business. It is particularly valuable in reporting business trends that can help determine the directions in which your market might go.

The U.S. Census Bureau is a treasure trove of information on everything from population to agriculture. While much of the information is abstracted in the *Statistical Abstract*, the basic census material itself is invaluable, even though it's compiled only once every decade. The *Census of Population*, for example, analyzes residents of the United States by age, sex, race, citizenship, education, occupation, employment status, income and family status—all categorized by state, city and county, and in large cities, by by census tract and city block.

The population census is taken every ten years, of course, but others are taken more frequently. The manufacturing census is taken every five years; others are taken every two years.

The Department of Commerce acts as a clearing house for all government-gathered information. It maintains a large staff of experts, available to the public, in its Washington, D.C. office and in regional offices throughout the country.

Comparable information is available from many state and local governments. Most states have departments of commerce, as do many larger cities, all of which make information readily available. Because their focus is local and regional, the information they provide can be particularly helpful.

In addition to the government and professional societies, a surprising number of other sources are available to professionals. Many universities maintain bureaus of economic research designed to help local business people. Local banks can be helpful, as can be other professionals. Lawyers have information that can help accountants, for example.

As an aid to their own marketing efforts in selling advertising, local and national media do an extensive job of market research, and frequently make the information available to prospective advertisers.

There are, of course, a great number of data bases available from private sources, such as Dun & Bradstreet and Standard & Poor's. Directories of data sources are available at any public library, but one outstanding directory is *Where to Find Business Information*, edited by David M. Brownstone and Gorton Carruth, published by John

Wiley & Sons, NY. It is a compendium of more than 5,000 sources of business information.

For those who have computers, access to data for market (or other) information abounds. Services generally available to the public, such as *Dialog*, *Lexis/Nexis* and *Dow Jones Retrieval Service*, offer access to extensive data banks that can be enormously helpful in market delineation, and particularly detailed information about specific companies or industries. Consumer oriented services, such as *Compuserve*, offer less sophisticated sources, but can be useful nevertheless. Given communication capability as part of a personal computer, an initial membership fee is paid ($25 for Dialog, about $75 for Dow Jones) and then hourly charges are billed as the system is used. Among the many data banks available are business news gleaned from business periodicals, regulatory information, company information of such sources as Standard & Poor's, and, in the case of Compuserve, historical stock market information, Value Line's data base, and demographic market information, including the complete 1980 census material. It can shortcut a great deal of research. Myriad other data bases, some more sophisticated than others, are becoming increasingly available, and at reasonable cost. NEXIS, for example, is a data base that gives you access to the full text of *The New York Times*, *Washington Post*, *Newsweek*, *Forbes*, *Business Week*, and more than 90 publications and news services. Smaller data bases, more specialized, contain more detailed or technical information.

Economic Input

Because the nature of the professional market goes well beyond mere demographics, a great deal of market definition depends upon keeping abreast of current affairs. The financial services revolution, for example, substantially altered the nature of markets for a great many professionals. It developed very quickly, and any professional in a position to serve that market who was not in on it from the beginning has a great deal of catching up to do. The professional who limits his reading to just professional journals, and doesn't pay close attention to economic changes, stands in great danger of missing significant market trends.

PRIMARY RESEARCH

Primary research—research you do yourself—should follow intensive secondary research in market delineation. In addition to sparing you duplicate effort, it serves to refine and focus information derived from secondary research.

Primary research should begin with an analysis of your own practice. Who are your current clients? What kinds of services do you perform for them and what kinds of services—particularly new services—are they demanding of you? Where do your clients come from? What factors, in a business sense, are common to the largest number of them?

An analysis of your own practice will tell you a great deal about your market as it currently exists, but at the same time, it will tell you a great deal about what you don't know. This, combined with the information derived from secondary research, allows you to move on to the appropriate form of primary research.

While there are many techniques of primary research, it's important to remember that no matter which form you use, whether you do it yourself or retain outside help, you must not abdicate your own intelligence, nor deny your own instincts.

Research is a skill that frequently requires experienced professionals, for both the research itself and the interpretation of the data. Before even the most astute professional market researcher can begin work, there must be a clear statement of research objectives and a complete understanding of how the research is to be used. As in your own practice, the professional market researcher must know what you're trying to achieve if he or she is to function effectively for you.

But while professional research can be extremely helpful, it is only one tool of many. You must supply the judgment that brings all research into focus to help you define your market and, ultimately, your approaches to it.

SURVEYS

The major tool in market research is the survey, in which your target audience is asked specific questions, the answers to which tell you a great deal (but never everything) you want to know.

Surveys can be simple or complex, depending upon what you're trying to find out. They can be in writing, in person, or by phone. Simple surveys that seek factual information usually require no great expertise, and can sometimes be done yourself, but accumulating any body of meaningful sophisticated statistical information may require the services of a professional pollster. There are subtleties within subtleties that are part of the realm of professional experience.

Designing a survey begins not with the questions, but with a clear delineation of the information needed. A survey works best if it's brief and to the point. Certainly, if you are doing the survey yourself, the fewer the questions the better. For more involved surveys that seek information that is detailed or subtle, or that deals with attitudes, professionalism is required if the survey is to be at all useful.

Whether the beneficiary of a survey—the party for whom the survey is being taken—should be identified or not depends upon the purpose of the survey. If clear objectivity is desired, then the beneficiary should be anonymous. But sometimes, a survey can be designed so that is in fact a marketing tool itself. To ask a question such as, "Do you feel that your tax return has ever been unfairly audited?" is to imply that the firm asking the question can be specifically helpful with that kind of problem. On the other hand, despite the marketing value of such questions as these, there isn't too much gained in the way of objectivity. It may be a tradeoff between getting information you can use and getting marketing value from the survey.

There are three basic ways to take a survey:

• By mail
• In person
• By telephone.

Mail surveys give the respondent the opportunity to answer at leisure, which is both an advantage and a disadvantage. The advantage is that answers may be more thoughtful. The disadvantage is that there is a diminished sense of urgency in returning the questionnaire, which is why percentage of returns on mail questionnaires is usually very low (about 25% is considered the average). There are a great many devices used to motivate people to fill out and return mail questionnaires, such as enclosing a dollar bill or offering to make a contribution to a charity in the respondent's name. But perhaps the most effective motivation lies in the covering letter, which delineates a specific benefit to the respondent, if one can be determined.

Person-to-person surveys are the most intensive and valuable, but also require the greatest professionalism. Interviewers must be carefully trained to deal with respondents, particularly where the information being sought is complex and therefore, presumably, most valuable. These surveys are obviously relatively expensive, and a great deal of preparation must go into their development. Each interview, remember, is an opportunity to learn a great deal from a respondent, and care should be taken in preparation that the opportunity is not wasted. Surveying, it should be noted, is one of those activities that always seems to be simpler than it really is. There is a great body of experience in the field, and a good professional knows many techniques that increase the value of the interview.

Telephone interviews, while best done by professionals, can still be done by non-professional researchers if the questions are kept simple, and there are not too many of them. It is also the lowest-cost of the surveys, because it eliminates mailing and higher-priced field surveyors. In the hands of an experienced professional, a telephone interview can elicit a great deal of information, because an experienced interviewer can strive to improve the quality of the response. And while every call will not be fully productive, it will give a greater return of responses than will mail.

THE FOCUS GROUP

A research technique that is being used with increasing effectiveness is the focus group, in which a proper sampling of six or eight people in a target audience are gathered for a group discussion. Under the direction of a trained leader, the group discusses the research problem, such as an attitude toward a service, or a broader description of service needs. The advantage of the focus group over the straight face-to-face interview is that the group dynamic quickly leads people to be freer in their expressions. Focus groups are usually held in studios specifically designed with recording devices and one-way mirrors. The one-way mirrors allow the client and the research professional to observe the group at work, and if warranted, to videotape the proceedings for further study and analysis.

Properly done, the focus group contributes a considerable amount of valuable material to the total research study. In a straightforward interview, even in person, people may tend to give answers they feel are appropriate or desirable, rather than those that express their true feelings. The dynamic of the focus group tends to break down that reserve, producing more valuable input to the total research project.

The danger in relying too heavily on focus groups is that under poor direction, one or two participants may tend to dominate or overpower the others in the group, thereby leading their answers. And of course, the sampling must be sound, if six or eight people are to contribute information that may be adequately generalized for an entire market group. The client, of course, is never identified. Obviously, to do so would compromise the objectivity of the responses.

Focus groups are not inexpensive. Aside from the basic research costs, each participant is usually paid a token sum for his participation, and that may be as much as $50 or $100 per participant. The sum should be enough to make it interesting, but not so much as to color the participant's sense of independence. And because they are so expensive, they should be used wisely.

THE SAMPLE

Professional researchers have complex statistical formulae for determining meaningful samples in research. For the informal survey, however, the sample need not be scientific, but it must be at least rational if the results are to have any value.

In developing a proper sample, don't lose sight of the fact that you are trying to determine those factors about your market that will help you to define and serve it best. You begin the process, of course, with a general concept of who your market is and, in terms of your service, the possibilities of what you have to offer.

A sample, of course, is a cross section of the population you want to survey that is presumably representative of the entire population. If, for example, you are trying to determine the specific needs for personal financial planning in your market area, it would be grossly infeasible to survey every one of your prospective clients. There may be hundreds or thousands. Too small a sampling might give you a skewed view of what the market really wants. Short of using the scientific formulae of the professional, you must make an estimate of the cross-section that would really be representative of the entire market. It may be a numerical percentage, or it may be a selection from the total group. For example, five small business owners, five professionals, five executives of large corporations, and so forth. The factors to consider, if you're determining your own sample, are size of the total universe (everybody the sample is supposed to represent), the nature of the information you're seeking, the breakdown of your market by categories that are distinctive, and, of course, the depth of the market you feel you must penetrate to get the answers you need.

CORRELATING THE INFORMATION

After having done both primary and secondary research, you will have accumulated a great deal of data. How does it become information you can use?

This is the point at which you go back to your original research objectives, without which you may find yourself overwhelmed by extraneous data. Analyzing data is much like editing copy. A good analyst begins by knowing what to toss out, and how to combine a fact with a fact to see a pattern.

The data must be correlated in terms of what you really have to know to define your market and its needs. You will find considerable extraneous data from both primary and secondary research. You will find data that, in conjunction with data from other sources, will have an altered meaning. But if all of the data is viewed with an eye toward what you really want to know, it should yield significant information.

At the same time, the information must be judged intelligently, and not used without interpretation. For example, the results of a survey on who influences decisions to choose an accounting firm showed that 37% of respondents were influenced by lawyers, and 9% were influenced by bankers. It would be very simple to assume that lawyers were the prime influentials, and to ignore bankers, but that would be a misreading of the data. The 9% of the sample that were influenced by bankers represent a substantial body that cannot be ignored in a marketing program.

And again, your own experience, instincts, and knowledge of your profession are a significant input. As has been noted, even with the best research, you don't abdicate your own intelligence.

SUMMARY

The purpose of market research is to define your market—to know who and where your market is, and the nature and kind of services your market wants and needs. Without a clear knowledge of your market, it's irrational to determine what your marketing efforts should be. Without understanding your market, your marketing efforts are diverse and unfocused, and your ultimate choice of marketing tools become random and expensive.

At the same time, market research must be done carefully and thoughtfully. It's all too easy, in market research, to become hypnotized and inundated in data, and to lose sight of why you are doing the market research in the first place. The aim of market research, after all, is to tell you what you need to know in order to develop a fruitful marketing program.

CHAPTER 3

Setting Objectives

No marketing program can be totally effective without a clear view of both firm objectives and marketing objectives. Absent clear goals, marketing efforts become random, diverse and expensive. With clearly delineated objectives, marketing programs become relevant and focused. They offer a test—a measure—against which all activities are laid. If a marketing activity doesn't clearly serve to meet a specific objective, it's usually wasteful, inept, and not cost-effective.

Developing a marketing program must necessarily begin with a clear view of objectives; a readily defined understanding of what the firm and its partners want, both in the near and the far term, and what they hope to have the marketing program accomplish. An overriding consideration is your decision as to the nature of your practice. What kind of firm do you want to be? How do you mean the firm to serve the personal and professional needs of you and your partners (and not to be overlooked, your staff)? How do you mean to be perceived by your clientele?

Perhaps no other factor contributes to the distinction among professional firms as do objectives. In professional services, which are so much more dominated by individuals than are corporations, objectives may be considerably more subjective, and can often be expressed more in terms of individual rather than corporate aims. A corporate objective might be to increase market share. A sole practitioner's objective might be to build a stable client base large enough to allow him to bring his son into the firm. A moderate-sized partnership's objectives might be to expand market base in a particular specialty or industry.

In setting your firm's objectives, perspective is important. The large corporation sets objectives of scope and magnitude, and may support those objectives with pages of documentation. The small professional firm is spared the need to go to these lengths; indeed, quite the opposite is necessary. Objectives, clearly defined as they should be, should not be overwhelming. Nor should they be adhered to slavishly. It is enough to know what you want to do, why you want to do it, and how you plan to get it done.

SETTING FIRM OBJECTIVES

In formulating firm objectives, it's important to recognize that objectives are a context and a direction, rather than a finite measure. They are not cast in concrete—they are dynamic. Circumstances change, and if the objectives are not able to be responsive to change, they become unattainable and unrealistic.

Obviously, the basic objective of your firm and your practice is to be profitable. Another objective may be growth—getting more clients and more revenue—although this may not universally be so. A single practitioner, or a small firm, may feel that it's already at optimum size to satisfy its partners. But even for this kind of firm, there's always the need to build for the future; to be able to readily replace clients that are lost through attrition.

A distinction should be made between retainer clients and project clients. A professional firm may have retainer clients as the largest part of its client base, with only a percentage on a project basis. A law firm that specializes (in real estate law, for example), or an accounting firm that does a good bit of consulting work, certainly have different objectives than do their counterparts with stronger retainer client bases. Doctors and dentists are in the same position as consultants. They may have a large body of loyal patients, but except for those with sustaining illnesses, a patient may see a doctor only once a year. Consultants find the largest part of their practice, for the most part, to be project work, and new projects must be generated constantly, from both existing and new clients. Architectural firms rarely have sustaining clients, although a project for a single client may last for several years. All of these firms have objectives that differ from those with heavy retainer client bases, and they differ from one another.

In defining firm or practice objectives, some specific factors must be considered:

Firm Environment. Nothing—not even profitability—is more important than the kind of firm you are or want to be. Without a firm environment that is satisfying and fulfilling to its partners and staff, there will be no growth or profitability.

Size. Businesses usually don't grow substantially by accident. It's almost invariably a conscious decision by its partners or owners, who then take steps to implement that decision. However, some professional firms may feel that they want to limit their growth, fully cognizant of the implications of growing, and of managing a large firm as well. Growth alone may not be of the essence—even a firm that chooses to stay at its current size must make that a conscious decision. But it should face the fact that in order to contain growth, it must take steps to sustain its size; it must perform marketing functions to overcome loss by attrition.

Profitability. Profitability, of course, is as much a function of margins as it is of volume, and so it's useful to know your costs rather precisely. In planning for marketing, you may decide to increase margins to allow for marketing to increase volume, or to accept a lower profit on the same margin. This means, of course, that you're going to want to define the time frame of your marketing program, both to limit the time of your reduced profitability or, more practically, to allow a realistic time for marketing efforts to show a return on investment.

Pricing. Pricing is as much an element of marketing as is advertising or promotion. Aside from the fact that it affects revenues and profitability, it also affects positioning. The classic question is, do I charge less and go for volume, or do I charge more and go for a more affluent clientele? This is a function of conscious choice, although, often, the choice is dictated by such other factors as access to affluent clients, the ability to supply the kind of service needed, or in some cases, simply the ability to ask for and sustain a high fee schedule.

Market. There are three aspects of a market that must be considered—its size, its needs, and its location, and all three must be viewed realistically in formulating objectives. How large a market can you realistically serve? What are the parameters of the market's needs that you're prepared to serve effectively? What geographical limitations are realistic?

Share of market. When a firm is in a rapidly growing market, or functioning in an era of rapid growth, share of market is not significant. Growth will come with the market. But when that market or industry slows its growth, and competition for existing business is the only possibility for growth, then share of market is crucial. If the only way to grow is to capture your competitor's clients, then obviously, your share of market grows as his diminishes.

Share of market is an equally important consideration in an industrially mature market area, where industry is either stagnating or declining.

Still, within those strictures that dictate strong competition or static markets, growth can come by offering new services to existing clients, or by offering new services to clients of other firms. If market share is meaningful, it is measured not only in terms of the total practice, but for specific services as well. A major accounting firm, for example, may be only the fifth largest firm in town, but it may have 70% of the market in small business services.

And of course, the two classic approaches to increasing market share are price cutting, which is fraught with danger, and improved marketing efforts, which is infinitely preferable.

Service concept. As a professional service, your relations with your clients dictate that they are served personally. But even within that function, there are degrees and options. A group medical practice, for example, may perceive of each patient as a patient of the entire group, in which case each patient may be treated impersonally, or it may decide to assign patients to individual physicians to establish strong personal relationships. A law firm may decide to give impersonal service to each client, particularly those not on retainer, or it may decide to devote a considerable amount of time and effort to client relations. A practice in any profession may be a 9-to-5 operation, or it may express a willingness to function around the clock, from both office and home, for its clients. One major accounting firm opened a second office in the Wall Street area of New York, ostensibly to serve the needs of its financial clients (and to expand its financial clientele.) Another accounting firm opened a branch office in suburban Dallas, to better serve the growing number of smaller businesses located there. The service option, of course, is the firm's, but it should be made a specific choice. If it's not, if it's arrived at arbitrarily, it sends a diverse message to clients, and is counterproductive to a firm's growth and success.

Objectives, then, should be realistic, as should be expectation for achieving them, or else they become wishes that will remain unfulfilled. If the aim is for growth that's greater than is realistically achievable, or for penetrating a market strongly overwhelmed by a competitor, and the expectations for achieving those aims are not substantiated by the elements, then obviously failure is in the offing.

It's always wise, also, to consider those elements that are beyond individual control. One can't control, for example, the national economy, which can throw the best formulated objectives awry. An entire legal practice can be created or destroyed by a legislative change. A major medical discovery can substantially alter a practice. Opportunities for professionals are generated or obliterated regularly. This is why objectives are never more than guidelines that serve to define a course of action, whether in marketing or otherwise.

There's always the danger, too, of successfully achieving marketing objectives too soon, and thereby outrunning your ability to serve a new or growing clientele. It makes little sense to do a successful job of increasing your tax business if you can't find a sufficient number of tax specialists to serve your new clientele.

FORMULATING MARKETING OBJECTIVES

If the marketing program is to be relevant, marketing objectives must stem from firm objectives. There are so many options and variables among marketing tools that without defined marketing objectives there's no way to rationally use these tools to optimum value.

The prime objectives of a marketing program can have rather specific broad-based goals. For example:

• To get new clients
• To strengthen relationships with existing clients
• To sell new services to existing clients, as well as to new clients

- To enter a new market for a specific service
- To introduce a new service
- To broaden a geographic base
    . . . and so on.

But within the context of these goals, the key elements to examine in setting marketing objectives are:

REVENUES AND RETURN ON INVESTMENT. Presumably, the objective is to increase revenues by increasing the clientele or the services to existing clients. But at what cost? In designing a marketing program, the cost of achieving a revenues goal—the return on investment—is a primary factor.

Merely to set an arbitrary figure or percentage increase is insufficient, without asking pertinent questions about what must be spent to achieve that goal. Nor is the expenditure in marketing dollars alone. The increased revenue, presumably from increased volume, must be serviced. Will new staff have to be added? How much will new staff add to overhead, in both salaries and support costs—space, secretarial and clerical help, support services, and so forth?

Thus, in setting a goal for increased revenues, the size of the investment to achieve that increase must be calculated, and from that must be determined the goal for return on that investment.

It must also be recognized, in this context, that in marketing, there is no one-to-one relationship between efforts and results. An ad that costs a hundred dollars cannot be expected to produce two hundred dollars in revenue the week after it's run. Marketing has a dynamic, particularly if it's successful. A well run campaign increases in effectiveness as it continues, and as the effectiveness increases, so does the return on investment. For example, an accounting firm may identify a need for a new service to banks. The firm must spend a certain amount of money to develop that service, and then to make it known to its prospective clientele. At the beginning, it's talking to a market that may be as unaware of the firm as it is of the service. But after a period of sustained marketing effort, the market is educated, and it takes less to sell more.

It should be noted, however, that the converse is not necessarily true. If the effort is diminished, there is no sustaining recollection by the market. Other competitors move in, and the value of the earlier efforts are lost. It's like a hoop. As long as you keep hitting it with a stick, it keeps rolling, picking up momentum. But when you stop hitting the hoop, it eventually runs down and falls over. It doesn't matter how far it's rolled or where it's been. It's down and out.

At the beginning of a marketing campaign, the return on the investment is smaller. But if the investment and the effort is sustained, the penetration of the effort is greater for the same dollar, and so the return on investment is greater.

CLIENT PERCEPTION. How do you want to be perceived by your clientele?

While the answer to that question is crucial to the marketing plan, it should be remembered that marketing alone cannot develop *images*—a perception that belies reality. No marketing program can convey an image of high service at low cost if, in fact, you are not *performing* high service at low cost. The acoustics of the marketplace are extraordinary, and what you are speaks so loudly that people can't hear what you *say* you are.

In developing this objective, there must first be a clear look at the reality of your firm and its practice. If your objective is to change the way you are perceived, then you must first change what is necessary to make your preferred perception a reality. Then, and only then, can you expect a marketing program to project those elements that will contribute to a realistic perception of your firm, and to a reputation that serves your marketing goals.

SHARE OF MARKET. If share of market is a significant element in your growth or competitive picture, then it must be generally quantified, and marketing plans must reflect the competitive values in your efforts.

PUBLICS. In every marketing program, the target audience must, of course, be clearly defined. The universe for every professional must be realistically defined by the service offered, as well as by the needs of the market. Obviously, a physician who specializes in arthritis is not addressing the same public as is the orthopedic surgeon. The accountant who specializes in tax work is not looking at the same public as the accountant who specializes in preparing financial statements for companies seeking financing.

Actually, in any market there are several publics. There are existing clients, whose needs for service must be constantly addressed, as must be their needs for new services. There are the prospective clients, who constitute as many publics as there are services you can perform for them. Your firm may serve one public with corporate services, another in the same market group with financial services, and a third in the same market with personal financial services. The three groups may be contiguous, but each may still be separate and distinct.

Defining a target audience is a function of determining those universal characteristics of the target group to which your services are most profitably addressed. The universal characteristics must include the ability to reach them in a uniform and economical way. For example, the best way to reach small businesses as a target audience is through such defined publications as *Inc* and *VENTURE* magazines.

TIME FRAME. A practical and realistic time frame in which to achieve specific goals is essential to establishing marketing objectives. Marketing must be given a reasonable time to work, and yet, if it's not working within a reasonable time, this should be recognized in time to make adjustments. Unreasonable expectations are a clear danger, in terms of both results and time frame. Marketing professional services has a longer time frame than does product marketing. A retailer placing an ad knows his results almost immediately, by the number of people who come into the store. In professional services, the results are felt not when the brochure or direct mail piece goes out, or the release is printed or the ad is run, but when the contract is signed.

BUDGET. There are a number of techniques for determining budgets, such as a percentage of revenues or a percentage of projected fees. But it is not a simple process, and requires a great deal of consideration. And again, it should be remembered that in budgeting, effectiveness—and therefore return on investment—will increase as the marketing program gains in penetration.

When the marketing objectives are clear, then there can be a clear view of the marketing mix—those several tools of marketing that, together, move the program forward.

SUMMARY

A marketing program should begin with a clear view of the firm's overall business objectives, and then a delineation of marketing objectives. Marketing objectives should reflect, and stem from, firm objectives. They should in all cases be realistic and attainable.

Key elements in establishing firm objectives are:

- Firm environment
- Size
- Profitability
- Pricing
- Market
- Share of market
- Service concept

The prime objectives of a marketing program can include:

- To get new clients
- To strengthen relationships with existing clients
- To sell new services to existing clients, as well as to new clients
- To enter a new market for a specific service
- To introduce a new service
- To broaden a geographic base

Key elements in setting marketing objectives are:

- Revenues and return on investment
- Client perception
- Share of market
- Publics
- Time frame
- Budget

CHAPTER 4

The Marketing Mix

Marketing is the sum of a great many activities—a thrust of the several marketing tools working together to accomplish specific marketing objectives.

It's not advertising alone that works, nor direct mail, nor public relations. Rather, it's a mixture of all tools, working in a balanced relationship.

In marketing professional services, the challenge is compounded by the very nature of professional services. Advertising doesn't sell professional services, nor does public relations, nor brochures, nor any other tool.

An ad may sell a product, but only an individual can sell a professional service. And it's usually the individual who is capable of performing that service.

An intensive advertising campaign can convey some compelling facts about your services, and even generate inquiries. But no ad was ever responsible for a client's signing a contract, without a personal discussion.

A well-conceived direct mail campaign can make your prospective clients aware of your ability to address a particular problem, but the client will not call you and say "Start tomorrow" without meeting with you, and assuring himself that you really can help him with his specific problems. Nor will any brochure, nor article, nor press release bring you clients. They will only educate your prospective clientele about you and your capabilities, and perhaps lead to direct inquiries. They will convey a great deal of information, leaving you free, in your personal contact, to focus on how your capabilities address his particular problem.

Yet, these tools of marketing are essential to a marketing program—to helping you meet your own objectives.

What role, then, do the tools of marketing play?

They serve to establish a context in which selling can be enhanced. They build reputation and focus a perception of a firm. They develop leads. They pre-sell. They educate the prospective client.

But only the professional who performs the service can actually close the sale.

If your marketing efforts were limited solely to selling, then the limits of your efforts would be the number of people you could reach in person, and then could persuade that you can address their problems more effectively than can any of your competitors. Assuming that you had sufficient contacts to meet a large number of prospective clients, you would be starting from scratch in explaining who you are, what you do, why you do it better, and so forth.

An effective marketing program, using the tools of marketing appropriately, does all that for you on a large scale. Then, when you meet the prospective client that's been produced by the campaign, you don't come as a stranger.

To accomplish this, it's important to know what each of the tools are, how each works, and how to use them, in balance—in a proper mix—to reinforce one another.

Each performs a different role, and each takes on a different quality when used in conjunction with others. Nor are they interchangeable. Advertising will not do what public relations will do, nor is public relations "free advertising". Direct mail will not do what display advertising does, nor is a brochure a substitute for an article about you in a professional journal.

Each of the marketing tools will be discussed in a separate chapter, but for perspective, an overview is useful.

ADVERTISING

Advertising is a practice and discipline that uses space or air time you purchase in media—print, broadcast, or any other of a number of possibilities—to deliver a message. An ad in a newspaper or magazine, or a message on a pencil or a calendar, or a radio or television commercial, in which the space or time has been paid for and the message supplied by the purchaser, is advertising.

If you've paid for the space, you can use it for any message you wish, as long as it doesn't violate basic laws concerning flagrant misrepresentation, or violate professional canons of ethics.

The major roles of advertising are to persuade and to inform. To be effective, advertising must engender in the reader or listener a desire to do business with you. If it informs, it should do so in a way that fosters a feeling of good will, and even enthusiasm, for what you have to offer. It should persuade the prospective client that you understand and are capable of solving his problem.

Each of the media used in advertising has a different purpose and value, and makes a different contribution to the marketing mix.

Institutional and Display Advertising. Display (or promotional) advertising is what is usually referred to in the general context of advertising. It is the display ad (other than that which appears in the classified advertising section of a newspaper) that takes a fraction of a page or more to deliver the sponsor's selling message. It is, in a sense, a description of a product or service and an offer of that product or service for sale.

When advertising space is used to go beyond selling a service—to promote a firm without selling a specific service—it's called *institutional advertising.* When a major accounting firm buys a full page in *Fortune* or *Business Week* to discuss its attitude toward government regulation, that's institutional advertising.

When IBM takes an ad to say that communications is good for America, and that IBM is a great company in the communications business, that's institutional advertising, too. When they buy space to say that IBM makes the best personal computers, that's display advertising.

There's not so fine a line to be drawn between display and institutional advertising in professional services as there is in product advertising. The professional firm that uses display advertising to discuss its qualifications and strengths is never just talking about a service it delivers—it is discussing the firm itself, which is a crucial element of institutional advertising.

Thus the differences between advertising a service and advertising a product substantially intrude upon the advertising process in a way that has rarely existed before.

Which is not to say that advertising doesn't play a significant role in service marketing. When used properly, and when key issues of structure, position and copy are addressed, its role is significant, no matter how large or small the firm.

Broadcast Media. Broadcast media—radio and television (including cable)—are rapidly coming into their own in professional service advertising. At first little used by professionals after the change in the canons of ethics (they were considered too blatant), more and more professionals are learning to use it tastefully, ethically and effectively.

Broadcast advertising has a very different quality than does print advertising. A reader may choose to overlook or not read a print ad; the listener or viewer has considerably less opportunity to overlook the broadcast ad. True, many people use the commercial as a time to get a fresh drink, but more people don't. One doesn't turn the radio off during a radio commercial.

Credibility and effectiveness in the print ad are a function of the degree of talent of a copywriter. In the broadcast media, that talent is tempered by the ability of the announcer and the effectiveness of the production. The announcer functions as a live and presumably persuasive salesman, whereas in print the copy must speak for itself. The television commercial has the advantage of motion, visualization and frequently, dramatization.

On the other hand, print media has a staying power not inherent in broadcasting. The broadcast message flees with time. The reader who is interested in any aspect of the print ad can peruse and study it at a leisurely pace. It can even be clipped and saved for future reference.

And so even in advertising, there is a difference in values by media, and therefore a difference in impact.

Direct Mail. Direct mail is the form of advertising that has the distinct advantage of bringing the message directly to the individual prospect. In all other forms of advertising, a measure of the advertising dollar is wasted because you pay for readership that includes nonprospects for your service as well as prospects. In direct mail, you have the opportunity to define a universe of prospects—those with characteristics most likely to be amenable to your services—and to write to them directly.

Used correctly, direct mail can be one of the most powerful vehicles for marketing professional services. It allows you to personalize your message, to aim it directly to your prospect, and to to talk to more people as individuals than you can possibly meet directly, in person or by phone.

Direct mail is also a vehicle. It can be simply a personalized letter, or it can carry a brochure, a reprint of an article, a case history, or even a reprint of a print ad.

It's crucial to realize, however, that the limits of all service advertising apply as well to direct mail. The effectiveness of a direct mail letter that sells a product can be measured by the number of order forms that are returned. Rarely can the effectiveness of a mailing for a service be measured in the same way. Its purpose, in marketing professional services, is to inform and to persuade and, in some circumstances, to invite inquiries. But like any other form of advertising for professional services, it cannot be expected to close a sale.

Because it goes directly to an individual whom you've identified as a prospective client, direct mail offers the potential for the best return on investment of all advertising media.

Classified Advertising. Classified advertising is advertising in space specially designated by category, such as *HELP WANTED*, or merchandise or services for sale. It's most frequently used by professional firms to advertise for staff. It's sometimes useful, however, to project facts about a firm to a target audience. For example, a display ad in the classified section of a publication, seeking tax accountants for hire, can be used to describe the virtues of the firm. This is useful for enhancing a reputation within the firm's profession.

Other Advertising Media. Any medium that can carry your message to a large and defined audience is valid to consider for advertising. There are circumstances, for example, under which billboards can be effective, and in fact, legal and medical clinics are using them now. They can be used tastefully and ethically, and can be cost effective. Pencils and premiums, as distant an advertising media as they may seem in view of the traditions of professional marketing, are still valid media, and any dentist who doesn't give his patients toothbrushes with his name on them is losing an opportunity. Transportation advertising has its uses as well.

The point is that no medium should be overlooked, simply because it has never been used before. Professional advertising has a short history, no tradition, and a future to be determined only by the imagination of marketers.

PUBLIC RELATIONS

The term "public relations" is a broad one, encompassing a great many activities. Publicity, the actual function of developing editorial coverage, is a part of public relations, but by no means the entire public relations function.

Literally, of course, the term means relations with the public—everything you do in dealing with the public. In fact, it's a group of activities designed to enhance the way people think about your firm and know about you. Public relations is the broader technique of creating a firm worthy of being publicized, and developing activities that are newsworthy. Inherent in public relations, as well, are all aspects of your public persona, from the way your phone is answered to your letterhead, to the way your office is decorated—all of which contribute to your reputation and the way in which you are perceived as a professional.

Public relations, and particularly the publicity aspect of it, uses the editorial media to reach its audiences. This can be accomplished by direct contact with the media, or by developing newsworthy devices (seminars, speeches, etc.) that have an inherent news value.

The basic technique of publicity is to cast the story you want to tell in ways that are newsworthy, and then to persuade the editors that the story is of sufficient interest to a broad range of readers. Successful publicity has the advantage of an implied editorial endorsement, because it's assumed that an independent and objective publication has chosen to publish it. It has the disadvantage of lacking control over the way the message appears, as we control the message in advertising. In publicity, we merely propose, others—the editors—dispose.

Publicity, cast as news or information, has no selling power, except under the most serendipitous circumstances.

It's value, however, is immeasurable in terms of its ability to inform, to build reputation, and to enhance credibility. A tax expert who's constantly quoted authoritatively in the business pages develops a reputation that substantially enhances any selling effort. A doctor with an unusual specialty makes that fact known by being interviewed and quoted frequently. An accounting firm or law firm whose partners are constantly quoted in a context of expertise quickly becomes known by name, and recognized as a source of that expertise.

Unique to the public relations aspect of professional services is the fact that the product is the individual who performs the service. Your firm is represented by every individual, from the senior partner to the lowest ranking associate, who deals with your clientele. Many a client has been lost because a very junior associate has behaved in some deleterious way.

PRINTED MATERIAL

Material such as brochures and newsletters are standard fare in professional services, and they are a crucial tool of marketing. Unfortunately, they are too frequently used ineffectively. And, as sometimes happens with direct mail, they are too often distributed without a clear view of the recipient. They are too often used as a sole marketing tool.

Printed material is an important part of the marketing mix, but again, only if used in conjunction with other tools.

THE PRACTICE DEVELOPMENT TOOLS

The traditional practice development tools still have an important place in marketing. Networking, joining organizations, the golf club, seminars, speeches, memos to clients that find their way to non-clients—all are integral to the marketing process.

And even though contemporary marketing brings something of a science to those techniques that professionals have instinctively used for so long, these techniques still rely upon the individual practitioner. The professional marketer may program the organizational memberships, or design the seminar, but the professional practitioner has to join the club and participate on the seminar panel.

The traditional practice development tools have always worked very well for those who used them assiduously. They work even better in conjunction with the new tools of marketing.

SALESMANSHIP

In marketing professional services, no marketing tool actually brings in the client except the selling skills of an individual. All of the other tools may develop reputation and create a desire to do business with you, and even produce inquiries about your service. But only an individual can close the sale.

Other tools enhance the sales effort, and even generate, through reprints, etc., sales aids. But in the final analysis, the personal contact must be made, the presentation, either written or oral, must be made, and the client must be persuaded to sign a contract.

It's important, then, to hone selling skills, and to plan the selling effort.

THE MARKETING MIX

In using the tools of marketing, there are several key points that should be kept in mind.

- All marketing tools should be used against a context of the marketing objectives. The best advertising, the most incisive direct mail campaign, are of nothing if they don't further the marketing objectives.
- There is no such thing as a bad ad or a good ad, or a good or bad public relations program. Judgment of each tool's value is always in terms of the degree to which it addresses the marketing objectives.
- The tools themselves are not of the essence—it is the mix that counts. Each has its purpose and its role in the marketing program, and each supports and contributes to the other.
- In choosing the marketing mix, effectiveness is important, but so too is cost-effectiveness. If there is a poor return on investment, in terms of meeting the objectives, then the program is ineffective, no matter how low the cost. Marketing works not by throwing dollars at the problem, but by using skill and thoughtfulness.

Keeping in mind the role that each of the marketing tools plays—the task it performs—the marketing mix is designed to use each tool and technique to support and reinforce the others.

Public relations, for example, builds the reputation, advertising backs the reputation with a selling message for the firm and its capabilities, practice development tools (including printed material and brochures) support the reputation for expertise, direct mail focuses on the prospect and opens the door. All have worked together to build a context that makes it infinitely easier to generate prospects, and against which to sell the prospect.

The degree to which each tool is used in the marketing mix is a function of several factors, all of which are flexible:

- Marketing objectives. I `ast growth is an objective, then all stops come out, with full-scale advertising, public relations, etc.. If the objective is simply to build name recognition, then public relations will do it faster and cheaper than advertising.
- Budget. Full page ads are very nice, but cost a lot of money. If you're not prepared to invest a large budget, rely more heavily on the less expensive tools.
- Accessibility to the skill or professionals who have the skill. If you can't afford to hire a top notch ad agency or public relations firm, don't settle for less than the best. Scale your program to the limits of the skill. If the talent is available in-house, use it to its limits, but not beyond. Having written for the college paper is a slender experience to bankroll as a copywriter for full page newspaper ads, even for a senior partner.
- Firm objectives. If firm objectives call for moderate growth, that hardly warrants large scale investment in expensive media blitzes. If firm objectives call for increasing share of market, then the choice of marketing tools is made accordingly.

Nor is exposure for exposure's sake particularly valuable. The objective, remember, is to serve the needs of the practice, not to build random and irrelevant reputation.

Time frame is also an important consideration. Any marketing program, particularly one embarked upon for the first time, requires time for penetration. The marketplace is noisy, and it takes a great deal of effort to be heard and recognized. But within a given time frame, there has to be careful monitoring, to be sure that if something isn't working, it's clear to you whether the fault is in the tool itself, or your expectations for it.

Expectations are, after all, key to monitoring a marketing program. Assuming a soundly conceived program, with realistic objectives, there should also be realistic expectations for each facet of the effort. If you execute a superbly crafted direct mail campaign, and expect more from it than it is capable of producing, then you are going to be frustrated with even the best results.

The answer, of course, lies in understanding each tool and how it works, and how it contributed to the marketing mix. And that is what the following chapters are about.

SUMMARY

Marketing is the sum of efforts of many marketing tools, working in concert. No one tool will serve the entire marketing program. Advertising will will inform and persuade; public relations will build and enhance reputation; direct mail will aim specifically at target markets with a direct appeal—but all serve only as a context for final sale, which must be made by an individual.

Each marketing tool is different from the others. Advertising uses purchased space and time to deliver your message. Public relations uses publicity—generating and reporting newsworthy or informative activities through the editorial pages to project skills—and sound business practices to engender a favorable attitude. Direct mail is a vehicle to use letters and other printed material to direct a selling message to individuals on a large scale. Traditional practice development techniques—joining organizations, giving speeches and seminars, using brochures and newsletters—still work, but work better in conjunction with other marketing techniques.

The marketing mix—the choice and balance of tools used in an individual marketing campaign—is a function of understanding the uses and values of each tool, and:

• The marketing objectives
• The budget
• The firm's objectives

- The time frame
- The expectations for the program, which must be realistic, in terms of objectives and the limitations of each marketing tool.

PART II
Advertising

CHAPTER 5

What Advertising Is

When the canons of ethics were changed, after so many generations of not being allowed to advertise, professionals walked around this new marketing tool as if it were a whale that had beached on the shores of Lake Michigan.

Everyone knows what product advertising is, of course—we see it all the time. But at the beginning, nobody knew what it was in terms of professional services, nor how it would work. And most significantly, nobody seemed to know what advertising could be expected to do for a professional service.

Even the advertising people were wary. Good advertising produces sales, and sales (over a period of time) are measurable in relation to the advertising dollars spent. The success of an ad announcing the availability of a product is easily measured by the volume of the products sold. The success of a campaign for a new product is measurable by sales, and perhaps by the share of the market it captures.

But will "X" dollars in advertising produce "X" dollars in revenue from new clients? Unfortunately, there was no experience to supply the answer. And so the first advertising for professionals was all test and conjecture.

Other problems surfaced. The changes in the canons of ethics allowed advertising, but still let stand prohibitions against the kinds of claims that are standard in product and nonprofessional service advertising. An accounting firm still can't say, "We balance books better"; a law firm can't say, "We do better divorces"; a medical clinic can't say, "We cure illness faster." Under the professional codes of some states, accountants may not use slogans in their advertising. Almost universally, professional ethical codes preclude any claims of superior ability to perform the professional tasks.

But if you can't use advertising to distinguish your firm's services from those of a competitor, or make the kinds of claims that persuade buyers, what, then, is the role of advertising in professional services?

Slowly, and after spending many thousands of dollars, professional marketers began to feel that the ability to advertise was less of a marketing advantage than they had at first thought. Moreover, it became clear that the techniques of advertising that had been so successful in selling products didn't quite work in the same way for professional services.

PRODUCT VS. SERVICE ADVERTISING

Where is the difference?

By definition, advertising is the marketing tool that uses purchased space (or time) to deliver a specific and focused message. It has the advantage of allowing us to say precisely what we want to say to a generally defined audience. It has the disadvantage of a credibility that's limited by the fact that readers understand that it's our space, our dollar, and our subjective claim, and the liability of competition for attention in a clutter of other advertising.

The traditional techniques of advertising that continue to be effective, are, for the most part, those that dictate good rules of copy, layout, media, frequency, and so forth. In that respect, a good ad is still a good ad.

But the differences between the old and the new are even more significant than are the similarities.

There is still the problem of how to distinguish one firm from another, when all firms in the same profession perform the same services, and where the distinctions between firms reside primarily in the ability of individuals who perform those services. All auditing firms do audits under the same basic principals. Under very few circumstances are there distinctions in the audit process that can be projected, one firm from another, in an advertising statement that's acceptable under the canons of ethics. Adjectives that are at the heart of most advertising—*better . . . stronger . . . creamier . . . healthier*—have no currency in advertising professional services.

An ad selling bicycles may be said to be effective if the number of bicycles sold increases substantially as a result of the advertising, But no one ever hired an accountant or a lawyer from an ad. Professional services, as we've seen, must be sold by individuals. And so, even the measure of ad effectiveness is different.

There are other problems.

You can sell a diamond ring with a picture of the ring, but how do you photograph a professional service? And in firms with offices in several cities, national advertising is too often precluded because the firm's capabilities differ from one city to another.

Advertising for professional services, then, has had to start, in many ways, from the beginning. It has had to develop an entirely new body of skills built upon elements of old and tested skills.

Of all the differences between the old and the new, the toughest problem in advertising professional services is to find a way to advertise distinctions between firms in the same profession. Too often the restrictions that remain in professional advertising generate situations in which what can be said for one firm can be said for any other in the same profession. One need only change the name of the firm, and not the message, and truth would not suffer. This puts a burden on all parts of marketing, since advertising will not carry the same weight as it does in product advertising.

Some approaches are beginning to emerge, and will be dealt with in the next chapter.

WHY ADVERTISE?

With all these distinctions and restrictions; with all these obstacles, professional services advertising continues to proliferate. It's taken almost a decade since the change in the canons of ethics for the reticence to diminish, but diminish it has. Tentatively at first, and then eagerly, accountants, lawyers, dentists, doctors, architects, consultants and others move forward to advertise their services.

What they're saying, in a sense, is that they have faith that advertising contributes something to the growth of their practice. They may not know what works—nor do their agencies. They may not know why it works. But they know it contributes something.

In this, advertisers are not wrong. It does indeed contribute something to marketing. Sometimes more, sometimes less.

THE ROLE IN THE MARKETING MIX

Despite all of these strictures and obstacles, advertising has an important role in the marketing mix:

- It helps to establish a professional presence
- It clearly delineates a firm's attitude toward the way its services are delivered
- It helps increase market penetration
- It enhances and supports a position in the market
- It helps define and project specific marketing objectives, based on a realistic perception of your firm and its services.
- It affords the opportunity to be persuasive, even within the limited context of professional advertising
- It can focus on a problem, and define how your service can help to resolve that problem for a prospective client
- It reinforces, and is reinforced by, the sound public relations program designed to build and enhance reputation, to inform, and to focus an accurate perception of your firm and its services.

Most of all, it functions well in conjunction with all other marketing efforts, such as public relations, direct mail and personal selling. It builds a foundation that can enhance the more active marketing functions.

With direct mail as a door opener, advertising serves as a pre-selling device; it sells your firm, so that you are free to sell your services.

And in the cold call, it helps take the chill off of ignorance about who you are and what you can do.

In the broader campaign, then, advertising's role in the marketing mix is consequential.

WHAT ADVERTISING CAN DO

What, then, can you expect advertising to accomplish? At least the following:

- To spread word of your existence, and to broadcast the name of your firm and the nature of the services you perform.
- To convey a favorable impression of the kind and quality of your services, and the way in which you perform those services.
- To develop a need for your firm's services by appealing to either the intellect or the emotions.
- To build a favorable context in which you can use other marketing devices and methods to urge and inspire people to take action in retaining your services.
- To announce or define a specific service you perform within the context of your profession.
- To strengthen internal pride and morale, by demonstrating to staff a visible, concerted effort to project the firm and its strengths to the public

Advertising, then, has three major purposes:

- To inform, and to reinforce that information
- To create an umbrella of favorable attitude toward you and your firm
- To either generate action, or to allow for a more favorable context in which other action may comfortably take place

WHAT ADVERTISING CAN'T DO

To understand its effectiveness, it's equally important to know what advertising can't do. For example:

- It can't supply complete objectivity or credibility. It's your space or time and your message, and readers know it. Readers also know that because you say something doesn't necessarily make it and so, and so all ads are read with a measure of skepticism.
- Not everyone who reads your ad is in the mood to be persuaded by its most logical or emotional appeals at any given moment.

- Advertising, with the exception of direct mail, can never limit itself to precisely the audience you want, and so a measure of it—and a measure of its cost—is always wasted. You may safely assume that by advertising in a journal for naval engineers, your ad will be read by people who are primarily naval engineers. But not all of them are in a position to buy nor to influence buying decisions. Under the best of circumstances, there is a great deal of slippage in reaching an audience, and certainly in the cost of reaching that audience.
- No ad can work entirely on its own and out of the context of a larger program. No matter how startling, exciting, new or valuable the service you offer in your ad, each ad fights other ads and editorial copy for attention, credibility and persuasiveness. The degree to which any advertising works is in proportion to a larger marketing effort.
- No ad can close a sale for you, particularly in professional services. An ad that offers a product can effectively sell products, and that effectiveness can be measured by counting products it sells. Clients of a professional service, on the other hand, rarely respond that way to an ad. The best that can happen is that an ad inspires your prospective client to inquire further of you, or even to send for a descriptive brochure, but that's not the same thing as making a sale or signing a contract.

If you have no total marketing program, of which advertising is just one part, and if your objectives in advertising are not clear, then you're not ready to advertise.

And if you can't back up the promise of your ad, in terms of delivering the service, or following up to sell what you're advertising, then advertising is not for you.

But if your advertising is correctly perceived, and conceived, and properly executed, it's an effective marketing tool.

Within the context of advertising there are several different categories that are distinctive. Each is different from the others, and each has its place in the total marketing mix.

CATEGORIES OF ADVERTISING

Essentially, advertising breaks down into several major categories:

Institutional advertising, sometimes (unfortunately) called "image advertising", is advertising designed solely to enhance the reputation of a firm without focusing on any specific service it performs. For example, a law firm ad shows a picture of the scales of justice. The headline and copy simply say that in an unjust world you need a good law firm to help you be treated justly, and that this is a good law firm. This is institutional advertising. It's not trying to sell or promote any specific service or capability. Rather, the firm is attempting to generate good will through its broader message . . . to project an "image" of itself.

In a sense, all good advertising—and most marketing activities—should have at least institutional overtones, in that no matter how specific the service described, the general feeling should be favorable towards the advertiser—the institution that's sponsoring the ad.

Institutional advertising for professional services can be useful, but has some very strong potential for danger. It's too easy to expect too much of it; to expect that the favorable impression it means to convey translates readily into new business. In this context, it tends not to accomplish very much. It can certainly be a poor investment if it's used for the wrong reasons, such as supporting the ego of the partnership, or for simple name recognition. If building name recognition is its sole objective, there are more effective and less expensive ways to do it (public relations, for example.) Moreover, the staying power of reputation built in this way is highly questionable. Generally, the staying power of institutional advertising is minimal if it's not sustained over a very long period of time, and supported by the facts and other marketing efforts.

Nevertheless, institutional advertising may have its place in a very large campaign in which it is one of a great many elements, and in which cost is not of deep concern. Still, if the same dollar can be used to promote a specific capability, then it becomes very difficult to draw the line between institutional advertising and the ego of the partnership.

No form of advertising is without a possible place in the marketing program. But to find a place for institutional advertising too often requires a long, long stretch.

Service advertising is display or promotional advertising in which a particular service or capability is described in a selling context. These are highly focused ads that describe a particular service to a clearly defined audience. This is the kind of advertising that would be used by the consultant who specializes in computerizing an office, or the accountant who specializes in'addressing the problems of emerging business, to sell these services.

In fact, it's the peculiar nature of professional services advertising that the ad limited to one particular service appears to have greater impact than the broad-based ad that attempts to sell many services at one time. For example, an accounting firm may have a broad spectrum of capabilities, but its advertising is more likely to be effective if each ad in a specific campaign addresses only one such service, such as tax preparation, or estate planning, or offers the solution to only one kind of problem to be solved by these services.

The reason this is so seems to reside in the fact that by the very nature of professionalism there is a paradox. All professionals do the same things on a broad scale with very little room for deviation. All audits, for example, conform to generally accepted accounting principals; all tax returns are filed under the same tax code; and so forth. The paradox is that the differences from one professional to another in the same profession elude distinctions that can be articulated. When a number of services are lumped in one ad, the focus on abilities becomes to broad, losing both credibility and selling power. There are approaches to resolving the paradox as we shall see, but the paradox remains.

Direct mail, in which letters (with or without enclosures) are sent directly to a carefully predetermined list of prospective clients, to sell a service. It's a particularly effective form of advertising in professional services because it is so precisely and directly delivers a specific message to a carefully defined audience. It can address a specific problem, and it can be used as a door opener to develop the opportunity to sell a prospective client personally. Like other forms of service advertising, however, and unlike product direct mail, it cannot be expected to produce clients by return mail.

Tombstone ads are the simple, straightforward announcements, originally used by brokerage firms to offer new issues of securities for sale. Eventually, they came to be used by all professional firms to announce major personnel changes, such as new partners, a significant event such as a merger (or the firm's role in a merger between two clients), an acquisition, or a new office. It may be simply a calling card (a simple ad that states only name, address and profession) to establish your name and presence.

While the tombstone may seem to be mundane and routine, it nevertheless has a place in the marketing mix simply because it's one more technique that supplies visibility and an impression to be conveyed to your perspective clientele.

Classified advertising. For many years, both here and abroad, when other advertising was prohibited, classified "Help Wanted" advertising was used as a frank marketing tool. A display ad in the "Help Wanted" section that was ostensibly placed to recruit personnel served as a marvelous vehicle for describing the features and benefits of a firm. Until very recently, when the rules prohibiting advertising changed in Great Britain, it was considered a primary form of advertising for both the accounting and legal professions. It was assumed that prospective clients read those sections, as did prospective employees.

Yellow Page advertising is yet another form of advertising that will undoubtedly grow in acceptance by professionals. The small, tasteful display ad in the Yellow Pages can be both ethical and effective, even though it must be devoid of the kind of selling message used for products.

It should be remembered that Yellow Page advertising has a life of a full year between issues of the directory, so that anything that's said in the Yellow Page ad must apply at least until the next issue.

Because Yellow Page ads are usually small, considerable skill must be used to get a logo or effective message into the limited space. Layout, use of logo, and type selection are all important, and it must be remembered that your ad competes with others in the same profession on the same page.

In larger cities you may want to consider advertising, or at least being listed, in several different categories. For example an accounting firm can be listed under *Accounting, Consulting,* and *Tax Services.*

Broadcast Advertising

Radio and Television—the broadcast media—are an entirely different advertising structure.

As in print media, the audience is definable. You need only look, for example, at the successful use of radio and television by the major computer and business machines manufacturers to know that radio can reach a business audience. Several of the law clinics throughout the country are already using broadcast media successfully. Tax preparers are experienced broadcast advertisers.

Obviously, then, broadcast advertising generally has its values as part of the marketing mix. It's useful to:

• Build reputation and to penetrate deeply into a market.
• Sell a specific service.
• Expand a market by reaching new people, or to move into a new market position.
• Visualize a concept through television.
• Dramatize a concept.

As part of a larger marketing and advertising program, broadcast advertising should work well for all professional services if it's used with the following in mind:

• As in all advertising, it should have a specific theme and be part of an overall program.
• Its objectives should be understood. For example, a print ad can tell a complicated story about your service because if the reader can be made to become absorbed in the ad, he or she will take the time to read it. A broadcast message is fleeting, and will be lost on the listener if the message is too complicated.
• The value of repetition in the broadcast media, particularly in radio, can be extensive in building name, reputation and recognition.
• Even though the primary advantage of television is to demonstrate, and it's difficult to demonstrate service, television can be effective. Henry Bloch successfully appears on television on behalf of his own company, H & R Block, to sell tax services. As the head of his own company, he projects a quality of credibility—his personal reputation is on the line. And as a result of repetition and ubiquitous appearance, Bloch is himself a celebrity, and commands attention.

Each of the broadcast media has some rather distinctive advantages of its own.

For example, in television:

• Television reaches more households in any given moment than does any other medium. About 80% of all adults are believed to see television at some time during the day and 95% during the average week.

- The diversity of television programming makes it possible to pinpoint a market somewhat more specifically than in newspapers. Programs are aimed quite specifically at defined audiences, as are magazines. Newspapers are aimed at a more broadly defined audience.
- Television is extensively and carefully researched, which means that a great deal is known about the target audience.
- Television has presence. It can demonstrate, it can illustrate in a way that no other medium can.
- Television rivets attention. When your commercial is on it's not competing against editorial matter or other commercials for attention.

Radio, as well, has its advantages and disadvantages. For example:

- It tends to be a more intimate medium, in that the announcer appears to be talking to the listener as an individual.
- As in television, although to a lesser degree, there is focus. While your commercial is being read or played, there is no competition with other commercials or editorial. It is, however, less riveting than television, and listeners can be doing other things, such as driving, at the same time.
- Radio programming tends to be more clearly delineated and focused on particular markets. Thus, you can choose the kind of audience you want through the programming (radio news, classical music, popular music, talk shows, and so forth).
- As a media buy, radio is the most flexible of all the media. You can buy a single spot or a series covering any period of time. You can move in and out of radio as your needs require.
- Radio production is relatively inexpensive and can be as simple (a single sheet of paper with a 30 second spot announcement to be read by an announcer) or as complex (an elaborate dramatization) as you want. It's a convincing medium that reaches a lot of people at very low cost.

And of course there are disadvantages as well in the broadcast media. In actual outlay of dollars, television is usually the most expensive of all media (although it may be more cost efficient in terms of viewers reached and impact). All broadcast media is limited by time constraints. Local television, and sometimes local radio, can sometimes be subject to clutter—a lot of commercials back to back.

Radio is limited by its reliance upon the spoken word for visualization. It can be heard but not seen. And while you can buy one or two spots, the repetition needed for impact requires many more.

But in the final analysis, more and more professional services are turning to radio and television, for its very specific advertising advantages.

There are, of course, other forms of advertising, such as billboards and calling card ads. But these forms of advertising will be spoken of in another context.

THE ELEMENTS OF AN AD

Producing a good ad, in any medium, is a combination of skill and art. There are indeed some basic rules. But as successful abstract painting frequently succeeds because of the ways in which it deviates from the rules, so does successful advertising succeed in altering rules through flair and imagination. Originality opens new paths and accomplishes new success.

Nevertheless, there are basic elements that are part of all good advertising, and that tend to produce good ads:

- *The objective.* A favorite game in any profession is to look at the ads of other firms in your profession and to find fault with them. The problem with that is that we rarely know the objectives of a campaign. If the objectives are clearly stated, and the ad is written to those objectives, then the judgment of the efficacy of the ad must be made not on its aesthetics, but in terms of the objectives.
- *Theme.* An ad must say something. Its story line, no matter how many or how few words are used, must go someplace very specific. The theme of an ad is its basic line of attack. No matter what kind of ad, in any medium, it should be consistent in all its elements In developing a theme, the basic question used to test an ad is "What do I want the reader to know or to feel after reading (or hearing) this

ad?'' If that question can be answered clearly, and the ad is responsive to the answer, then it is more likely to be successful.

An ad with no theme, on the other hand, tends to become diffuse, and fails to make its point. It lacks unity and won't hold a reader's attention, much less serve any marketing objectives.

- *The headline*. The purpose of a headline (in print ads) is to capture the reader's attention by saying something meaningful or startling. The headline must be relevant to the rest of the ad—to its theme and text. Merely to capture someone's attention and then not follow through with a consistent selling message destroys the value of the ad.
- *Copy*. The copy is the text of the ad and usually contains the selling message. Copy, as everybody knows, should be simple, terse, clear, concise and credible. It should say as much as possible in as few words as possible. But that's as far as the rules go. Any copy that captures the reader's attention and imagination, and moves the reader in ways that fulfill the objective of the ad, is great copy no matter how it's written.
- *The layout* is the position of the various elements within the print ad. The way the elements are laid out should attract the reader, be appealing, and contribute to the reader's becoming absorbed in the ad's message No matter how little copy or illustration you put in an ad, the words or the picture still have to be carefully sized to fit the space, the typeface must be selected, and it must all be laid out effectively in a defined space. A well-designed ad is easy to read, focuses the reader's eye where you want it, is easy to digest and to understand, and from a reader's point of view makes the whole process of dealing with an ad painless and even enjoyable. A poorly designed ad, on the other hand, with the wrong typeface, or an illustration that overwhelms the copy, can be a disaster, destroying the effectiveness of what might otherwise be superb.
- *Logo and Identification*. While it seems obvious that the firm name and address should be present, there is a clear advantage in using a logo to build a visible and readily identifiable identity for your firm. A logo (short for *logotype*) is a design factor that may use any of several design elements, including a distinctive typeface.
- *Media*. Media are the vehicles in which the ad is placed—newspapers, magazines, radio, television, billboards, etc.. Media should be

appropriate to the prospective clientele As you will see in Chapter 8, selecting media in which to place ads is a highly refined technique. It's important to note here, however, that an ad should at least be designed to keep a medium's audience in mind. Nothing is sillier than seeing an ad written for one audience appear in a publication clearly subscribed to by a very different audience.

- *Placement.* While it's not always possible to indicate where in a publication your ad will appear, to the extent that it is it should be considered. If you're practicing sports medicine, you may want an ad to appear in the sports section. If you're practicing corporate law, the sports section may be precisely where you don't want your ad. In broadcast advertising, placement is a function of where in a program your ad fits.
- *Production* is the physical preparation of the ad. It should be meticulous and professional.

The success of any ad campaign is more than the clever headline or the catchy illustration. It is, rather, the sum total of the effectiveness of all of these elements.

But most significantly the effectiveness of any advertising depends upon its ability to fit consistently into the total marketing program, and to carry its weight as an element of that program.

SUMMARY

Advertising is the marketing tool that uses purchased space or time to deliver a message to the consumer that informs and persuades, to help sell the service.

- It allows us to say what we want to say, but . . .
- It lacks full credibility because the reader knows that space is purchased.

There are profound differences between advertising a product and advertising a service, which affect the techniques of advertising a service. The differences include:

- Difficulty in distinguishing one firm from another, because ethical codes still prohibit touting skills as superior to those of other professionals.

- Personal and intangible nature of professional services means nobody buys the service from an ad; it must be sold by an individual.
- A service cannot be illustrated, as a product might be.
- In multi-office firms, national advertising tends to be precluded because all services not universally offered—or purchased—in all offices.

Still, advertising has strong role in the marketing mix:

- Helps establish professional presence
- Describes a firm's attitude toward how it delivers its service
- Helps increase market penetration
- Supports market position
- Helps define and project marketing objectives
- Affords opportunity to be persuasive
- Can focus on a problem, and offer a solution, to prospective client
- Works well with other marketing efforts

Advertising can:

- Broadcast your name and nature of services
- Convey a favorable impression of your firm and your services
- Appeal to intellect or emotions to develop a need for your services
- Build a favorable context to sell
- Announce or define a specific service
- Strengthen morale

Advertising has three major purposes:

- To inform
- To create favorable attitude
- To generate action or context for action, such as purchasing your service

Advertising can't:

- Supply objectivity or credibility
- Work on its own, with larger marketing program
- Close a sale

Categories of advertising are:

- Institutional (or "image") ads
- Service (display or promotional) ads
- Direct mail
- Tombstone ads
- Classified ads
- Yellow pages
- Broadcast (radio and television)

Broadcast advertising's role is to:

- Build reputation and penetrate a market
- Sell a specific service
- Expand a market
- Visualize a concept (television)
- Dramatize a concept

Television's advantages are:

- Broad market reach
- Programming diversity helps focus target market
- Markets usually carefully researched
- Can demonstrate and illustrate
- Rivets attention

Radio's advantages are:

- More intimate medium
- No immediate competition with other ads
- Most flexible media buy
- Programming sharply focused on target audiences
- Production can be inexpensive

The elements of an ad are:

- The objective
- Theme
- Copy
- Layout
- Media
- Production

CHAPTER 6

Advertising Strategy

Because we are just now beginning to understand advertising's role in the marketing mix, the opportunities to let imagination soar are vast, and the prospect of finding new pathways is exciting.

And not excluded from this experimentation is the drive to explore the limits of professionalism, and how the public will accept these new limits.

When the first major accounting firms began to think of advertising, they were concerned that their clients might have reservations, or take a dim view of it. As it turned out, these fears have been unwarranted to a large degree. The client companies, after all, had been advertising for years. What was the big deal? Nor were there any complaints that advertising costs were increasing fees. Most client companies were too sophisticated for that. The professionals, its seems, in their anxiety at doing something new, were projecting their own inexperienced perceptions of marketing.

Other professions have faced different perceptions, and acted accordingly. Doctors and lawyers, except for the clinics, have encountered some resistance to advertising—some clients and patients seem to feel that it diminishes the sense of professionalism. This may mitigate as experience, fueled by increased competition, erodes public resistance. So far, any change in attitude has been subtle and barely perceptible. Dentists, on the other hand, seem to be thriving on advertising. And consultants as well seem to have found approaches that work.

But as in any pioneering effort, efforts to find an advertising strategy that works have run a broad spectrum. At the one extreme, full page campaigns, using such media as *Fortune* and *Business Week*, attempted to proclaim an accounting firm's concern for the national issues faced by its clients. At the other extreme, the first ads for legal, medical and dental clinics were blatant and blaring, startling and chilling staid traditionalists. At the middle ground, some fine and successful advertising has been produced.

But these problems and negative reactions are at best transitory. They will change as the needs of the marketplace dictate more aggressive marketing, as the prospective clientele gets used to what it sees, as marketers find an appropriate voice.

EFFECTIVE ADVERTISING

What do we know now, however, about what really *works*? Certainly, not as much as we know about product or nonprofessional advertising, but still, much more than we knew a few years ago. And more than enough to begin to use advertising with confidence. The evidence is just beginning to come in, but it's coming in fast.

We know, with certainty, that because advertising can't sell professional services the way it sells products, ads can't work on their own. They must be part of a larger marketing program.

A campaign in which each ad is devoted to describing a service that addresses a particular business or legal problem seems to capture the attention of prospective clients. And if the campaign consists of a series of ads that are integrated, the institutional effect seems to take over in a most positive way. An example is a series of ads in which each ad addresses an aspect of small business management. By the end of the campaign, the consciousness of the prospective clientele is well penetrated, and there is an impression that the firm has an expertise worth listening to.

There are some other basic strategies that have demonstrated a measure of effectiveness:

• Sound basic advertising principles work—or at least, nothing works in their absence. Advertising must still be well-conceived and executed. Objectives must be clearly delineated, campaigns must be well-planned, ads must be well-planned and designed, media must be intelligently chosen.

- It is absolutely crucial that all advertising must be cast in terms of the clients' needs—not the firm's wishes. There is a strong tendency to want to advertise what you want to sell, not what the client wants to buy. And despite the fact that this is a classic advertising theorem, even the most creative advertising agencies still make this mistake (possibly because touting the product on its own merits sometimes works so well in product advertising.) The idea is "This is your problem, and we understand it, and we can solve it." The other way, "We know how to do tax returns," just doesn't seem to make an impression. Of course you know how to do tax returns, or file briefs, or do audits. So does every other accounting and law firm.

- Except in those rare—very rare—instances where institutional advertising is indicated, keep each ad as tightly focused on a single service as possible. With the ethical limits on characterizing the quality of your service, the broader the focus on the services you offer, the more likely the ad is to be diverse, bland and ineffective.

- If you have a multi-office operation you have to be very careful about the services you describe in a national or regional ad. You may be able to perform those services in one office, but not in another, in which case regional or national advertising can be dangerous and potentially counterproductive. Advertising seems to work best, even for a national firm, when the ads are localized. They work even better if there's a clear understanding of the distinct nature of a local community's business practices. In Dallas, for example, research showed that the drive for success, among smaller business, is unique. A successful business person may be an absolute newcomer to the community, but he'll be more readily accepted than an unsuccessful old timer. Knowing this contributed to the success of one firm's ad campaign.

- A strategy that has demonstrated effectiveness in its impact is based on timing. If by offering a service, or defining it in a new way, you can imply that you are the first to offer it. then you have a strong chance to beat the competition. The competition must then face the possibility of being perceived as an imitator or a follower in the marketplace rather than a leader. This is a bit of slight of hand discussed further in the chapter on copywriting.

• Repetition is a crucial element in all advertising. The reader of display advertising is a random reader, and is rarely searching the pages of a newspaper or magazine looking for your ad. Repetition is necessary to ingrain your name and message in his mind. Moreover, advertising for professional services is very often for the future—the casual reader may not be looking for a doctor or a lawyer or a consultant at the time he reads the ad, and so the ad's message must have staying power. The ad must offer the kind of recognition that stays in the mind for that time in the future when the doctor or lawyer or accountant is needed, or when you make direct contact with him in some other context. We know as well that no one absorbs or retains the contents of a single ad. Repetition, then, becomes extremely important, and if it can't be built into an ad campaign, then advertising of any magnitude should not be considered at all.

• Ads compete for attention against other ads. Print ads do not stand alone. They are surrounded by other ads, sometimes for your competition, as well as by editorial matter. Each element of an ad is important. Superb copy in a poor layout or with a badly conceived headline is wasted. A magnificent ad set in unreadable typeface or running in the wrong medium can be a total disaster.

• Slogans, normally a mainstay of product advertising, are either proscribed by local codes or turn out to be irrelevant or ineffective. How to carry through a common thread of identification, then? One successful campaign did it with an unusual layout, which by the second or third ad in the series became readily identifiable with the advertiser.

• The basic media rules still apply. Newspapers do what newspapers do, broadcasting the same, and so forth. The rules of media haven't changed, and each requires its own advertising approach. At the same time, there is no medium that hasn't demonstrated some value for some aspect of professional advertising, including billboards, transportation advertising, and even premiums. All media should be considered in planning a campaign.

• It takes a lot of words to describe a service. And while the fewer words the better, this should not, on the other hand, breed a fear of text. If the ad is addressing a prospective client's problems, and offering him a solution to his problem, large blocks of text will be read and understood.

We know that the call to action must most frequently be supported by an outreach by the professional. Nobody every hired a professional by coupon. In one of the greatest fiascos of contemporary professional services advertising, an overwhelmingly successful ad campaign for a firm resulted in an extraordinary inundation of returned coupons—*not one of which was followed up*. Thousands of dollars in advertising went down the drain, along with the firm's reputation.

Indeed, the impression made by professional service advertising is fragile. This may be because it's so difficult to make the distinction between two firms' ability to perform the same service. Thus, selling efforts must be made while the iron is hot, because the iron cools off quickly. And keeping it hot without striking can be tremendously expensive.

But beyond that, your ads must distinctly recognize the unique nature of professional services marketing, and your creativity (and, of course, that of your agency) must reflect that. Advertising strategy is limited not so much by rules, and certainly not by experience, but rather, by sheer imagination.

WHO DOES IT?

Experience dictates that professionals who are new to advertising, or who feel that their firms are too small to involve outside agencies, should accept the fact that ads should be professionally written. There is simply too large a body of experience in designing advertising, even though not necessarily for professional services, for the inexperienced ad designer or writer to know how to do it instinctively. An amateurish ad for a professional firm is worse than no ad at all.

Successful advertising always looks easier than it really is—and the better the job the more effortless it looks. Just as the professional accountant, doctor or lawyer knows his or her skills, so does the marketing professional.

At the same time, in all advertising there must be a strong collaborative effort between the client and his marketing services.

Professional advertising is so new that you're unlikely to find an agency that's ever worked for a firm like yours (a situation that's rapidly changing.) Here, your constant and patient input is crucial.

And the fact that advertising for professional services is so new too frequently means that even the best advertising professional is not aware of some of the problems in advertising professional services. For example, most advertising professionals are trained to talk about product advantages, which too frequently don't exist on a tangible basis in professional services. Thus, the collaboration between client and agency must be greater than in any other kind of advertising.

In the collaborative effort between the client and the agency, the client's role is clear-cut:

- You must be absolutely open in describing your service to your agency. They must be made to understand, as clearly as possible, what you do, who you do it for, the kinds of problems you address for clients, the kinds of solutions you bring to those problems, the nature of your practice and your overall service concepts
- You must be sure that your agency recognizes and understands the ethical constraints in your profession, including, if applicable, state and local regulations. While the law regarding these ethical constraints is still murky and in many areas untested, it is important that your agency understand that they exist.
- Most professional services are partnerships. To subject your advertising agency to the full force of constant criticism and oversight by all of your partners is to court disaster. Designate one partner, or at most a committee of a few partners, to take the responsibility of dealing with the agency. When it comes to advertising, everybody is an expert and everybody has an opinion. What is most dangerous is that not everybody recognizes the professionalism in marketing and from this springs subversion of good marketing. The ideal solution, of course, is to have a knowledgeable and well-trained marketing professional on staff.

Slowly but surely, there is a new breed of marketing professional emerging. Now few and far between, the tribe is increasing. These specialists are marketers who come to know and understand the nature of their firm's profession, and how to best apply sound marketing principles to professional service marketing.

Not only do these marketing professionals bring great skill to the firms they serve, but they act as translators between the the firm's professionals and the outside agencies. The savings on wear and tear is tremendous. More significantly, the quality of the marketing that results is superior.

ETHICS

Despite the new ability of professionals to advertise, both common law and ethical codes still apply. In some cases the ethical codes are governed by state bodies or professional societies, and should be carefully observed. In all cases overall ethical considerations are extremely important if advertising is not to be counterproductive. The clients of any profession expect ethical behavior of professionals.

Obviously, the overall ethical constraint against lying or misrepresenting applies. There are also a number of laws pertaining to advertising generally, covering such practices as misrepresentation, offering merchandise or service that doesn't exist, or can't be delivered within a reasonable amount of time, and so forth.

But beyond that it would simply be taken amiss to advertise in any way that would be unethical within a profession in other contexts. This might include promising results in areas that are beyond your control—winning a case, curing an illness, even saving money on a tax return. And even if you could deliver on these promises, to make them so subverts professionalism as to strain credibility and to be counterproductive—much less to risk the wrath of professional bodies. The imaginative boundaries allow more than enough room to advertise and market within ethical considerations.

MEASURING RESULTS

There are some technical methods that can be used to judge advertising. For example, surveys can be taken both before and after a campaign to determine such factors as:

- *Name recognition.* How many people knew and recognized your firm's name before and after the ad campaign?
- *Attitude.* What was the perception of your firm before and after the ad campaign?
- *Penetration.* How many people actually saw the ad and remember it?
- *Knowledge of your services.* How many people read and understood the ads and retained an understanding of what it is you have to offer.

Surveys of this kind can and should be taken professionally if the size of the advertising program warrants it. In a smaller campaign, however, simple surveys can be designed with a sample of at least a hundred people to give you a sense of the answers to these questions.

In fact, you'll get plenty of feedback about your advertising—from clients, friends, and even competitors. If the campaign has any impact, positive or negative, you'll hear about it. The information may not be scientific, but it will contribute to your own reaction.

Judging the effectiveness of an ad or an ad campaign is primarily a function of understanding at the outset what you expect that campaign to accomplish and then judging whether that mission has been fulfilled. Presumably, your expectations will have been realistically and clearly delineated. Unrealistic expectations can sing the followup of an otherwise successful campaign, and warp your valid judgment of it.

But ultimately, a successful ad is one that meets its objectives, no matter what they are.

But within that context, a successful ad:

- Will be seen and read, or heard and listened to
- Make its points clearly and quickly, with nothing obscure. Relate and be responsive to the needs of the prospective client who reads it
- Cause or contribute to a change in knowledge, in attitude, in proclivity, no matter how subtle, or to action, if appropriate. But if the reader is totally untouched, unchanged, then the ad is a failure

SUMMARY

Because professional service advertising is so new, we are far from the limits of our knowledge about strategy. Most clients seem to be free of prejudice against professional advertising.

What seems to work best is:

• Sound basic advertising principles
• Ads must be cast in terms of clients'—not advertisers' needs and wishes
• Each ad should address only one service at a time
• Ads should be local, not national, even when firm is national or regional
• Defining service as if you were first to offer it
• Repetition
• Each element of an ad is important and warrants close attention
• Thematic identification can sometimes by accomplished with layout
• Basic media rules still apply, and each has its own approach
• Ads should use as few words as possible, but not too few to tell the story

Advertising strategy is limited by imagination, not rules.

Advertising should be done by professionals, although close liaison with partners is important. A staff professional marketer can be particularly helpful. In the collaborative effort between client and agency, the client's role is:

• Be absolutely open in describing your service and your firm to your agency
• Be sure agency understands professional and ethical constraints
• Designate only one partner, or professional staff marketer, as liaison to the agency

The ethical codes of each profession are supplemented by the ethical codes of advertising. They should be understood and observed.

Results can be measured, using surveys, on the effects of advertising on such factors as:

• Name recognition
• Attitude about your firm

- Penetration of the market
- Knowledge of your services

Judgment of the success of a campaign should be made against predetermined realistic expectations.

A successful ad:

- Will be seen and read
- Make its point
- Be responsive to needs of the prospective client
- Cause or contribute to a change or to action

CHAPTER 7

Direct Mail

Direct mail is a marketing tool that has long proven its ability to sell products. But its ability to contribute to selling professional services is extraordinary. When it's properly used, direct mail fills a role that can, in most circumstances, make it the most effective of all professional service marketing tools.

It has an exceptional track record as a primary tool for developing personal selling opportunities. It can substantially increases the number and effectiveness of personal selling opportunities. It's highly flexible, and has the ability to focus on any or all of several aspects of a professional service's capabilities. Its ability to address the problems that a professional service might solve is singular.

And it works exceedingly well to support other marketing efforts.

THE ADVANTAGES OF DIRECT MAIL

The rationale is deceptively simple. If I want to write you a personal letter to persuade you that I understand the nature of a particular problem you may have, and that I have the solution, then I have an extraordinary opportunity to get your attention. But if "you" are a potential client, then there are many more of "you" than there are of me. But when I mass mail that letter, and it's properly personalized, and cast and presented in a way to increase the likelihood that "you" will actually read it, then the effect of the relationship established is the same as if I were to send "you" the one personal letter.

Properly done, then, direct mail has significant and clearly discernible advantages:

- It allows the target audience to be carefully defined and selected. Unlike display advertising, where the limit is the broad demographic base of a publication's readers, direct mail allows you to select and define your target audience to the tightest possible parameters.
- It aims a highly personal and individualized appeal or sales message to a carefully defined audience. It functions as if you were writing an individual letter to an individual, even though it's a mass mailing.
- It has the space and flexibility to deal with complex or technical problems and solutions.
- It's useful in reaching both large and small audiences. If the letter is perceived as a personal letter from you to the recipient it makes no difference how large your audience is.
- It's particularly effective in preselling a service and a service organization, particularly to people who don't know you or your service.
- It can sum up in a very few words a specific problem faced by the prospective client and, in a very few words, explain why your service can help solve that problem.
- It's *relatively* inexpensive and cost-effective, in terms of return on investment. With a highly focused message to a clearly defined audience, the likelihood of getting a broader return is greater than in other more diverse advertising.
- It's timing can be carefully controlled. You can send out letters at any time that's to your advantage, and you can time the letters to your ability to follow up.
- It eliminates absolute cold calls by serving as an introductory device.

Clearly, then, there are profound advantages to direct mail in selling professional services.

WHEN DIRECT MAIL IS INDICATED

As with any marketing tool, direct mail won't be effective without a clear rationale within the marketing program. It's important to distinguish those factors that are most conducive to using direct mail effectively and those that dictate when it is not practical.

Essentially, direct mail is used when a specific service is best sold directly to a specific individual or company; when it's the first step in directly selling to an individual, the second step of which is the actual face-to-face selling effort.

It's particularly useful in selling a single service as a solution to a specific problem. It's even more effective if the problem or the solution is complex or technical. For example, if you have a system to help small companies manage surplus cash, then direct mail is a natural. You know the problem, you have the solution, you know your target audience.

Direct mail should be used when there is:

- A *clearly defined market*, in terms of the need for the service you're offering, and your ability to reach that market effectively and efficiently (usually through the use or availability of mailing lists).
- A *clearly delineated product or service*, particularly in your defining both a specific problem and your specific service to solve that problem. Vagueness or a too-general description of what you have to offer produces confusion and poor results.
- The *capability to follow up* on mailings, in terms of direct contact and selling. No one sees an ad or gets a letter and decides to retain you. The best that can be expected is that it will help develop a personal selling opportunity. Therefore direct mail should be used only when there exists the capability to follow up on mailings to develop a selling situation.
- *Distinctions between national and practice office capabilities.* In a multi-office operation, the distinction should be made, as in print advertising, between the ability to perform a service nationally and to perform it on an office-by-office basis. Not to make that distinction poses the danger of offering nationally a service that can be performed only locally, in selected locations.

When at least these factors are not favorable, then using direct mail may well be contraindicated.

ELEMENTS OF A SUCCESSFUL PROGRAM

Perhaps one of the disadvantages of direct mail is that it appears so easy to use that it's often misused. "After all," you might say to yourself, "I've been writing letters to prospects for all these years."

In fact, the professionalism involved in using direct mail effectively goes well beyond merely writing a letter.

Experience tells us that at least the following elements comprise a successful direct mail campaign:

- The marketing objective for the program must be clearly stated and understood. A program begins not with the letter, but with the marketing objective.
- There must be an integrated relationship between the direct mail program and other marketing efforts. Direct mail doesn't stand on its own. If it's not integrated with other marketing efforts, the likelihood of its success is substantially diminished.
- The selling message must be clearly delineated. Writing the selling message in the letter may ultimately be an art form that depends upon the skill of the writer, but before it demands art, it demands technical marketing skill.
- The service being sold must be clearly defined in terms of the audience's specific needs, and presented in terms of advantages to the prospect. It's not a question of what you want to sell, but rather what the prospect wants to buy.
- Each direct mail program must be tailored to the specific service being sold and to the specific audience. There is no such thing as a standard program or a standard letter.
- The mailing package must be carefully designed, including the letters and enclosures. Each envelope that goes out has a great many options in what it can contain—the letter, brochures, reprints of articles, and so forth. Each element is as important as the others, and all elements must support and complement one another.
- The timing of the mailing must be meticulous, in terms of the ability to follow up, the spacing between letters in a multiletter campaign, the timing of a market's needs, and so forth.
- There must be assiduous followup. Again, a letter doesn't—sell people do. A campaign comprised of the most effective letter and mailing material will accomplish nothing if there isn't followup to

the prospect to establish a meeting and to make a presentation to close the sale.

Ultimately, making the contact—softening the market to accept the contact–is best done by direct mail.

EXPECTATIONS

Without clearly understanding what you may rationally expect from direct mail there stands a danger that a successful campaign— one in which exceptional entree is gained into the potential market— may be perceived as a failure. This is why the results of direct mail must be judged differently for professional services than for products.

Because direct mail is a relatively new tool for most professional services there's a tendency to think of its potential in the same context as in selling products. A direct mail campaign to sell books, for example, can be expected to sell a number of books in proportion to the number of letters sent out. Numbers like 2% or 5% return are usually heard.

In professional services, however, the role of direct mail is to presell. Thus, there is no direct sales return. Nobody receives a letter and sends a check, as in product sales. Nobody responds to a letter by calling and retaining the firm (although there is sometimes an inquiry.)

Therefore, the measure of success in direct mail resides in the degree to which the direct caller is accepted—the ease and frequency with which the individual professional is able to make a personal presentation.

In a successful direct mail program, phone solicitation followup should result in 30 to 50% acceptance of offers to make a personal sales presentation.

PLANNING THE DIRECT MAIL CAMPAIGN
AND PROGRAM

Planning the direct mail campaign begins, as you might expect, with a clear understanding of the campaign's objectives. These objectives should be more sharply defined than merely to sell your service. Therefore, the best tactic for determining your objective is to clarify the problem that the service you are offering is capable of solving, and to focus on selling the solution to that problem.

For example, one successful campaign for a consulting firm began with the understanding that fluctuating interest rates created a problem of great magnitude for banks, and had a strong potential for adversely affecting their profitability. The banks' problem was to keep track of portfolios with loans with mixed interest rates and differing maturities. Many banks were not able to constantly monitor and control their mixture. The service the consultant had to offer was a system to monitor and control these diverse portfolios.

Moreover, the consultant was aware that the problem was most prevalent in medium-sized banks, which, in fact, tended to be unaware that the problem existed until it was too late.

Thus, the primary objective of the program was to make the target audience—medium-sized banks—aware of the serious problem, and to make them aware that the consultant had a solution. A second objective was to generate a context of receptivity that offered the opportunity to sell the consulting service. A third objective was to develop inquiries, if possible.

It was determined that the decision-maker for retaining the consultant was the bank's chief executive officer. This might not have been the case with larger banks, where responsibilities are more diversely spread among a larger management group.

The decision to write directly to the chief executive officer dictated both the strategy and the tone of the letter. The strategy was that a series of letters were to be sent, alerting the bank's officers to the problem, advising that a solution existed in the consultant's service, and soliciting a direct response for further followup. (Despite the fact that each letter was to be followed by a phone call.)

Two letters were planned, with a third to be used if needed.

Why More Than One Letter

In most programs, more than one letter is necessary for at least the following reasons:

- Despite the highly personalized nature of a letter, it's still a direct mail piece, and one of many to arrive every day. While the well-designed letter and package enhances readership, it must be assumed that readership of the first letter is at least cursory. However there is frequently a subliminal retention of the firm name and logo, which makes the second letter more acceptable because it comes from a source that the reader now recognizes or finds familiar.

- In many cases the letter is coming from a source unknown to the recipient. Credibility and knowledge doesn't begin to build until the second letter.

- If the second letter doesn't do its job, a third letter affords you the opportunity for a stronger sell and greater risk in a hard sell. After all, if the prospective client hasn't demonstrated interest after two letters, you have nothing to lose by pushing a little harder.

In a situation like this, the first letter should focus heavily on the problem itself and the dangers inherent in not recognizing it. The letter then indicates that there is a solution to the problem, and that the consulting firm writing the letter offers that solution.

In the campaign to the banks, where the problem is so acute, the brochure describing the services was not included with the first letter. To do so would be to divert the focus away from the problem.

The second letter, on the other hand, indicates the problem, but focuses heavily on the solution and the firm's ability to help. In this case, the brochure is included.

The third letter, should it be needed, is more balanced between the problem and the solution than were the first two, and is a much harder sell.

Considering the problem and the target audience, the tone of the letters was that of senior executives talking to senior executives. The letter was written on the finest stationary that the firm has, with the first letter no more than one page. In its delineation of the problem it was quietly alarming, offering the solution in the broadest terms as a comfort factor, and soliciting an inquiry.

The mailing list in this case was developed by direct research of prospective clients, rather than a standard list bought from a mailing house.

The first two letters were spaced three weeks apart.

Because the campaign was for a firm with offices in several cities, the campaign was tested in two cities, each of which was selected because of its ability to control the followup. Initial mailings were in batches of 50, so that the responses may be coped with effectively.

The signer of each letter was the person who will be in the best position to deal directly with each response.

The campaign was a rousing success, with more than 50% of the addressees allowing the sales presentation to be heard, and a large portion of that number buying the service.

The Program

No direct mail campaign should be started without a clearly delineated program to give it form and direction. The program should include at least the following elements:

- *The problem*. This should be a clear statement of the problem faced by the market—its needs, as seen in terms of the firm's ability to meet those needs and to solve the problem. This is a crucial element of a direct mail program—that it stress the needs of the prospective client rather than focus on the service you have to offer.
- *The objective*. A primary objective of the campaign should be developed in terms of persuading the prospective client that your service is capable of solving his problem. The second aspect of the objective is to decide what it is you want the prospect to know, think, feel or do after he has read your letter.
- *The strategy*. Each campaign should have a distinctive strategy that relates the campaign to the overall marketing objectives, and that addresses the configuration of the specific market. For example, a campaign may recognize that the decision-maker is the chief executive officer, and that he must be the recipient of the letter. The campaign strategy must be designed to present the letter to him in a way that increases the likelihood of its being read. At the same time, another campaign strategy may dictate that the letter be aimed at a lower echelon decision-maker, in which case the strategy for reaching him is different. In any event, this strategy must be detailed.
- *The letters*. A decision must be made about the number of letters, the style and tone of writing, the copy platform and the balance in each letter between the clarification of the problem and the statement of your ability to solve the problem. Examples of tone might be senior executive talking to senior executive; formal versus informal; technical or lay terms.

- *The timing*. How often will the letters go out, how many go out at each mailing, when the letters go out, the amount of time between letters.
- *The list*. A complete description of the mailing list, its composition and its source should be included.
- *Tactics*. This is the plan for the campaign itself. Should it be tested? In how many cities? How many letters in the initial mailings and in each batch? Should separate but simultaneous letters be sent to influentials and decision makers? Who signs? Who copes with responses?

WRITING THE COPY

While the basic general rules of copywriting will be discussed in the next chapter, direct mail for professional services has a distinctive body of elements that do and don't work, as well as a number of elements that have not yet been tested.

A good measure of the hard sell we have come to expect from direct mail for products is precluded by professional ethics. Words like "guaranteed" or "your money back in 30 days if not satisfied" simply have no place in this kind of marketing.

Some of the other devices, such as multicolored letters, jazzy headlines, and extremely strong claims tend to be counterproductive, in that they're considerably less than the public expects from professionals. It diminishes credibility.

At the same time, there are some devices that can be used that have the appearance of simply making the letter and its point more readable. For example, the indented paragraph. Underscored words to make a point. The headline-like sentence before the salutation. These are some of the devices that, if tastefully used, strengthen the letter without diminishing the appearance of professionalism.

As you will see in the chapter on copywriting, there are really very few rules that are so hard and fast that they can't be broken or used experimentally.

If there is such a thing as a hard and fast rule, it is that the letter must focus on the prospect's problem, and not on your service. And there can be exceptions to even that rule. Can you imagine a reader not reading through a letter that begins, "I have found the cure for the common cold."?

But unless you have indeed found the cure for the common cold, the letter must be cast primarily in terms of the prospect's needs and anxieties as a lead-in to the solution you have to offer. Thus, the first paragraph should get directly to the heart of the matter in delineating the problem in its most dire form. And it should be done in a way that doesn't state the obvious, merely as a platform for your argument.

For example:

"Everybody has a problem in choosing the right computer to solve small business accounting problems," is merely a statement of an obvious fact. Very dull.

"When you know that choosing the wrong computer can be more expensive than choosing no computer at all, then you understand the high cost of being confused." This is a statement of fact that's designed to hit a nerve and to generate anxiety, without dwelling on the obvious.

And the second paragraph should say, "Our firm can help."

In writing a direct mail letter the questions that should be foremost in your mind are:

- Who am I writing to?
- What do I want them to know, think, or feel after reading the letter?
- What do I want them to do after they have read the letter?
- Are there any questions that go unanswered, except those that I mean to have go unanswered?
- And then comes the first crucial question before writing—"What is the most startling, riveting, attention-getting thing I can say in the first sentence?" The first sentence, incidentally, should never be a question that can be answered negatively. If you ask, "Do you have a problem with your taxes?", and the answer is "No", then you can bet that the rest of your very fine letter will go unread.

The answer to these questions dictate the nature of the letter, the copy platform, its tone and its content.

Aside from the emotional appeal of the first paragraph, and the beginning of the sell in the second paragraph, the subsequent paragraphs should succinctly describe the service being offered, your qualifications to perform that service, and a call to action—even if you plan to call.

MAILING LISTS

Mailing lists are the bane of everybody's existence. Mailing list brokers, who can be found in the Yellow Pages in any major city, seem able to supply rather precise lists in every category except the one you want. A good list house will usually qualify its list (purge it of out-of-date names and addresses,) charging more for guaranteed up-to-date lists. Standard Rate & Data Service has a directory of mailing list sources that's invaluable.

But if direct mail is to be properly used in marketing professional services, the chances are it will not be an extensive list. Few professional services will be doing national mailings. And so the lists should be qualified not only by the mailing house, but by your own sense of where your potential clientele lies. In fact, if you've been in practice for any length of time, the chances are that you already have a mailing list of current, former and potential clients. This should take precedence over any purchased mailing list.

It might be useful to understand where mailing houses get their lists.

The sources range from subscriber lists of specific magazines to extensive research by the better mailing list houses. Mailing lists made up of subscriber lists are useful only if the publication that served as a source rather precisely covers your potential clientele. This is not likely to be the case however under most circumstances. Other mailing lists may be derived from successful mailings of other vendors.

For example, you can buy a list of purchasers of books by direct mail. How, on the other hand, can you get a qualified list of prospective dental patients without very carefully describing your own criteria for clientele?

In fact, you don't really buy a list—you rent it. Reusing a list, particularly if it's more than a few weeks old, is a poor idea because in most cases many of the names on that list will have become obsolete, even in that brief period of time.

A qualified list, guaranteed to be up to date and with a very high percentage of accuracy, is worth the price. Inaccurate lists are expensive, and mean wasted postage and production costs. The larger the list, of course, the less likely it is to be accurate, since people move, change their circumstances or interests, change their jobs and so forth.

ASSEMBLING THE PACKAGE

There is always a question as to what goes into the envelope in a mailing. The answer depends upon what you are trying to sell, to whom you're trying to sell it, and the strategy you've chosen.

If you mean to personalize the mailing so that letter is you speaking to each prospective client as an individual, the chances are that the less you enclose the better. Quite the opposite is true in direct mail campaign for products.

For example, if you're writing to describe a rather specific service to the chief executive of a corporation, then you want it to look as much like a personal letter as possible. You'll use monarch size stationary, the letters will look as if they're individually typed, and there will be no enclosure—at least in the first mailing. The enclosures—the brochures, the reprints of articles, etc.— should in most cases be saved for the second or third mailing. It should be assumed that the first mailing sparked the interest, the second mailing will have a higher readership, and the third mailing is hard sell.

The letter and the brochures and other enclosures should complement one another, and no piece should be expected to do the job of another. The letter is the sales message, the brochure is the description of the service, the reprint of the article or clipping is the support. This is where the emphasis should be. The letter may describe the service, and the brochure may have some sell in it, but focus on each piece's primary job.

If each piece of the package is seen in this way, then judging what goes into each mailing is a function of what you want each mailing to accomplish.

It's important, then, to tailor the package to do only the job it's supposed to do.

TIMING AND FOLLOWUP

The timing for a mailing is dictated by two factors:

• The ability to followup.
• External circumstances.

The external circumstances would be those that might normally limit attempting to sell a specific service at an unpropitious time. For example, just as you would sell a tax service within a reasonable proximity of tax filing time, you might not sell a hay fever test in mid-winter.

The ability to follow up is yet a different matter. It's a function of your ability to schedule phone or personal visit followups within two weeks after the letter has gone out. In a multiletter campaign this should be a minimum of two weeks and a maximum of four weeks between letters, to allow for a continuum of impact.

MEASURING RESULTS

Among the advantages of direct mail is the ability to test aspects of it inexpensively. In print advertising, only those advertisers with large budgets can afford to try several different approaches, in different media. A direct mail campaign, however, can be tested in several ways:

- Different letters can be sent to different segments of the mailing list.
- Separate mailing lists can be tested with one letter.
- Different packages (one with, one without a brochure) can be tested.

You should remember, when testing a direct mail campaign, to keep careful records so that you can score results and use them for subsequent campaigns.

Ultimately, the best test of results is the response you get to phone followups. If the campaign has been done properly, and is effective, a significant number of phone calls should demonstrate recognition of your firm, recall of the letter, and the willingness to meet with you personally for further discussions that can lead to closing the sale.

For moving your service directly to the potential client, direct mail, properly conceived and executed, is an unparalleled marketing tool.

SUMMARY

Direct mail, with its excellent selling record, is one of the most effective of the professional services marketing tools. Its advantages are that it:

• Allows for a defined audience
• Aims a highly personal appeal—the personal letter
• Is good for large or small audience
• Can focus on a target company's problem and offer solution
• Is relatively inexpensive and cost-effective
• Allows timing to be controlled
• Eliminates cold calls by serving as introductory device

Essentially, direct mail is used when a specific service is best sold directly to a specific individual or company, and when there's:

• A clearly defined market
• A clearly delineated service
• The capability to follow up letters
• A complex problem and a complex solution
• Local office selling structure, even in national firm

The elements of a successful program are:

• Objective must be clearly stated
• Integrated relationship between direct mail and total marketing program
• The selling message must be clearly delineated
• Service must be clearly defined
• Program must be tailored to the specific service being sold and specific audience
• Mailing package must be carefully designed
• Timing must be meticulous
• Must be followup

Expectations for results are not direct response in new clients, but hospitable climate for personal sales presentation, and favorable response to personal followup. A successful campaign should achieve that from about 30 to 50% of letters followed up by phone.

A campaign plan and strategy should include:

- Specific objectives
- Target audience
- Definition of audience problem, relative to solution offered by your service
- Target letter recipient
- Copy platform
- Package content
- Number of mailings
- Followup

Copy should be cast in terms of target company's needs—not the service offered. Letter should begin with a statement of the problem in a mode to exacerbate anxiety. Second paragraph should offer to help solve the problem.

Mailing lists should be carefully selected to assure closest possible fit to the target audience. The choice of mailing lists, which can come from mailing houses or your own culled list of prospects, can make or break a campaign.

The mailing package can contain just the letter, or brochure or reprints of articles or ads. Choice is subject to objectives and strategy.

The timing of mailings is determined by the ability to follow up and to external circumstances, such as seasonal considerations for the service offered. Multiple letter campaigns should be spaced with between two to four weeks between letters.

Testing can be done, with different lists and different mailings to the same list. Results are measured against reasonable expectations, and assuming that a campaign is properly followed up.

CHAPTER 8

Copy, Design and Production

Essentially, an ad is a vehicle for a message.

And while a number of elements contribute to presenting that message, and controlling its quality, the burden is usually carried primarily by *copy*—the words—the text.

To try to define the art of copywriting is as futile as trying to define the art of painting like Michaelangelo. Nevertheless, there are the mechanics of copy, a view of which can help to understand what it is and how it functions to do its job.

And whether you do it yourself (which is difficult for the inexperienced nonprofessional copywriter) or you must judge the work of those who do it in your behalf, the rules and limitations of copy should be clearly understood. They should be understood even if they are to be honored in the breach. Even the most abstract artist knows which rules he violates, so that it can be done with control, skill, and aesthetic strength.

The limits of copywriting are essentially the limits of the medium. You can't write 10 minutes of copy for a 30-second radio spot. The mechanics of writing for one medium are too infrequently translatable into another medium. You can't put 50 words of copy on a billboard alongside a high speed highway and expect the message to be read.

And yet there are times when originality, imagination, and skill dictate that all rules be violated. Fifty or 100 words on that billboard may be just the ticket if the headline is something like, "There are not enough words to describe . . . "

THE OBJECTIVES OF THE AD

Writing advertising copy begins, as you might expect, with defining objectives—of the campaign, of the marketing program, of the specific ad. These objectives will be unique to you and your firm, to each campaign, and to each ad. They dictate that the copy—as well as all other elements of the ad—are focused and relevant.

ELEMENTS OF A GOOD AD

The elements that constitute a good ad include at least the following:

- *Attention.* In the clamor and clutter of sight and sound, and the competition for the reader's eye, ear, and heart, it is imperative that you compete successfully for attention. If you can't capture your reader's attention then your copy may offer the formula to transmute base metal into gold, and no one will notice. There should be some element in the ad—whether it's the headline or the illustration or the layout—that attracts the eye or ear and arouses sufficient interest to warrant attending to the message. And the copy itself must sustain that attention.
- *Promise of Benefit.* There must be an element in the ad that promises the reader or the listener some benefit that will accrue from accepting the ad's premises.
- *Credibility.* The premises of the ad must be believable, and credible within a context that the reader can understand. To speak the truth is not sufficient; it must be believable as the truth.
- *Persuasiveness.* The ad should be persuasive and reasonable in its selling message. It should sell the need for the service you offer, and project your service as superior. And if that need isn't immediately apparent, it should generate the need.
- *Interest.* Once you've captured the reader's attention you've got to say something to sustain his interest. If this isn't accomplished, then once again, your message will not be heard.
- *Desire.* The ad must generate a desire to accept what you have to

say about what you have to offer; to want to do business with you. It must generate a favorable atmosphere in which you can function to sell your service.

- *Action*. Basically, the ultimate aim of an ad is to generate action on the part of the reader or listener; to cause him to want to do something that you want him to do, such as buy your product or service. But as we've seen, the nature of professional services marketing precludes that, beyond generating an inquiry. Even in those situations in which an ad might inspire an ultimate action (for a specialized clinic, for example,) there is almost invariably an inquiry and discussion before the decision is made to become a patient. But even a call to be aware of something is an important call to action.

It can be said that an effective ad is one that achieves a preconceived objective. It's difficult to judge an ad on the basis of it's ability to generate inquiries if the objective of the ad is to enhance name recognition. In marketing, serendipity counts for a lot, but you can't build a career on it.

THE FOUNDATION FOR COPY

Copywriters know that ads work best when two elements exist:

- *Know your prospect*. Understand not only who your prospect is, but what his or her needs are. Do you know what kind of service your prospective clientele really wants, and what kind of problems they'll depend upon your service to resolve? If you don't understand your prospects, and can think only in term of what you do and what you have to sell, then it becomes impossible to develop an ad or an advertising program that will effectively reach them.
- *Know your service*. You know, of course, what you do and how you do it. But in an ad, the way you present what you do must be in terms of your prospective clients' needs, not your needs. The important distinction is to know your service in terms of what the prospective client is willing to buy, not what you're offering to sell.

Even within the context of professional limitations there are differences in the way you and your competitors perform the same services. These are differences in approach to a problem, in organization, in service concept. Nothing must be taken for granted in analyzing just who you are and what you do. The view of how your way of doing things differs from the ways of others must be realistic.

Here, there comes into play a catalog of who you really are and how you function as a professional. What's unique about what you do, or about the way you do things that aren't of themselves unique? What are your strengths and weaknesses? What can you realistically offer your prospects, and where are your shortfalls? What are the physical dimensions of your capabilities in terms of service, personnel, technical skill and so forth?

In other words, what is your service really about, beyond the mere definition of your profession?

In good copywriting the clearest answers to these questions will produce the most effective ads.

COPY STRUCTURE

Although there may be deviation for sound reason, ad copy usually consists of a headline, text, and signature.

The Headline

The basic purpose of a headline is to attract attention and to bring the reader to the ad. It usually accomplishes this by promising, by imparting news, by direct address, or by being clever or funny. It's usually in larger type, designed to jump out of the page to catch the reader's eye and interest. If the headline is the device your ad uses for this purpose (it could just as well be the illustration), then it must have power. If its purpose is to promise, then the promise must be made clear. If the purpose is to be clever or funny, then clever or funny it had better be. A headline that offers nothing to the reader in terms of either benefit or interest may effectively mask the cleverest ad, and one that's offering the most useful service.

The Text

It's extremely important that the text should spring from the headline, and follow through the promise it offers. It should explain and clarify the facts and claims. And no matter how long or short the text, it should be a logical progression of ideas. It should cover all of the points you mean to cover and exclude no information of importance.

Copy can be either factual or emotional. It can appeal to the intellect and reason, or it can appeal to the emotions. It can do both, of course, but the choice and effort should be knowledgeable and conscious—you should know why you're doing it.

Call for Action

The text should lead naturally to a call for action. What precisely do you want your reader to do? Call now? File for future reference? Send in a coupon? Send for a brochure? Remember something? Experienced copywriters know that the call for action works. It's not so much that when readers are told to do something they do it. It's that when they're not told to do something they're less likely to do it.

Logo, Signature and Slogan

The copy usually ends with a logo and a signature for identification and impression, and sometimes also a slogan.

Slogans in advertising professional service can be very dangerous. A slogan is a battle cry, and is in fact derived from the Gaelic words that mean battle cry. It's usually a simple statement extolling the virtue of a company or its product which, when repeated over and over again, gains currency. It's the repetition that turns an ordinary statement into a slogan that has selling power, assuming that the slogan says something consequential to begin with.

The danger in relying on slogans in professional service advertising is that it fosters a tendency to move attention to the service rather than to the needs of the prospective client. An extensive ad campaign for a major accounting firm, based on a slogan, cost hundreds of thousands of dollars. Its impact on improving the practice, according to many of the firm's partners, was negligible. Moreover, the slogan was remembered long after the advertiser's name—and message—was forgotten.

There is another caution to be observed here, in that in some states, the canons of ethics of some professions still prohibit the use of slogans in advertising.

THE COPY PLATFORM

In facing the prospect of writing copy for an ad, the professional copywriter usually develops a concept, sometimes called the copy platform, which is a clear statement of the copy objectives, focus, and approach. This is an attempt to articulate, as clearly and as simply as possible, what the copy shall say and how it shall say it. Shall it be extensive or brief? What tone shall it take? Shall it be breezy and light, or formal? What message shall it try to convey? What is the rationale behind the approach?

The purpose of this copy platform, whether it's specifically articulated on paper or merely understood in the copywriter's mind, is to serve as a guide to actually writing the copy. Many copywriters use it to present to their clients for a clear understanding of how the ad will come out.

UNIQUE SELLING PROPOSITION

Copywriters frequently speak of a concept called the Unique Selling Proposition (USP). It's simply one approach to advertising that attempts to focus an ad or an ad campaign most effectively.

The concept suggests that you find the most effective product distinction you can discern, and use that as the basis for the entire campaign and as the thrust for the copy. The USP is then supported in every aspect of the ad, including the illustration, design and layout, and the selection of the media. With a product, it's a product distinction that sets the product apart from its competitors. In marketing a service, a USP can be extremely difficult to find. But does this mean that the concept of USP will not work in professional marketing?

In fact, quite the contrary is true. In order for advertising to be effective in marketing a professional service, a USP is absolutely essential.

But in a context in which basic professional services are indistinguishable one from another, from wherein does the USP derive? There are several possibilities:

- Presenting material in an original way. A classic example is the Arthur Young advertising campaign, "We take your business personally." Here the layout, copy theme, and subject matter is done so originally and with such enthusiasm that despite the fact that it makes no overt distinction between its service and and that of its competitors, the personality of the firm is crystallized and conveyed as unique.
- The configuration of services, in which several different aspects of classic service are presented in ways that appear to be unique.
- The unique presentation of a single aspect of service, in which one aspect of the service is described as if it were developed yesterday. It's presented as if no other firm has it, without actually saying that. "Now you can have your taxes done by a tax professional" says one thing. "Now, *at last*, you can have your taxes done by a tax professional" says something else. (Something, by the way, that you can't ethically say.)
- The new service, in which a new approach to solving a problem, or a new solution to an old problem, is presented for the first time. The first firm to announce it effectively wins the field, and all others subsequently offering the same service are perceived as merely followers.

The unique selling proposition frequently springs from the position you take in the marketplace—your approach to serving your clients—and should certainly relate to it. The fresher the view you take of your own services and how you perform them, the more likely you are to perceive a unique selling proposition.

WRITING THE COPY

The artistry of advertising lies in the ability to manipulate symbols and ideas in order to inform and persuade people. As in any art form, there are no rules that can guide you in doing this, except to list those factors that seem to work most consistently. And yet, some of the most successful ads are those that violate the rules. In all likelihood, the rules are best violated when they are best understood.

Two universally accepted axioms are that an ad must be simple, and it must look and sound as if it's worth paying attention to. And obviously, it must be complete—it must contain all the information you want to convey. These axioms—if indeed they are axioms—spring from the fact that few ads are successful when these rules are ignored. Beyond that, clarity is essential. No matter how an ad is written it must be understood and easy to read.

It should be grammatical—despite the fact that there are many examples of successful advertising that are clearly ungrammatical. A breach of grammatical rules, however, should be deliberate, and designed to serve a specific purpose. The rules of grammar are not arbitrary, nor are they engraved in stone. But the purpose of the rules of grammar is consistency, understanding and clarity. Unless there is a conscious reason to do otherwise, copy should be grammatically sound.

There are some other guidelines that professional copywriters also find useful:

- *Talk to the reader, the listener, or the viewer.* Don't announce, don't preach. And don't get carried away by words and lose sight of the message.
- *Write short sentences*, with easy and familiar words. You want the reader or listener to do the least possible work to get your message. Even when you're talking to very bright people, communication is of the essence, not language manipulation.
- *Don't waste words.* Whether you use three or a thousand words make sure each is exactly the one you need. Make sure each word is exactly the right one to convey your meaning.
- *Try to avoid being formal.* You're talking to people as people. You're not writing an insurance contract for lawyers. An ad is information and persuasion.
- *Use the present tense and the active voice* ("All professional copywriters have extensive experience in preparing material," rather than ". . . extensive experience in the preparation of material."). If you do want a formal style it should be deliberate, and you should have a clear idea of why you are using it.
- *Punctuate correctly.* Punctuate to help the reader, and not merely to follow specific rules. The less punctuation the better, within the bounds of clarity, but don't be afraid to use it if it helps the flow of an idea. Don't be afraid to use contractions and personal pronouns,

just as you would in chatting informally with a prospect. After all, that's what you're trying to accomplish in your ad.
• *Watch out for cliches.* They turn some people off. More significantly, people don't hear them as they pass automatically through the mind, and the point you're trying to make is lost. (Again, unless you're doing it deliberately.) Try to use bright, cheerful language that keeps the reader alert and maintains attention. To be enthusiastic and exciting is to be well along on the way to being interesting.

Writing is not the manipulation of words—it's the expression of ideas. Words, grammar and punctuation, are merely the tools and devices we use to express ideas most clearly. To think of copy as a configuration of words is the same as thinking of a symphony as a configuration of notes.

COPYWRITING FOR OTHER MEDIA

While these rules and concepts apply generally to all copywriting, obviously different media have different copywriting requirements.

A print ad may successfully consist of little more than a solid block of copy with perhaps as many as 1,000 words. A billboard, on the other hand, allows you only five or six words to tell the entire story. Nevertheless, these five or six words should follow the same basic concepts of all copywriting, in terms of objectives and so forth. They should begin with a specific thought, which then becomes words, and not with just an arbitrary choice of words that might be clever. They should be consistent with the thrust of the total campaign. Billboards seem to offer a greater temptation to be cute or funny than do other media. There is nothing wrong with that, unless the funny line is neither funny nor relevant to the point you are trying to make.

The strictures of broadcast copy stem from the fact that the words are heard rather than read. The added element is, of course, the speaker. If the copy is to be dramatized, then the rules of dialogue and drama weigh more heavily than if the copy is merely to be read. There is a vast difference in the skills necessary to write copy to be spoken, and copy to be read. Timing, phrasing, punctuation, all tend to be different from one medium to the next. For example, the experienced radio writer tends to stay away from longer words that might work well in print, and from words that are difficult to pronounce or that have too many "S" sounds. Rarely does a print ad read consistently well on radio.

Copy for direct mail is a lot more personal in its appeal and should be written as if it were an individual talking to an individual.

AD DESIGN AND LAYOUT

The cohesive force that makes a print ad work—that pulls together all of the elements of copy and illustration in a way that attracts the reader—is the design. The elements are laid out in a total configuration to make the ad stand out in a busy page, and engage the reader's attention.

In designing an ad, the art director is concerned with three basic things that make the ad work as a sum of its parts:

- *A sense of unity.* The art director tries to see the ad as a totality, rather than as a mere collection of individual parts. To an experienced and competent art director, an ad is not a headline plus an illustration plus copy. It's a total unit that achieves the complete visual effect to fulfill the ad's objective. Everything must relate to everything else—the headline to the copy, and the illustration to the total ad.
- *Balance.* The elements of an ad should be balanced, both in the proportion of each element in relation to all the other elements, and in their location in the space. An ad in which elements are out of proportion to one another is as awkward and unattractive as might be an elephant's head on a giraffe's body. Typefaces of the wrong size, or that don't complement one another, or that give the wrong graphic feeling to the message, can make the reader grossly uncomfortable, and destroy the best written ad. The balance can be formal, in which every element is centered in relation to the others, or it can be deliberately informal. To the art director, each form has its purpose in conveying a mood, a feeling, an attitude.
- *Flow.* The reader's eye must be attracted to the ad, and then flow logically from the headline to the text to the signature and logo.

This makes the ad more effective by making it more compelling, more readable and, in a sense, more hospitable.

A well-designed ad, one that succeeds in these three elements, functions better in achieving its objective, and competes successfully against other ads and editorial material on the same page.

THE DESIGN ELEMENTS OF AN AD

There are ads without headlines and ads without illustration and even ads without text. But the various elements that an art director might have to put in juxtaposition with one another in designing an ad include:

- *The headline* The headline, usually in a larger or different typeface than the text, sends out a signal to the reader that says something particularly interesting or attractive. Visually, it supplies the emphasis and the drama.
- *The subhead.* Usually in a smaller typeface than the headline (but still different or larger than the text), it is sometimes used to expand or clarify the message of the headline.
- *The body copy.* This is the text of the ad.
- *The illustration.* It could be either a photograph or a drawing—or even a painting.
- *The caption.* Sometimes used to describe an illustration, and separate from the body copy.
- *The logo.* This is the distinct design, emblem or typeface that identifies the advertiser, and is sometimes different from the signature.
- *The signature.* This is the name of the advertiser, the subject of the ad, the company that's sending the message.

Naturally, few ads contain all of these elements at one time. Some ads use no illustrations and some use no headlines. But no matter which of the elements are used in any ad, the art director must lay them out effectively.

Even an ad that consists of only a few words poses a design problem. What typeface should be used? How large should the type be? Where in the space should the words be placed? A glance at any magazine, much less a book of typefaces, tells you that there are hundreds of different typefaces, and many sizes in each face. The art director knows that each face has its different values and uses. Some faces are more dramatic, some more subtle and flowery. Some shout, others whisper. Some are official looking, and others are more informal or humorous. Some are great for headlines but difficult to read in smaller sizes when used in text.

In a display ad, there's no right or correct way to design an ad in which you're looking for a particular feeling. Some ways work better than others. But the wrong layout, the wrong balance, the wrong typeface—any of these can spoil an otherwise excellent ad in which the headline is brilliant and the copy superb.

PRODUCING THE AD

Ad design usually begins before the copy is written, and uses the same concepts and objectives as copywriting does as a point of departure. An ad is conceived in its totality, so that design and copy complement one another. Design and copy must be coordinated so that the art director understands how much space is needed for copy, and the copywriter understands how much space he has for copy. If the type is smaller, there is room for more words, and so the copywriter must know the size type to be used. If the copy is written first, or must contain a specific amount of information, the art director knows how much space he must allow for it.

After the ad is conceived, the art director usually does a rough sketch—called a thumbnail sketch—indicating the approximate size of each element in proportion to the others, and where it will go in the space. When the sketch is approved, preparation of the final ad begins.

The copywriter works on the copy. If a drawing is to be used, an artist must be set to work. If it's to be a photograph, the photographer must be assigned. If stock art or photos—art already done and available for reproduction—are to be used, then files must be searched to find the right material.

When all of the elements are approved, the art director does a comprehensive layout—called a *comp*—in which a drawing of the ad is done that's as close to the finished ad as possible. A rough sketch of the art or photograph is used, the headline is hand lettered, and the body text is indicated with straight lines. This enables everybody to get a good idea of how the final ad will look. It also serves as a guide to the technician who will put the finished ad together.

In the meantime, the other elements are completed. The copy is written and approved, final illustrations purchased and so forth. The type is then ordered, usually from an independent typesetting firm. All of the elements except photographs are then pasted down in place on a special piece of cardboard, using the comp as a guide. This is called a *mechanical*. It's this board that's photographed to make the plate used to print the ad. Photography is keyed in to indicate location, but shot separately because it must be screened—photographed through a screen that reproduces it in dots rather than in a continuous gray scale.

When the mechanical is ready, it's either sent directly to the publication, or a special photo is taken of it for the publication, depending upon the physical requirements of the medium.

WHO DOES THE DESIGN?

Because of the technical skills involved, a measure of experience, as well as talent, is needed to perform the task of the art director. The art director may work for your agency, for your firm, or for an independent art studio. In some cases, the publication itself will supply design and layout help, but this should be accepted with some caution. Few publications—newspapers or magazines—maintain sophisticated design staffs for their advertisers, and so you're not likely to get the best work. And if you let the publication set the type, you're limited to the typefaces the publication has available, which is usually not a wide variety.

There is very little money to be saved by using less than professional ad design services, since a poorly designed ad can negate the best advertising concept. At the same time, learning the elements of ad design is important to the advertiser, to judge the quality of his own advertising.

PRINT PRODUCTION

While most of the functions of production in a print ad are performed by technicians, the successful planning of an ad can very well depend upon your understanding the mechanics of the production process. If you understand the process, then you understand the creative routes that must be taken, and the options you have for designing a better ad.

Typography

At the heart of both the design and production process is typography. The evolution of typefaces since the ancient Chinese invented movable type centuries ago has resulted in a complex art form. The vast array of typefaces available today offers a variety of values in readability, mood and pure aesthetics. The variety of techniques available for setting type has, in recent years, undergone a revolution that's resulted in new, better and cheaper techniques.

Some typefaces are new and modern, and new ones are constantly being redesigned. Others are as old as printing itself, and are still in use. Each face has its best uses and purposes, from the simulated handlettering style of the Middle Ages, to the old style Roman letters with their classic, formal but highly readable look, or the contemporary faces, with their crisp and futuristic look. This book is set in Times Roman.

In some typefaces the letters are graceful, with varying thicknesses in the lines of the letter, and ornamental *serifs*—short lines at the ends of each letter. Others, without the serifs (called *sans serif*) are more contemporary, and sometimes look like block printing. Each face has its own look, its own feel And each purpose has its own most effective typefaces. The boldfaces—in which a letter in a typeface has heavier lines—seem to work best in the larger sizes, and are most frequently used for headlines. The same typeface, in a smaller size, may or may not work for body text. It can be Roman, a name which can be applied to any typeface in its normal fashion, or italic, which means that the letters are slanted slightly for emphasis, as the word *italic* is in this sentence.

All the letters of a style are called a font, which includes all of its sizes, bold, italicized and roman, and numerals and punctuation.

Typefaces of one font can be mixed with faces of another in the same ad, but some faces complement one another and others clash.

The measure of type size is a point. There are 72 points to the inch, which means that a 72-point letter is one inch high. Typefaces up to 18 points are usually used for text. The smallest type size commonly used is 6-point, too small for body text, but sometimes useful for picture captions. The most common sizes for the text of ads are 8, 10 and 12-point. In these sizes, text is easier to read without distracting from the message the text is trying to convey. This book, for example, is set in 11 point type. Type that's 24 points or larger is called display type.

The spacing between lines also affects readability, and therefore the choice of type size. The spacing, called leading, is also measured in points. This book, set in 11 point type, has 2 point spacing between lines. Printers refer to it as 11/13 or 11 on 13.

The width of lines of type is measured in picas. There are six picas to the inch. The lines of this page are set 28 picas wide. Picas are also sometimes called ems. A half pica is an en. When all the lines of a body of copy are even to the margins on both sides, they are called justified. When they are on just one side, they are called (depending on the even side) flush left, ragged right, or flush right, ragged left.

In newspaper advertising, and in some magazines, the height of the ad on a page is measured not in inches, but in agate lines. There are 14 agate lines to the inch.

How Type Is Set

For centuries the only way to set type was by hand, one letter at a time. This is called foundry type, and is used today only for very special and rare fonts.

With the invention of Linotype, type was set by huge machines, with a keyboard like a typewriter. When a key for a letter is pressed, a brass matrix for that letter slides into a holder. When a complete line has been set, hot molten lead is forced into the matrices, and a line of type is cast. Machine type set this way is known as *hot type*.

Today's technology, both in typesetting and printing, has made hot type almost obsolete. Most type is set by computer photo composition, called *cold type*. A typist works at a keyboard that looks like a typewriter and the copy is displayed on a screen like a television set. Corrections are made by proofing the copy on the screen and pressing correction keys. Justification right and left is done automatically by the computer. When the typesetter is satisfied with the copy on the screen, another key automatically starts the photo composition process, and out comes the finished copy, printed on a piece of paper, camera ready for the art director. By simply changing a computer disc, the computer can set thousands of different fonts.

Today, with so much writing being done on word processors, type is frequently set by taking the writer's own data disk, with the text corrected and formatted, and feeding the data directly to the typesetting computer. This saves the considerable time and expense needed to re-key a manuscript on the typesetting machine. This book is set in exactly that way, from the author's computer disks.

Because any kind of cold type can be photographed for printing, it can also be set on a typewriter. The wide range of typefaces available on typewriters that use interchangeable fonts makes it relatively inexpensive, although not as versatile as computer type.

Printing

There are three basic methods of printing. Letterpress is the oldest method, requiring either hand set or hot type. The type is locked into a metal form, and mounted on the press. The type is then inked and impressed on the paper. In larger plants, where whole pages are printed, such as newspapers, a more advanced form is used. The entire page of type is pressed into a fiber matrix, hot metal is poured into the matrix, and the entire page is cast as one form. This is used primarily on rotary presses where the single form is curved to fit a roller. A rotary press that prints from a continuous roll of paper is called a web press. A rotary press can also be fed a single sheet at a time. A flat bed press, in which type is set in a flat form, is sheet fed one sheet at a time.

Most printing today is done by a newer technology called offset lithography. The matter to be printed is photographed on a photosensitized metal plate. When the plate is developed, a barely perceptible raised surface remains for the matter to be printed. On the press, which is rotary (either sheetfed or web), the plate is treated with a chemical. When the plate is inked, only the raised surface accepts the ink, which is then transferred to the paper. Because offset lithography uses cold type, it is considerably less expensive and more efficient than letterpress. Today, even major newspapers are printed by offset lithography, and it's rapidly replacing all other printing methods.

A third method of printing used for special purposes, such as engraving or printing on certain kinds of paper, is intaglio, more commonly known as rotogravure. The material to be printed is etched into the plate. The plate is inked, and then the entire surface is wiped. Ink remains only in the etched depressions. When the plate is pressed to the paper, the ink in the depressions is transferred to the paper.

Color printing is done by making separate plates, one for each of the three primary colors (cyan, magenta and yellow and one for black). Each plate is printed separately, either in individual press runs or, on larger three-color presses, with one roller for each color. As each color is printed, it either stands separately if the color is needed in its basic form, or is overprinted to blend the various shades (blue and yellow in various combinations of intensity, for example, make different shades of green). The printing technician must be sure that the paper passes through the press in exactly the right place, so that all colors register exactly where they're supposed to be.

Regardless of the printing process used, almost all advertising is supplied to the printer in camera-ready form. This can be either the pasted-up mechanical, or a fine quality photograph called a *velox*. In offset lithography, the mechanical or velox is photographed directly onto the litho plate. In letterpress, it's photographed on a plate to make photoengraving.

The two main types of photoengraving are line and halftone.

Line plates can be used only for drawings or other illustrations that use solid lines or masses, but with no shades of gray. Photographs and paintings, however, have a spectrum of shades, and must be engraved by the half-tone process.

The half-tone process uses dots in clusters on the printing surface. The more dots—called screening—per square inch, the darker the area will print. A photograph or painting to be printed consists of a combination of dots in different densities for the different shades, which gives the impression of the finished photograph. In color printing, the density of dots on the different color plates makes it possible to combine them, in the final printing, to give the various shades of color.

These dots are achieved by photographing the original artwork through a screen made up of a crosshatch of some 50 to 150 hairlines per square inch. This forms little windows—from 2,500 to 25,000 of them—through which the light passes. The greater the number of hairlines per square inch, the more dots the plate will have, and the finer will be the finished picture. Newspapers tend to use a coarser screen because newsprint absorbs ink more quickly, and finer dots would tend to blur. The better papers, sometimes coated with a material (usually a clay) to make them harder on the surface (and glossier), absorb less ink, and can take finer dots. this is why artwork in magazines or on coated stock looks better than in newspapers.

The screens are standardized. Newspapers, for example, usually use a 65 screen (65 dots to the square inch), and magazines usually use a 120 screen.

When the same ad is to be used in a great many newspapers, an inexpensive form of duplication called a matrix, or mat, is made. This is done by pressing a raised type and photoengraved form into a papier-mache mat. The printer then pours hot lead into the mat to reproduce the raised letters for letterpress printing. For offset in many different publications, each printer is supplied with a velox rather than a mat. Either the velox or the mat can be sent through the mail.

These basic processes are used in the production of virtually all advertising, whether it's in newspapers, magazines, poster billboards, brochures or handbills. The advertiser who understands the process invariably finds that it's easier to design ads, to judge ads designed by others, and to schedule their production.

SUMMARY

While copy—the words in advertising that convey the message—is governed by several basic rules, it's essentially an art form that allows the rules to be bent to accomplish its mission. Copy, ultimately, is governed by imagination and skill.

Key elements of a good ad include:

- Promise of benefits
- Credibility
- Persuasiveness
- Generates interest
- Creates desire
- Call to action
- Meets predetermined objectives

Ads work best when the copywriter:

- Knows the prospect's needs and desires
- Knows the service he is selling

The copy structure for a successful ad usually includes:

- The headline
- The text
- The call for action
- The logo, signature, and (sometimes) slogan

A copy platform serves as a guide to writing copy. It includes a clear statement of the copy objectives, focus and approach. A *unique selling proposition* is frequently developed or discerned, in which the theme of the copy stems from some unique approach to the service being advertised.

In writing copy, some basic rules include:

- Talk to the reader
- Use short sentences
- Don't waste words
- Try to avoid being formal
- Use the present tense and the active voice
- Avoid cliches

Writing is not the manipulation of words—it's the expression of ideas. Words, grammar and punctuation are just writer's tools.

Copy for other media follows the same general principles, adapted for the medium. Broadcast copy is written to be spoken or acted; billboard copy must make its point in a few words, etc..

The design of an ad pulls together all of its elements—headline, text and illustration—to make the ad more attractive, readable and effective. The designer seeks a sense of unity, balance and flow.

An ad is usually conceived as a totality, so that design and copy complement one another. The art director does a rough sketch that generally indicates where each element goes, then, following acceptance of the format, a comprehensive (more detailed) drawing of the ad indicates the exact location and size of each element. When the elements are assembled in their final form, they are pasted in place for the camera-ready mechanical.

The production of an ad uses technology in typography, photographic reproduction and printing. The range of type styles and sizes, each of which serves its own purpose, gives a designer a great many options. Type may be cast in lead (hot type) or produced by the increasingly popular computer (cold type) method. Printing may be done with letterpress, which uses raised type, or by lithography, the more popular photographic printing method. Photographs and artwork are reproduced by rephotographing through a screen, which produces minute dots in various densities to match the shades of the art. Color is printed by making separate plates for each of the primary colors, which are then overprinted to blend shades and colors.

When the same ad is to be used in many different publications, matrixes are used—inexpensive molds from which entire ads can be cast by each publication.

CHAPTER 9

Media

The choice of vehicles to carry your advertising to the public—the media—is extensive. That means that with so many options available to you, the media you choose must be thoughtfully considered. Each medium has its advantages and disadvantages, measured in terms of circulation, readership, audience, effectiveness and cost.

The selection of media is made simple in only one way. The media, in their eagerness to sell space or time, supply a great deal of demographic information to the prospective advertiser.

Your primary objective in selecting media is to get your message to the largest possible audience of prospective customers and clients, as effectively as possible, at the lowest cost that brings you the best return on your advertising dollar.

In the last statement, the effective factor is *return on the advertising dollar*, not lowest cost. In buying media, cheap can be expensive, if your ad isn't seen by the very people you most want to reach.

Selecting media, then, is a function of more than buying space and time. As in every other phase of marketing, your choice of media must be predicated on the marketing objectives. And as in all other aspects of marketing, media choice is always a mix—a balance of many factors to reach the appropriate, as well as the larger, audience; the cost-effective smaller but more select audience; the audience most responsive to your own position in the marketplace.

As in copywriting, there are rules. But as in copywriting, few of the rules are inviolable. For example, what rule of cost-effectiveness can preclude the wisdom of buying an ad in a fraternal organization's journal that reaches very few people, but gives you more than your money's worth in good will?

THE RULES OF MEDIA BUYING

A media plan is much like a portfolio of stocks, in which you balance growth stocks that give you a consistent but low return, with speculative stocks, in which you have a higher risk but a higher potential return.

Consider the following pertinent factors when judging media:

Circulation. Circulation is the number of copies of a publication that reaches the public. In the broadcast media, it is the number of viewers or listeners at any given moment. Publications may be sold or given away free. They may be sold on newsstands, by subscription, or delivered door to door. They may be distributed free at supermarkets or shopping centers. Circulation figures must be supplied by the publication. Circulation figures for most newspapers and magazines are audited and certified by newspaper and magazine trade associations.

But even audited circulation figures must be taken with a grain of salt, since it's impossible to know that every copy of a publication that leaves the printing plant will land in the hands of a reader. Mail subscription figures are perhaps the most accurate, and most newspapers and magazines accept and credit returns of unsold copies from newsstand dealers. But still there's a lot of slippage. In a media plan, circulation is important—but of itself it's the least important of all the elements.

Audience. Audience is more important than circulation, because who reads the publication is more important than how many people read it. Business Week magazine is a powerful advertising medium, with a huge circulation. You would hardly use it to sell the services of a local medical clinic or a small local civil law practice. The audience of a publication is its demographics—the educational and economic levels of its readers, their ages, their locations, their purchasing habits—are what's important. While no medium (with the possible exception of direct mail) can define its audience precisely, each medium is directed at a specific and clearly defined group. It accomplishes this by controlling its editorial matter, or in the case of broadcast media, its programming. In New York City, for example, *The New York Times* is read by people who generally have a higher income and higher levels of education. *The Times* is read by white collar workers, professionals and government and industry leaders. But it's also read by students and academics, who have less purchasing power. *The Daily News*, on the other hand, has a much wider circulation, but is read predominantly by blue collar workers and people with generally lower income. *The New York Post* is read mostly by middle income groups.

The Times, because of its higher income readers, is the preferred medium for most professional services advertising. But the *Post* and the *News* also reach an audience that might be appropriate for mass-market legal and medical clinics, or tax services. All three have reasonably large circulation, but in choosing one over the other as an advertising medium, the distinction is clearly in terms of audience, not circulation.

Readership. A newspaper or magazine that enters a household is counted as one unit of circulation. But the publication may be read by two or more people in that household, each of whom is a potential consumer. A magazine in a dentist's office may be one unit of circulation, but may be read by fifty people. Thus, circulation is tempered by readership, and a publication with a small circulation may have a large readership. It's also possible that, in terms of advertising readership, a publication with a large circulation might have a small ad readership. This is why most larger magazines and newspapers, and such organizations as the Newspaper Advertising Bureau, conduct frequent readership surveys. The surveys help advertisers to know the degree to which their ads are being seen and read. One word of caution. All advertising research—readership, audience and circulation—should be viewed skeptically. It is rarely scientific, and is usually weighted to favor the publication that supplies it.

Cost and return on investment. There is a distinct difference between cost and return on investment. Simply put, a $100 ad that nobody sees is no bargain. A $1,000 ad that generates $2,000 in commissions is a profitable investment. There is no such thing as good, cheap advertising, if low cost buys you a low return. In budgeting for a media plan, then, cost must be seen in terms of effectiveness.

Size and frequency of the ad. Size is important in print advertising because your ad competes with others on a page. But size can be tempered by frequency. For example, an eighth or a quarter-page ad that appears in the same space regularly for a long period may have greater impact than might a larger ad that appears only occasionally. Even a calling card-sized ad that becomes a fixture in the same space for a long time has the power to establish identity and name retention. And repetition, remember, is crucial to effective advertising.

Frequency of publication. Newspapers come out daily. Magazines can be weekly, semiweekly, biweekly, monthly and even annually. Some community newspapers are weekly. There is a close relationship between a publication's frequency and its audience, dictated by the frequency with which each publication feels it must deliver its editorial content to its readers. Sometimes an annual reaches a specific and clearly defined audience that may be in the very market you want to reach, and annuals tend to have staying power; they're usually kept and referred to frequently.

Newspapers and other publications frequently have special feature days. For example, Thursday has traditionally been the day that newspapers feature food and recipes editorially, with heavy food advertising. Some papers feature real estate advertising one day a week. Circulation and readership tend to be higher for the audiences targeted on those days.

In the context of these guidelines, media should be bought by the advertiser, not sold by media salespeople. Each media salesperson who calls on you will be persuasive, and armed with data about his publication. But the judgment to buy should be made in the total context of a media plan that meets your marketing objectives.

THE MEDIA

Each medium has its purpose, its audience and readership, its place in the marketing mix. Within each category of media, each publication or broadcast vehicle has its own elements of value and disadvantage, and is competitive with others in its category. This competitiveness is an advantage to the advertiser, of course, because it keeps each vehicle working to improve itself—its circulation, audience, editorial content and so forth. And the competition frequently takes the form of keeping you better informed about the nature of the market, as each develops more information about itself to use for its own sales efforts.

Here are some of the values, advantages and disadvantages of each medium:

NEWSPAPERS. There is virtually no community in the United States that isn't served by a newspaper of some kind, and perhaps three-quarters of all adults read newspapers. Their journalistic quality ranges from the meticulous professionalism of the influential big city papers, such as *The New York Times* or *The Washington Post,* to the sometimes (but not always) casualness of small town weeklies. Unique is *The Wall Street Journal,* which is not only a specialized financial newspaper read much beyond the environs of the financial community, but is the country's only national daily newspaper.

Because the editorial content of newspapers—news—concerns nearly every resident in a paper's market area, newspapers are widely read by people of all ages, economic status and education. In communities served by more than one daily paper, there's usually a distinction among the several competitors. Each one takes a position in the market; *The New York Times* reaches for the more affluent and better educated reader while *The New York News* is written for the less well-educated and less affluent reader. There is occasionally a distinction, other than the currency of that day's news, between morning and evening papers. In a community in which there are a great many commuters, for example, the morning paper might tend to feature advertising of items and services for which the breadwinner makes the buying decision, and evening papers might focus on advertising food and furniture for which the buying decision is made by the housewife. Not a hard and fast rule, but one you might look for in your own community.

Except for classified advertising, which is sold by the line, most newspaper advertising is sold by the agate line or the fraction of a page (quarter-page, half-page, two-thirds page, etc.). Newspaper advertising costs are usually in proportion to the circulation and audience, with the major city daily papers charging considerably more than the weekly community paper. Rates are frequently calculated on the basis of dollars per thousand readers.

The disadvantage of advertising in daily newspapers, in addition to the cost, is that advertising readership is usually a small proportion of circulation. Of the readers of 100,000 copies of a newspaper, for example, only a small portion—perhaps 10 percent—may be prospective buyers or sellers of your service. In addition, newspaper advertising competes with other ads and editorial material on the same page. Any one ad can be overlooked or only glanced at by the very people you want to reach.

Two ways to overcome this are by repetition—running the ad or the campaign on a consistent, frequent basis—and ad positioning. Many newspapers and magazines will, for a premium, guarantee to place your ad in a specific part of the newspaper. This may be in the business or financial section, a special real estate section (which is sometimes sold at a discount rather than a premium), or in the sports section (a favorite for cars, for example), on the first page of the second section (wider readership) or opposite the editorial page (also wider readership).

Though suburban and community weekly newspapers usually charge considerably less for advertising, they are still valuable advertising media. Their editorial material is generally local in nature, and geared to community interests. Advertisers are usually local stores and services, although some weeklies have a large enough audience to garner some national advertising. The advantage in advertising a community or suburban weekly is that it's easier to judge the demographics of its readership, since you can easily come to know the community.

MAGAZINES. National magazines reach a national audience, and the cost of advertising in them is proportionately high. Only the professional with offices throughout the country, or a valid national market, should consider national magazines an effective medium. But many national magazines sell regional editions, some of which break down to fairly small areas. You can buy *Time, Newsweek* or *Business Week,* for example, for just the New York City edition. This allows you the prestige of the major national publication to reach a specific market area at a comparatively reasonable price.

For most professionals, however, the city or local magazine affords the prestige and access to specialized market of magazines at a cost-effective price.

Not all cities or regions have local magazines, of course, but their number is increasing. Almost all major cities—New York, Chicago, Philadelphia, Albuquerque, San Francisco, Dallas—have publications that range from fair to superb. Their markets are clearly defined geographically, as well as by audience. Most local magazines are editorially slanted toward a more chic and affluent audience—some, in fact, are particularly trendy—and so make excellent vehicles for professional advertising.

DIRECT MAIL. While the structure of direct mail is obviously different than for publications, direct mail is nevertheless a medium. It's a way to get your advertising, whether a brochure or a letter or a display ad, to an audience. The advantages of direct mail are that you have a wide choice of the material you can send the reader, and you can more carefully select the lists of individuals to whom you mail.

The disadvantage is that direct mail can be expensive, when you add up the cost of contents, lists and postage. Direct mail is also considered "junk mail" by many people, and is sometimes thrown away unopened. On balance, however, direct mail can be very effective, since a large percentage of recipients do read it.

The secret of success in direct mail advertising lies in sending the right piece to the right audience. In direct mail, the right audience is found by purchasing the right mailing lists, usually from list brokers. List brokers are found in the Yellow Pages of any major city.

The list broker gets his lists in a number of ways. He may buy the subscription lists of magazines or newspapers. he may develop them from directories, or from companies.

Lists may be broken down in hundreds of different ways, such as a publication's subscription list (if you know the publication then you know the audience the list will reach); by zip code; by economic status; by individuals who have purchased by direct mail in the past; by profession; by age—a broad range of categories that should encompass any conceivable category within your target market. Some lists are unqualified, which means that they haven't been "cleaned" recently of people who may have moved or otherwise changed status. Others are qualified, either by having been cleaned and updated in recent mailings, or by containing names of people who have specifically responded to a direct mail appeal. The more highly qualified the list, the higher the cost.

Lists can be purchased in part, which is sometimes done for testing. If you wanted to test the response of a list of 5,000 chief financial officers in a particular zip code, for example, you might use every fifth or tenth name. If the list brings you the response you want, you then mail to the entire list.

With the increasing cost of printing and postage as well as the labor for handling, direct mail must be used with increasing care. Few advertisers can any longer afford to use unqualified lists, or to be cavalier in the choice of materials to be mailed.

RADIO. Radio, as was noted, has the advantage of knowing a great deal about its audience by virtue of each station's specific programming. You might then consider that a classical music station, AM or FM, is likely to appeal to a better educated—and therefore probably a more affluent—audience. The size of the audience may be smaller, but with its demographics more easily definable, it might give a better return on investment. A rock and roll station, on the other hand, would have an audience of predominantly teen-agers, hardly a market for professionals.

The entire country is covered by radio, with few areas reached by fewer than five or six stations. The more powerful the station, the more expensive the time. And the more people it may reach outside your market area. Most radio stations, however, have useful information available to advertisers about their audiences and their markets. If a market is clearly delineated, the relatively high cost of radio (as compared to newspapers or magazines) still gives a good return on investment. And the cost of production for local radio can be reasonable.

TELEVISION. Television coverage is geographically as broad as is radio, although there are not as many stations. And unlike radio, television programming aimed at different audiences changes from program to program, rather than from station to station.

Television time costs considerably more than local radio, even on a local basis—perhaps as much as five or six times as much. For the professional who can afford it, though, it's a very effective medium.

The growing cable television industry may ultimately make television advertising more feasible for the smaller professional firm. It's more localized, its audience is more readily identifiable (from subscriber lists), and its advertising more localized. Currently, only a small percentage of the country is covered by cable television that accepts advertising, and it may be a few years before this situation improves.

OTHER MEDIA. It's been said that any public place that can sustain an ad is a viable medium. One wag even suggested selling advertising space on the tails of attractive dogs.

The number of vehicles for advertising is infinite. Penny savers, the free publications distributed by supermarkets and shopping centers, proliferate. They vary in quality and distribution, and so are hard to categorize in terms of price and value as advertising media. Special publications, such as the journals of church and fraternal organization, offer opportunities for reaching clearly defined audiences, even as the act of buying an ad in them is an act of good will. Trade journals can be useful to reach a particular profession—engineers, doctors and so forth. But no matter what the medium, the same factors apply for judging the appropriateness of the medium within the framework of your objectives and your budget.

HOW ADVERTISING IS BOUGHT

Almost all media supply rate cards, indicating the purchase arrangements, costs, production limitations and deadlines.

Standard Rate and Data Services, Inc., simplifies the job for larger advertisers by publishing directories that contain standardized media rates and other information in an exceptionally useful form. They are comprehensive and up-to-date, providing information for media buyers, production people and others in advertising.

Display advertising is somewhat more complicated. The rate card lists the costs by agate line or fraction of the page, with discounts for the same ad repeated or for multiple space buys for a campaign. Production limitations usually allow a great deal of latitude, because most display ads are supplied camera-ready. Extra charges may include ads that bleed (are printed to the edge of the space, without margins) or that require half-tone illustrations. Deadlines for display ads are frequently longer than for classified, because larger space has to be set aside. Costs for publication-set ads are usually clearly spelled out.

Classified advertising is perhaps the simplest of the major media. The classified ad is almost invariably sold by the line, and the advertiser is limited to the typeface and style of the publication. Logos, for example, are rarely accepted by daily newspapers. Type sizes are usually limited to a body type size, a headline size and occasionally a boldface. Deadlines are usually pretty tight—two or three days in most cases, and Thursday for Sunday's papers. Usually, discounts are available for multiple insertions of the same ad.

All print and broadcast media buys are discounted 15% to accredited agencies or to individual advertisers who make prior arrangements. Rate cards also spell out guarantees for mistakes in publication costs for special positions or edition, and terms for prompt or delayed payment.

HOW RADIO AND TV ARE SOLD

Television is sold by network, by region of the network, and a spot basis or locally. Spot television means selecting key markets and purchasing the time for individuals through station representatives. There are innumerable purchase options.

Time on an individual television station is usually sold in 10, 20, 30 and 60-second spots. The 60-second commercial allows time for a miniature dramatization. The 10-second spot allows time for little more than a quick message and identification.

Television rates are usually based on time classification, with class A time—from 7:30 to 11:00 PM—the most expensive; and class B time—all other times, less so. Local stations may, for example, have a finer breakdown depending upon their market and sell accordingly.

Every station has its own rate practices, all of which are quoted on a rate card supplied by the station. Standard Rate and Data Services, the media buying publication, publishes the rate cards for all media, including radio and television.

Radio, too, is sold on local and spot basis. Prime time for radio is usually automobile drive time, which would be 6:00 to 10:00 AM and 3:00 to 7:00 PM. This is obviously when most people are listening. Daytime rates from 10:00 AM to 3:00 PM are usually lower and evenings from 7:00 PM to midnight, which is television prime time, is lower still.

While broadcast media has not achieved total acceptance in professional advertising, it's ability to focus a message to a carefully defined audience make it certain that it will ultimately be used as a primary medium.

WHO BUYS MEDIA

Buying a classified or a single display ad requires no special skill, and you can easily do it yourself. And while buying display advertising sometimes requires a measure of paperwork to clarify terms, positions, etc., it isn't too much of a burden.

Buying space and time for a full campaign, on the other hand, can be a little difficult, and requires some specialized skill. Large buys, for example, can be negotiated, particularly if an agency buys a lot of space from a publication for several clients. Instructing the publication on complex scheduling and production techniques, and following up, can be a full-time job.

In radio and television, some agencies specialize in bartering goods and services for radio and television. They can often make time buys at bargain rates, but these are complex arrangements that should be done by professionals.

The media staff of an agency usually includes traffic experts, who are trained in the techniques of scheduling and guiding advertising from the advertiser to the media.

The complexity of media buying is a function of the schedule and the number of media involved, as well as the number of different ads involved in the campaign. To the experienced media buyer, however, a great many complex activities become almost routine.

Media planning, however, requires a full understanding of the objectives of the marketing program, of the campaign and of the ad. It requires knowing target markets, and the options available to you for reaching them.

But whether you do it yourself or use a professional media specialist, you don't abrogate your responsibility to keep the plan and all its elements within the framework of your own objectives.

SUMMARY

Each medium for advertising—the vehicle for carrying ads—has its own values in getting your message to your audience. But the most important factor in media selection is the return on each advertising dollar, not lowest cost.

The important factors in selecting media are:

- Circulation—the number of copies of a publication that reaches the public (or listeners, in broadcast media)
- Audience—who actually reads the publication or listens to the broadcast
- Readership—the degree to which the publication and its ads are actually read
- Cost and return on investment—how many actual clients you ultimately get for your advertising dollar
- Size and frequency of ad
- Frequency of publication

Each medium has its purpose, audience and readership. Newspapers are widely read, but each tends to serve a particular audience geographically, intellectually, economically and in news coverage.

A great many magazines are local or regional, rather than national. Most trades or industries have their own publications.

Direct mail, in which your message is sent directly to a carefully selected mailing list, avoids reaching an audience that's not part of your market.

The broadcast media reach a defined audience by the nature of their programming. Radio has the advantage of focusing attention on your message. Television has the advantage of being able to visualize and dramatize.

Most media supply rate cards that indicate purchase arrangements, costs, production limitations and deadlines.

Media buying for a large schedule can be complex, and is usually done by professionals. Small ads can be purchased with no particular expertise for a purchase, although only accredited advertising agencies are granted a 15 percent discount by most publications.

Careful media selection is as consequential to a good marketing program as is any other element of marketing.

CHAPTER 10

The Advertising Agency

There are, as you've seen, a great number of skills and techniques involved in putting together even the simplest ad. The ad that you write yourself requires knowledge of many things that go beyond your own profession, and the fact that you may be able to write and place your own advertising is testimony not to the simplicity of the process, but to your own capabilities.

But for the larger campaign, particularly one that uses several media, a great many skills and specialties are required. The coordination and teamwork required is extensive, whether that team consists of one multitalented person or an individual professional for each skill.

A fully staffed, full-service advertising agency may, then, include a team made up of at least the following people:

- Account supervisor
- Account executive
- Creative director
- Research director
- Copywriter
- Art director
- Media buyer
- Production director
- Traffic director

163

- Art buyer
- Agency administration
- Administrative personnel

If you write, produce and place your own ads, you are all these people rolled into one. If you use a one-person agency, that person must either have all these skills, or subcontract those he doesn't have. In a larger agency, at least one person, a specialist, performs each of these tasks, all of which you should understand.

In a full service agency, fully staffed, each person functions in a particular way.

The account personnel. The people responsible for the day-by-day operation of your account may not be specialists in any of the creative or production skills, but they must be thoroughly familiar with how each skill is performed, and how it contributes to the finished ad. The account supervisors, or the account executives who report to them, must also be marketing specialists. They must understand your business and its objectives. The account people must be experts in costs and budgeting. And ultimately, they must be able to communicate your marketing program to the various specialists who will implement it.

In some agencies, a marketing specialist helps in developing the overview; in others the account supervisor or the account executive performs that function. Your account executive is your direct link to your advertising agency.

The research director. The research director is responsible for every aspect of marketing research, from defining the target audience and its demographics, to evaluating readership of ads. The research director and his staff supply the basic material that allows the account personnel and the creative director to function intelligently and relevantly to your needs.

The creative director. In an agency large enough to have a creative director, that person is usually a heavily experienced copywriter or an art director, with talent for designing and creating the thrust for the campaign. The creative director is the conceptualizer. He visualizes and articulates the best approaches and techniques to be used by the specialists in developing the campaign and its individual ads. And perhaps his most important role is to maintain creative quality control in all areas.

The copywriter. In larger agencies, the copywriters may specialize in different media and sometimes in different industries. In most agencies, the copywriter is the real creative force.

The art director. The art director is trained in the visual aspects of advertising—its design, layout, typography and illustration. Art directors may also specialize by media. The television art director is concerned with the visualization of the TV commercial—the scenery, costumes, camera angles, and in color television, the color balance. The print art director and his staff are also responsible for buying the typography and illustrations, and pasting it up for the camera-ready mechanical.

The media buyer. The media buyer is responsible for understanding the options among all media, and the effectiveness of each medium that might possibly be used in your campaign. This means knowing circulations, audiences, rates, timetables, and production schedules and limitations. The media buyer must also be experienced in negotiating with media sales representatives for schedules, rates and positions, and must monitor the delivery and appearance of the ad.

The traffic specialist. In a busy agency, or in a large campaign, a great many elements must be coordinated. This is the job of the traffic coordinator. Schedules must be adhered to so that all of the elements of the ad—design, copy, layout, typography, etc.—are delivered at the appropriate time, and that the ad is ready for the publication or broadcast station on the proper schedule.

The production director. The production specialist is responsible for the physical production of the ad, from typesetting to printing in print advertising, from filming and recording to reproduction of tapes and film in broadcasting.

Administrative personnel. An advertising agency is a business. Its personnel must be managed, it must bill its clients, it must pay its own bills. It must keep track of its suppliers, including media, and pay them. The larger the agency, the more elaborate the administrative staff and its organization.

Other specialists. Larger agencies will include staff specialists in other areas, such as promotion or public relations. Some agencies specialize in specific media or industries. An agency that specializes in direct mail, or classified advertising, must have specialists in those fields. Agencies that specialize in specific industries need other specialists as well. For example, a fashion agency might have fashion coordinators on staff. A retail agency might have specialists in merchandising.

Should you choose to use an advertising agency, the options of specialties and specialists are numerous. This makes it possible for you to choose the agency that can best serve your needs.

AGENCY COMPENSATION

The commission system of agency compensation seems to have grown up with the advertising industry and has become an integral part of it. Originally, this system was quite simple. The media discounted the cost of the advertising space to the agency by 15 percent. The agency billed the client at the full rate, and the 15 percent became its commission.

While this system is still used to some extent, the growth of advertising, the increase in the variety of media, and the elaborate techniques of advertising have resulted in developing new compensation structures.

The straight agency commission, in its traditional form, is still used most often. But now, in some cases, publishers allow an additional 2 percent cash discount for prompt payment. This brings the commission to 17 percent. The 15 percent discount applies to broadcast media as well, but they don't pay the 2 percent cash discount. Outdoor advertising operators usually discount 16 2/3 percent to advertising agencies.

A significant difference in current and past practice is that in the early days, the 15 percent commission was sufficient to cover all production costs. This is no longer the case, and agencies now pass along the cost of production plus a service charge of 17.65 percent (which is actually 15 percent of the gross cost of production). This arrangement is made by prior agreement with the client.

In recent years there's been a tendency toward direct fee compensation, rather than commission. This change came about because many agencies found that the amount of time and effort it takes to service two different accounts that bill the same amount is not always the same for each account. Some accounts require more time and effort than others. Under the direct fee structure, the agency usually predicates its fee on a formula based on its own cost for overhead, etc., plus a fair profit margin. These fees are then negotiated with clients. Agencies on a fee structure usually bill the clients separately for production costs and expenses, adding the 17.65 percent markup.

The many services supplied by the modern full service agency go so far beyond just placing advertising that there are few campaigns that continue to warrant the straight commission basis, and it seems just a matter of time before the straight commission basis is replaced completely by the direct fee.

HOUSE AGENCIES AND IN-HOUSE CAPABILITY

The traditional advertising agency structure today has many variations, including house agencies and in-house capabilities for larger companies.

Some large advertisers maintain subsidiary house agencies as full service profit centers owned by, and servicing, only one company. They have only their parent company as a client. A valid concept only where there is a great volume of advertising, the house agency has both advantages and disadvantages. The 15 percent commission pays for the operation of the agency, and sometimes even shows a profit that can be passed on to the parent company. There is complete control of the agency's personnel and complete focus on the advertiser's problems. Agency personnel have the opportunity to become totally immersed in the advertiser's products or services and markets, without the distraction of other clients. On the other hand, there is the lack of input that comes from working on a variety of other products and services. There's also the tendency for the house agency to become immersed in the advertiser's corporate structure, which usually results in the agency's being unable to attract the best talent and to compete effectively in the marketplace of ideas.

The in-house staff agency is usually just a staff of advertising specialists on the company payroll. It's not a separate profit center. The in-house staff rarely has a complete complement of agency personnel, and relies instead on outside services for such various elements as research, copy, art, media buying, etc. The in-house concept has grown in recent years as these services improved, and independent groups known as boutiques came into existence. The boutique uses the talent of creative specialists in small firms that specialize in only one or two aspects of advertising, such as copy or art. This has been further enhanced by the growth of modular system in full service agencies, in which individual services such as copy, art or media buying may be purchased separately from other agency services. An in-house advertising staff can frequently produce high-quality advertising by judiciously using independent outside services to supplement its own capabilities.

There has also been substantial growth in independent media services, which do in media buying what the boutique does in the creative field. While they function in all media, they're of greatest value in television and radio, where buys can be more complex than in print media. Their growth in recent years is predicated on the fact that the media have become more aware that advertising space and time are ephemeral. When they're not used, they can't be recaptured—they're lost forever. Thus, the media are frequently willing to make arrangements with these media services that go beyond the standard rate card. So many of these deals are possible that it takes an independent organization to keep track of them, and thus serve both the media and the advertiser.

The independent media service functions as an intermediary between the agency or advertiser and the media. It does media planning, scheduling, negotiating, buying and monitoring. These companies save both time and money for both the small advertiser and the larger company, and can supply a great deal of valuable expertise at reasonable rates. There tends to be no standard method of compensation for their service, and arrangements differ for each deal. Sometimes it's a straight media commission, sometimes a fee based on total billing, and sometimes a fee based on the amount of money the service saves the advertiser.

AGENCY OR DO-IT-YOURSELF

Your decision to do your own advertising or to use an outside agency depends primarily on three factors—the amount of advertising you do, the skills you have or are available to you, and your confidence in your own ability to do what needs to be done effectively. If your advertising budget limits you to classified advertising and an occasional display ad, and if you feel perfectly capable of doing it yourself, then by all means do so. You can, after all, supplement your own efforts by using outside services and boutiques.

If, on the other hand, you recognize the need for a broader, more effective campaign, and feel that you lack the expertise to do it yourself, then by all means consider an outside agency. And remember that no matter how capable you are, performing the advertising function takes considerable time that you might better apply to other aspects of your business.

SELECTING AN AGENCY

Finding an agency need not be difficult, even if you're located in a smaller community in which there are few choices. There's no rule that says that your agency has to be right in your own community. If your marketing plans, and the size of your budget, warrant it, an out-of-town agency can work as well for you as can a local one. Lists of accredited agencies (accredited by the media, and therefore entitled to media discount) are readily available from regional or national advertising trade associations, or from the Yellow Pages.

Selecting an agency, on the other hand, requires some thought and foresight. First, marketing professional services with any degree of sophistication is relatively new, and few traditional agencies can be expected to understand it without extensive orientation. And second, as a professional, you perform a service. An advertising agency also performs a service. You understand the service concept. On the one hand, you know how difficult it is to forecast how a service will perform for you. On the other hand, this knowledge should make it relatively simple for you to understand the agency's service concept, and to judge its ability to develop and produce your marketing program.

Prior to asking agencies to make presentations to you, it may be useful to spend some time with each of the candidates explaining your agency and your profession, including some of the ethical strictures. It will save a considerable amount of time, because the more the agency knows about you, the more likely that it will zero in on what you really need.

Beyond this, there are a number of specific things you should look for in selecting an agency:

Reputation. An agency's reputation can be checked by discussing it with media representatives in your market area, or with other of the agency's clients. Certainly, any reputable agency would be delighted to give you references and a list of its clients. Reputation should be based upon service, creativity and integrity.

The agency's client list. The list should include a large number of clients whose advertising budgets are the same as yours. That can be more important than their having other clients in similar fields. If you're the small client in a shop with large clients, are you likely to get as much attention as the larger clients do, or be assigned superior account or creative personnel?

Range of services. Does the agency have the capability to perform the services you need for your advertising and marketing program? If the capability is not on staff, which are the outside services it uses, and what's their quality of work?

Creativity. What's your own impression of the work it's done for other clients? And not just the ads, but the full range of marketing services? How effective has the work been? Can you get references from other clients that attest to the fact that the agency's work produces results that are equal to the creativity, or does the agency just produce prize-winning ads that don't really sell?

And even more important, what's your feeling about the way it understands your problems and marketing needs? What sorts of questions does it ask you?: Are they routine, or searching? Simply because an agency has been successful in a campaign for one kind of product or service doesn't mean that it can grasp and understand your objectives, and successfully translate them into a great campaign for you.

Of course, the really crucial question is whether the same team that produced the great ads they've just shown you will be the one that works for you.

Service. Who's going to service your account? How much of his time will you have available to you? Do you personally like the account executive, and are you impressed by him in your initial conversation? Advertising is not only a creative business it's a personal business, and you have to work well with the person handling your account.

Fee arrangements. Are the fees reasonable for the service the agency says it can offer you, or are they too high or too low? Are they realistic in terms of your own budget?

In the final analysis, the best evaluation of an agency comes, unfortunately, only after an expenditure of time and money. Does it get results for you or not? An agency must be allowed a reasonable time to prove itself, and the time should be agreed upon at the outset. If after that time you feel that the agency hasn't worked for you, then don't hesitate to change. It's no reflection on either you or the agency. Sometimes a perfectly good agency can't perform as well for you as it has for other of its clients. There's no onus in facing the fact if everybody's been given a fair chance to perform. A fair chance means as well, that you've been cooperative with the agency.

SUMMARY

Producing an ad, from conception to publication, requires a great many separate but coordinated skills. Few individuals have all of the skills, although a capable individual or small advertising agency may supplement with outside experts. A full-service agency may have the following specialists:

- Account supervisors and account executives, who are responsible for planning and managing your advertising program
- Creative director, who is responsible for the creative concept and management of the creative effort of your campaign
- Research director, who is responsible for market and readership research
- Copywriter, who writes the ad copy
- Art director, who designs the ad
- Media buyer, who schedules and purchases media space and time
- Production director, who supervises the technical aspects of ad production
- Traffic director, who oversees the flow of all elements of an ad, from conception to production
- Art buyer, who buys artwork for ads
- Agency administrator and administrative personnel, who are responsible for running the agency

Agencies are compensated either by keeping the 15 percent discount on media purchases and billing the client the full amount, or by a flat fee. All services are usually marked up to the client by 17.65 percent.

Some firms may be large enough to have *house agencies*, complete subsidiary advertising agencies they own to service only their own firms, or *in-house* agencies, which have staff advertising capabilities, frequently supplemented by outside services. Smaller firms can sometimes run their ad campaigns with a small in-house staff, or even do-it-yourself with outside help retained on a project basis.

In selecting an agency, it should be remembered that few agencies can have had extensive experience in advertising for a professional service. It's helpful to recognize, as well, that advertising is a service, just as other professionals offer a service, which should be a guide in judging an agency. Other factors to consider are:

• Reputation, supported by references
• Client list, with an eye to accounts of comparable size
• Range of services
• Creativity
• Service concepts, and the individuals who will work directly with you
• Fee arrangements

When retaining an agency, be sure to specify your objectives and the time frame in which you expect them to be achieved.

PART III
PUBLIC RELATIONS

CHAPTER 11

Public Relations

The term "public relations" is best understood if the words are taken literally. Public relations is the way you meet and deal with the public, and in turn, how you are perceived by the public. The public, of course, is your clientele and prospective clientele.

As broadly used as the term "public relations" may be, it is prey to considerable misconception and mythology. For example, public relations is too often confused with publicity, which is just one of many tools of public relations.

And too often, public relations is seen simply as a manipulative discipline, sometimes with sinister overtones. True, public relations is indeed sometimes used that way. But rarely successfully, since that's not it's value or purpose.

IMAGE

The word "image"—another myth—comes to mind.

There is no concept in marketing more misconstrued, more mis-used, more deleterious to ultimate marketing achievement, than the concept of image. It implies that facts or symbols can be manipulated to offer a representation of a company or an individual that's in any way different from reality.

Truth told, facts and symbols are not often successfully manipulated, and misrepresentation to the public rarely works in the market-place. The acoustics of the business world are much too good to allow flagrant misrepresentation to pervade over any extended period of time. In the real world, this concept of "image" very quickly falls apart.

On the other hand, if the reality of your firm is reasonably favorable, that reality can frequently be focused and projected in ways that clarify a perception of the best of your firm, and that enhances your reputation as a superior practitioner. If this is what's meant by "image", then the word is used well.

And if the word "image" is indeed appropriately used, then public relations is the discipline that focuses on the reality, sharpens the perception, and enhances the reputation.

Public relations is the discipline, as well, that generates an atmosphere in which more people want to do more business with you.

Thus, by affording the public the opportunity to think well of you, thereby making the market more receptive to your sales efforts, public relations enhances your selling effort.

Like advertising, public relations can't of itself sell professional services. It's activities serve to educate your prospective clientele about who you are, what you do and how you do it, and may even generate inquiries, It can enhance your relations with existing clients by projecting an attitude of service, and a willingness to serve, that adds enthusiasm to the idea of doing business with you. But, as with most other marketing tools, it can't close a sale.

Public relations considerations dictate how you do what you do. This includes every aspect of your public persona, from the way your office is decorated to the way your letterhead looks, to the way you and your staff dress; the way you structure and conduct client meetings and client communications; the visible aspects of the way you manage your firm. In sum, the way you do business. It's this projection of the reality of a sound firm that builds credibility for everything you do or say, in either a professional or a frank marketing context.

In essence, then, effective public relations resides in the classic observation that what you are speaks so loudly that people can't hear what you say you are. The most effective public relations program projects the best of what you are.

ROLE IN THE MARKETING MIX

In the marketing mix, the major role of public relations is primarily to strengthen reputation within the context of professional expertise.

It uses publicity through the media to reach its audiences, both by direct contact and through activities such as seminars, speeches, etc. that generate newsworthy exposure. The basic technique of publicity is to cast the story in ways that are newsworthy, and then to persuade editors that the story is newsworthy for their readers. Publicity may have the advantage of an implied editorial endorsement, as well as ubiquitousness. But is also has the disadvantage of lack of total control. You propose and others—the editors—dispose.

Advertising works only when there are advertisements. Public relations' many facets, beginning with an attitude about service that's ingrained in a practice, works constantly. It works, even without publicity, on a day-to-day basis, with positive effects compounding.

Strategically, in a marketing mix public relations is used primarily to build reputation and enhance perception of a firm's skills and abilities. Although strategy differs in each case, ideally an ongoing and persistent public relations program would be used to generate a broad-based knowledge of a firm and its skills and to build credibility. Advertising would be used to focus the message and to add selling strength. Direct mail would be used to bring the firm closest to the sale, which ultimately must be consummated by an individual.

Public relations supports and extends the value of advertising in several specific ways. It should be made clear, however, that public relations is not free advertising, even though it may use publicity that results in telling a great deal about your company through the editorial pages of a publication.

Public relations, with it's ability to build credibility, is particularly important to professional services marketing. In an arena in which product distinctions can't be made, credibility takes on an increased value in enhancing reputation.

And when a public relations program succeeds in developing a favorable attitude towards your firm, it makes your advertising and sales claims more credible. Successful publicity efforts contribute to this because they have the added advantage of the implied editorial objective support; the third person endorsement of the publication, which appears to be saying, objectively, that because you are newsworthy, you are to be viewed favorably.

When your public relations efforts succeed, then they succeed on all fronts—improved client relations, improved perception of your abilities, enhanced reputation, and a broader base of understanding of what you do and how well you do it.

ELEMENTS OF PUBLIC RELATIONS

Public relations functions, essentially, in several basic areas:

Attitude and basic service concept. How do you perceive and project your own role in serving your clients?. To what extent will you extend yourself in their behalf? How significant is it for you to deal with your audience—your clients and potential clients—in ways that exude a willingness to serve in their behalf, rather than to perform what you do in ways that serve only your convenience? Do you consciously favor quality over expedience?

That aspect of public relations that projects the concept of service, and delineates your firm as one that is substantial, is an ongoing and never-ceasing affair. It should be a constant in any business.

But public relations is more than just an attitude of "niceness," or even of service. It must function in a realistic context of sound business practice and genuine excellence. News of poor practice or business techniques will travel further and faster than you can possibly offset with any kind of publicity campaign or manipulative "image".

At the same time, the good things you do, the services you perform, those activities that contribute to the very reputation you'd like to have, all travel well. And while everyone makes a mistake from time to time or makes an enemy, or mishandles a situation, the balance sheet also travels.

Publicity. This is the communications function in public relations. It's the skill—and sometimes the art—of communicating to the public, through news media and other devices, those factors that focus attention on you, your firm, your expertise and skills, your service concept—all those elements that ultimately enhance your reputation as a superior performer and outstanding service organization.

In a highly competitive marketing situation, publicity should also be ongoing. In publicizing a professional service it's never sufficient merely to expose the name. The essence of publicity, in this context, is to project expertise.

But publicity, and reputation, are very much like a hoop. As long as you keep beating a hoop with a stick it keeps rolling. The minute you stop, it falls over. So it is with reputation. The effort must be sustained.

Being publicity-minded doesn't mean being brash or unduly forward. Rather, it means being thoroughly professional in the sense of being a reliable source of expertise for the business press.

At the same time if public relations is to function effectively as part of the total marketing mix, and if it is to contribute to meeting marketing objectives, then the publicity program must be designed with the marketing mix in mind.

Newsmaking events. Frequently, a good measure of public relations consists of activities you generate to focus attention on the firm, its members, and its expertise. In many cases, it will serve as a basis for most of the publicity you garner.

A seminar for clients and prospective clients serves a valid purpose in marketing. But when that seminar deals with a subject in a way that's new or unique, it serves as a basis for publicity—for making news. When a new approach to solving a problem—a new audit technique, a new computer control system, a new legal service—is developed and presented to the public, this is a newsmaking event that's been generated in a way that affords special attention and news coverage. Speeches, and even participation in trade shows and conventions, serve in the same way.

The range of newsmaking events is limited only by the imagination. Special studies, seminars, community service—all these and more can be invented legitimately to serve as newsmaking events.

Professional relations. There are few industries that serve their members so well in public relations as do professional societies. Lawyers, doctors, accountants—all owe a large measure of the favorable public view towards their professions to the public relations efforts of their societies. The tangible value to professionals of this achievement is a public perception of probity, ethical behavior, reliability and integrity. That is pure money in the bank to any professional.

At the same time, good public relations demands that a professional comply with the ethics of his or her profession. Ethical codes remain a major factor in sustaining the somewhat elevated view of the professions, and good public relations demands the public perception of ethical behavior, as well as the reality of it.

Community relations. Long a cornerstone of professional practice development, serving the community is still a crucial part of marketing professional services. The public expects the professional, in his exalted stature, to be a pillar of the community. This, of course, has public relations overtones. It also gets clients.

As with all aspects of marketing a professional service, public relations does not function in the abstract. No agency, no matter how effective, can perform the public relations function without the total participation of the people in your firm who perform that service.

OBJECTIVES

The objectives of a public relations program, and particularly one that relies heavily on publicity dictate the nature of the program and the techniques that are to be used. Generally, a public relations program should build a structured capability that would:

• Expose and project the firm's capabilities, and those of the people who comprise the base of the firm's expertise, to its target audience—on a consistently high level of quality.
• Focus on the firm's greatest strengths and capabilities.
• Develop activities that increase exposure.
• Compete successfully for exposure against the public relations activities of the firm's competitors.
• Give a measure of feedback on how the firm is being perceived by its target audiences.
• Develop editorial reprints that inform and magnify the implied editorial endorsement.

The mechanics for achieving this are dictated by the nature of the profession and the firm itself. The broad range of the firm's activities, and their predominantly technical nature, frequently dictate a strong in-house capability. Even with a good external agency, the program must be driven internally, because it would be exceedingly difficult and expensive to expect an outside firm to be fully aware of even a fraction of the public relations possibilities of the activities generated by a professional firm on a day-to-day basis. Nor could they have the technical understanding of these activities without expensive and time-consuming participation by the firm's professionals.

Of all marketing activities, public relations is the one that requires the most consistent attention. Your firm and its people, after all, are constantly in the eyes of your clients, and should be for prospective clients as well. Even if you don't have an active publicity program, all other aspects of public relations—the way you deal with and present yourself to the public—are as crucial to developing your practice as are your technical skills.

No one marketing tool of itself comprises a program, but of all of them, public relations can supply the greatest mileage for the marketing dollar.

SUMMARY

Public relations is more than just publicity, it's the total approach to the way you meet, deal with, and are perceived by everybody you want to do business with. It is not an "image"—a manipulation of facts and symbols to present a perception of your firm that belies reality. It's a function of doing things well, and making the things you do widely known in a context that makes more people want to do more business with you. While it cannot close a sale, it effectively supports other marketing efforts.

The active elements of total public relations include:

• Attitude and service concept
• Publicity
• Community relations
• Newsmaking events, including speeches, seminars, etc.

The basic objectives of a public relations program should include:

• Project the firm's capabilities to its target audience
• Develop activities that increase exposure

- Compete successfully against competitors for exposure
- Supply feedback on how firm is perceived
- Develop editorial reprints that magnify implied editorial endorsement of publicity

Because of the complexities, technical and multifarious nature of most professional firms, a program must be internally driven, even if it uses a good outside agency.

Public relations, in conjunction with other marketing tools, can supply good mileage for the marketing dollar.

CHAPTER 12

Publicity Techniques

Public relations, as we've seen, is the sum of a great many factors designed to give your public—your markets—an impression about you and your company that's favorable, informed and conducive to doing more business with you. It's an ongoing attitude that should pervade every aspect of your business.

But doing the right thing, doing interesting and newsworthy things, is only part of the effort. The other part is to communicate what you're doing to your target audience. This must be done in a way that not only informs, but enhances your reputation as well. You want to be known, but for those things that will directly or ultimately help your business.

The technique for doing this—the tool of public relations that makes this happen—is called publicity.

Unlike advertising, in which you purchase the space for your message, publicity depends upon a presumably objective third person—the editor—who is more concerned with meeting the needs of his publication than with meeting your needs to inform. If the editorial thrust of a publication is not successful in consistently meeting the needs of its readers, it will lose circulation, diminish its value as an advertising medium, and go out of business. This is as true of the smallest community newspaper as it is of the *New York Times* or the *Washington Post*. It's as true of the smallest and most remote radio station as it is of the largest network.

Publicity, then, must be structured to meet the editorial needs of a publication or the broadcast media. The person to be persuaded, in the first instance, is the editor, not the ultimate reader.

WHAT IS NEWS?

In any newspaper, or any newscast, all news is relative. It's more than just the report of an event or an activity that has never been publicly reported before. Each day, editors of even the largest newspaper must review all reported events and make a subjective judgment as to which of those events will concern or interest their readers sufficiently to warrant the allocation of rare and precious space. On any given day, the news of a major airplane disaster will garner more editorial interest than the news of a major urban redevelopment plan. The urban plan, in turn, may preempt in importance the announcement of a company's decision to build a $5 million plant in the community. And this, in turn, will preempt the news of plans to build a 200-home development of middle-income homes. Lower down on the list would be an announcement of the appointment of a new partner of an accounting firm. Yet, sometimes, if not very much has happened that day, (or if it's precisely the kind of information for which the publication is read), the new partner news may be the most exciting thing the newspaper has to report.

Even feature material—general background or general interest stories, or service stories such as new techniques in estate planning or how to select a doctor in a strange town—has its editorial stringencies. Even the feature story must have its news hook—a focal point of immediate interest that serves as a fresh basis for writing about a familiar subject.

Moreover, every segment of the press, even broadcast news, has its own target audiences, and therefore its own point of view. The big city newspaper usually focuses on international and national domestic news, with local or regional news relegated to a secondary position, except for matters of citywide significance. The community newspaper focuses entirely upon news of interest to the community, which means news about the community.

Even television news is targeted to a clearly defined audience.

Some stations position their newscasts to reach a mass audience that's more interested in sensationalism than in politics. Others focus more heavily on government and national news. Some publications are large enough to be departmentalized, so that financial or economic news becomes the province of the business editor. Only occasionally is financial news considered by news editors to be of sufficient interest to the larger audience to be put in the general news section. Other newspapers make no distinction of news by industry, and a business story will compete for space with a school budget story. Sometimes the accounting or legal story is considered to be business news, and falls under that editor's province, and sometimes it's considered to be of interest only to other accountants and lawyers, and so is relegated to the back pages.

Newspapers and magazines have limited space and broadcast news has a finite amount of time. Each day an editor must make fast decisions about the priorities of what news should be given that precious space and time, and how much of that space and time should be devoted to each news item. Any information you have that you believe to be newsworthy, then, must compete against all the other news about which the editor must make a judgment for the next edition.

And so, the basic techniques of publicity are designed to help you compete successfully for the editor's attention and win a judgment in your favor in the competition for space and time.

Even in the smallest newspapers, news is categorized, with an editor assigned to each category. For example, a major city newspaper may have a separate staff for international news, another for national domestic news, another just to cover the activities of the federal government. Other departments might include city news, business and finance, real estate, sports, automotive, art, theater, music, women's interest, foods, etc. The smallest community newspaper, with a staff of only three or four people, may categorize news by special interest, such as city-wide news that affects the community, school news, real estate news, sports, news of people and so forth.

THE MEDIA

The media for disseminating news, and particularly news that serves your market, are not confined to just your local newspaper. You have at least the following options:

Daily newspaper. Every community is served by at least one, and usually several, newspapers. Larger cities may have two or more competing daily newspapers, and sometimes a morning and an evening paper. Smaller cities and towns usually have a daily paper for the city, and in some cases a county or area-wide paper. In many cases, smaller communities are served by both a local paper and the newspaper from the nearest major city. Many communities are served by local papers, most of which are published weekly. Because newspapers have the broadest news coverage they are the prime outlet for distribution of publicity material.

Radio. Most radio news is limited to small segments of time during the course of the day. This means that most stations will be concerned primarily with news of broader interest to most of its listeners. From your point of view, the only news of your profession that might concern a radio station is either a professional story of such magnitude that it affects the whole community or feature material that might interest a larger audience. Smaller radio stations, however, frequently pride themselves on local coverage and could very well be interested in direct, on-the spot coverage of an interesting event that you might stage or sponsor, such as a seminar.

Television. Television stations, except for the smaller ones and cable TV, devote remarkably little time to news in proportion to the total broadcast day—and particularly to news of activities that concern very few people. Some stations might pick up events or feature material that would add a human interest or informative angle to a newscast, but in all cases that would depend entirely upon how heavy the news day has been. If it could be measured statistically, television as a publicity outlet ranks a poor third after newspapers and radio, particularly for most business or professional news.

Trade Journals. Most trade journals rely heavily on publicity sources for news. If the readers of a journal in a particularly industry are in any way a part of your potential market, trade journals can be an excellent publicity outlet. A typical news story might address legal, medical or accounting techniques that particularly concern the chemical industry. This might be of interest to the chemical trade press. Trade journals number in the thousands, with some industries being served by several publications. These journals are listed in several directories (see Appendix).

Magazines. There are two general categories of consumer magazines that you might consider—city or regional magazines and national magazines. City magazines are a natural outlet for feature material because of their geographic distribution and their editorial slant. The narrower the geographic distribution, the greater the likelihood that the editors will be interested in news and feature material from a local source. Most of the city magazines are fairly sophisticated, however, and are not often concerned with the kind of routine information in which people might be interested as members of a small community. Yet, these publications offer the opportunity for general feature material, citing you as a source, on subjects that spring from your expertise, and that affect or interest the general public. This might include, for example, how to choose a tax specialist, new techniques in curing cancer how to get a mortgage, and so forth. National consumer magazines, on the other hand, including news magazines such as *Time* and *Newsweek*, are not interested in any but the most unusual news that a professional might generate in the normal course of affairs. But the size of a professional firm's operation doesn't preclude his considering opportunities to submit articles under his own name to appropriate consumer magazines, even though the distribution is far afield from his market. In this case, it's the reprint that counts. An article on "Five Ways to Finance a Home in a Tight Money Market" under your byline in *Family Circle* makes you a national authority. And reprints of it are better (and cheaper) than any brochure.

Penny savers and shoppers. There are literally thousands of such publications distributed throughout the country at shopping centers, supermarkets, and sometimes door-to-door, that include editorial material as well as advertising. The editorial material is usually chatty and loaded with items of interest to community residents. They are a natural outlet for publicity to a very local community.

Other media. Other vehicles for publicity consist of any media distributed to the public. This includes the house organs and newsletters of other companies (and even their bulletin boards), the journals of fraternal or church organizations and even the ads of other companies. When IBM runs an advertising campaign for its personal computers, using a small professional office as an illustration of the kind of business that can use the computer, it's an ad for IBM but publicity for the professional.

It's a basic rule in publicity that before you consider publicity in any medium you should spend time acquainting yourself with it. Each publication has its own editorial requirements and point of view, and you should look at several recent issues to try to fathom exactly what kinds of news or feature material each publication uses. *Harper's* or *Atlantic Monthly* are not likely to use news of four new partners, and in fact neither of those magazines uses news at all. Some daily newspapers publish a great deal of information about individual professional activities, and others publish news of only major consequence, such as a merger. If you sent a photograph to *The Wall Street Journal* to accompany a story you'd be wasting your time—*The Wall Street Journal* doesn't print photographs in its news pages. Knowing a publication's requirements is crucial.

A second major rule is that with rare exceptions, there is a high, thick wall between a publication's advertising and editorial departments, and if that wall is sometimes breached, it's never through an open door. Few consequential publications, and certainly none of any editorial quality, will make a regular practice of *quid pro quo* publicity in exchange for advertising. The fact that you're a major advertiser in any publication doesn't entitle you to breach the editorial independence of the paper except on the merit of your news or feature material alone. While it's true that advertisers sometimes have greater access to editorial pages than do nonadvertisers, any publication that allows its advertising department to influence its editorial department would rapidly lose its readers and its credibility with its audience. And since the value of editorial publicity is the implied editorial third person independent endorsement, using advertising clout for editorial space can be self-defeating. Even in the smaller publications such as some community newspapers, penny savers and so forth, where the practice of catering to advertisers is fairly common, the news should still be capable of standing on its own. Poor publicity is not better than no publicity at all.

THE EDITORS

The person responsible for selecting and publishing or broadcasting news is an editor. Some editors are giants of intellectual and journalistic perspicacity; others are not. Some are skilled and knowledgeable in the professions they cover; others are remarkably unsophisticated in those areas. But regardless of the publication, or the editor's professional capabilities, every editor has the same responsibility—to find news or feature material to meet the publication's readers' (or listeners') needs in terms of editorial position, to prepare it for publication within the context of style and format, and to publish it. This must be done with fresh material every day or week or month, depending upon the frequency of the publication. He may be the editor responsible for the entire publication or for just a department of it. Editors are aided in their task by reporters—journalists who are trained to gather news and write it in the publication's style. Sometimes editors do both editing and reporting.

In publicity, the important thing to remember is that the editor's responsibility is to give his readers what they want to read. What is consistent with the editor's needs is not always consistent with yours. The techniques of publicity are designed to make your needs consistent with the editor's.

NEWS AND HOW TO MAKE IT

In publicity, as in most other aspects of marketing, the strategy for a successful program for professional firms is somewhat different than it is for product or non-professional service campaigns.

While there are always many avenues to take, the one that seems to have proven most successful thus far is to use publicity to project expertise.

And even if the primary objective is to enhance name recognition, it's still best done within the context of projecting expertise.

Projecting Expertise

The reasoning is that by offering expertise to the press, the public perceives the source of that information to be the worthy and knowledgeable practitioner.

For example, a campaign in which your firm's tax experts are constantly quoted as a source of information on various aspects of a new tax law results in several tangible effects:

- That you are willing to supply this help to the journalists who must report on tax practice encourages them to turn to you as a regular source. Thus, the program begins to feed on itself, and the more you're quoted, the more you're asked to be quoted.
- Frequently being quoted in the press not only builds name recognition, but does so in an aura of knowledgeability. The frequent appearances say to the reader, "This must be a knowledgeable firm, because the press quotes it so widely."
- It's a strategy open to the smallest, as well as the largest, practitioner.
- It's a strategy that allows you to expose the expertise of each individual member of your firm, as well as the firm name. It encourages your staff and your partners, and displays the strength of individuals. Perhaps not important in non-professional services, but crucial in professional service marketing

Essentially, this kind of campaign uses all of the devices of publicity, from press releases to interviews to by-lined articles to speeches and seminars. It's based upon a strategy in which each area of your practice is explored for opportunities to function in this context. Moreover, it springs from capabilities and expertise that, presumably, you already have.

The Issues Campaign

Many lawyers and other professionals have long known the practice development advantages of politics, community activities, and other highly visible public activities. The *Issues Program* is emerging as a parallel activity with comparable advantages.

Issues management, which is a specialty within public relations, considers the role of major issues in public and business life. This includes how these issues affect constituencies, and the role that individuals or companies can play in either swaying positions in the issues or educating the public about them.

For the professional, they offer a singularly prestigious opportunity for public exposure under the best possible circumstances.

While the techniques of full scale issue management are extensive, and require considerable professional skill to execute successfully, there are several considerations that can be examined:

- In selecting an issue, is it of sufficient magnitude to concern a large enough audience to warrant a substantial effort? And is the magnitude sufficient to have a longevity that will allow you to make an impact before the matter is resolved or becomes passe?
- Is the issue relevant to your profession? For example, air pollution may be a matter dear to your heart, but not exactly relevant to your accounting practice. If you head a medical clinic, however, it's an issue to consider.
- Is your expertise sufficient to give you credibility on the issue?
- Are you prepared to commit the time and dollars necessary for an investment in a professional issues program?
- Do you have the staff, internal or external, to run the program? This includes researching the issue and constantly updating the research, developing your position, developing the platforms, preparing the material (speeches, articles, press releases, panels, etc.), and publicizing your activities in behalf of the issues.

Given a favorable answer to these questions, an issues program might serve your purposes very well.

The News Categories

Within the media structure, there are several news categories that offer publicity opportunities for the professional; that serve as a framework for the strategies for publicity for a professional firm:

Straight news. In the course of your daily activities any number of things might happen—or be made to happen—that are sufficiently different, sufficiently out of the ordinary to warrant interest by the readers and listeners of the news media. Certainly, if you win a landmark case in the Supreme Court, or merge your practice with a big national firm, that might well be news for the local paper as well as other media, and might well be considered newsworthy by local media. Depending upon the size of your firm and the size of the community in which it functions, some personnel news can be newsworthy as well. If you're the largest firm in town in your profession, and you've made one of your associates a partner, editors might like to know about it. If you're a small firm and just added two new associates, editors of publications covering your market area might well consider that important enough to publish. By reading the local media carefully—the media that service your market area—you can get a fair idea of the kinds of activities and events that might warrant publication.

Manufacturing newsworthy events. With the absolute caveat that no attempt should ever be made to lie to or mislead a publication—it can ruin your chances for ever being successful in publicity—you can do a great many things to develop or manufacture newsworthy activities. Speeches and seminars are primary. Sponsoring community events often serve well. But publicity is more successful with ingenuity. For example, surveys of attitudes or preferences within your expertise—attitudes toward a particular law, or high-rise vs. low-rise buildings, or group vs. private medical practice—all of these are likely to interest editors. If they are well done, and well presented to the press, they will be reported.

But this kind of information must be assembled and presented to them. This is manufacturing a newsworthy event in the same way that having your staff dress in period costumes to commemorate a holiday might attract the attention of the local press. Again, this is a function of understanding the media that serves your area.

Feature material. Newspapers aren't run on news alone. They have an educational function as well. The service article on how to get the most from a legal clinic, or how to chose an architect for a store front, or when it's safe to throw away old financial records, is as important to a newspaper as is the front page. This is feature material. It's the kind of story that serves as the backbone of most professional service publicity. As a professional, you're in a marvelous position to use your expertise to develop these very features.

By-line articles. Magazines, Sunday supplements and sometimes newspapers are delighted to consider articles written by outsiders who have expertise. Local media are constantly looking for service material to help their readers function as better consumers, and their business readers to function as better business people. This would include articles on any appropriate subject in which you have expertise and authority.

DELIVERING PUBLICITY

Given an understanding of the media, and of the quality of newsworthy or feature material, it must be delivered to the publication in a way that's acceptable to editors; that's most likely to succeed in garnering the publicity. There are several specific techniques for accomplishing this.

DIRECT CONTACT. The simplest way to deal with the press is by contacting the appropriate editor of a publication and discussing the story with him. Experienced publicity people know that the order of accomplishing this is:

Make sure you know what your story is. Get it clear in your mind, read the publication and be sure that your format for presenting the story on paper is consistent with the publication's own techniques for reporting similar stories.

Choose the media. Not every story is for every publication. The news of a merger between two small firms is of interest only to those publications that serve the community involved. Unlike the news of a merger of two large national firms, it's not a national story. Winning a landmark decision, on the other hand, can be of interest to even the largest newspaper. Know your media so that you can determine what story is right for what publication.

Find the right editor. In a small community weekly it's easy—there's usually only one editor. At a larger newspaper there are many editors covering different departments. If your local papers have editors covering your profession, you should make it a point to know who they are, and to meet them and let them know you. This is best done, however, by having a story for them on first contact. Your story may be a business story, in which case you'll want the business editor. It may be the kind of feature that should go to an appropriate features editor. The simplest way to find the right editor is to call the publication and ask for the name of the editor who covers the kind of story you have.

Contact the editor. Start with a phone call, remembering that editors are tremendously busy people. They are constantly facing deadlines and are besieged by people like you who have story ideas for them. Introduce yourself, explain that you have a story, tell the gist of the story in as few words as possible and ask to come to see the editor. He will tell you very quickly whether the story's of any interest and whether it warrants further discussion. It may be a news item the editor can take over the phone or, if it isn't an absolutely timely story that will be stale news within 24 hours, he may ask you to send it in writing. In that case, deliver it by hand, trusting the mail only for stories that will be as newsworthy a week from now as they are today. If the editor is interested in the story, you'll be asked to come down to the publication and discuss it, or if it's big news, the editor may assign someone to come to the site of the story to cover it. Ultimately, you'll want to establish a personal relationship with as many editors as possible. If an editor thinks that you have a large enough story or, more important, that you might be a fairly consistent source of news, he'll be delighted to accept an invitation from you for lunch or a drink after work. Most editors are professionals and build personal relationships slowly. They are not swayed by gifts or elaborate presentations. Just the story will do. Then you're doing your job and he's doing his.

Does a personal relationship with an editor make a difference? Only in that you're more likely to get a hearing for a story you have for the publication. Few editors will allow a personal relationship to affect their judgment of what's acceptable to their publication, nor is the friendliest editor likely to print a story as a favor to you that's not consistent with the editorial needs of his paper. Remember the competition for news space is extraordinarily keen. Editors receive five or ten times as much news as they can possibly print, and so the form of presentation of news to a publication is extremely important. It must attract attention for its essential news value in the shortest possible time. To ask a journalist to give you valuable space because of friendship rather than because of the quality of the news is to take unfair advantage of the friendship and jeopardize his position on the publication.

THE PRESS RELEASE

The press release is the standard form for distributing news to the media. The form of press releases is deceptively simple. Properly done, it looks easy.

In fact, it's not simple at all. It's a complex form of journalism, in which the press release writer competes directly with the professional journalist, and other press release writers, for scarce space or broadcast time. It competes, as well, with every other press release issued at the same time, and it competes in an arena in which the initial recipient, the editor, is not particularly receptive.

The physical form should be that which is accepted and traditional in most newspaper city newsrooms. It should be remembered that most city newsrooms receive hundreds—sometimes thousands—of releases every day. The editors charged with going over those releases grumble over the volume they receive, and invariably most releases end up in the wastebasket. They appreciate, however, those releases that are professionally prepared and which make their arduous job simpler.

Succeeding with press release lies, primarily in understanding the journalistic process. There are some basic rules:

Printed news release letterhead. The subject of the printed release head versus the blank sheet of paper is a matter of more debate than one would find at a philosophers' convention. Obviously, there's an element of silliness in the printed head that has the big words "NEWS FROM XYZ, CPAs" and then reports that John Jones has just joined the firm as a junior accountant. This is hardly earthshaking news for a paper the size of, say, the *New York Times*. The printed news release letterhead, on the other hand, is valuable if you're dealing with editors who have come to know you as a regular source of information. Printed letterheads are also acceptable from public relations firms that are well known by publications, and particularly if they're known to send news with a high percentage of acceptability.

If you choose to use a printed letterhead, then every release must have at its top the date and the words, "FOR IMMEDIATE RELEASE," unless it's an advance story where the information is not to be released until a later date; in that case the line should read, "FOR RELEASE [date]." If a printed release head is not used, then the same statement goes at the top, but so too does the name, address and telephone number of the source of the news, including the name of the particular person to be contacted if more information is required. In any event, the release should be written (typed, of course, on one side of the paper only.)

The Headline. Newspapers write their own headlines. Furthermore, the headline is never written—except perhaps in the smallest newspapers—by the person who writes the story itself. The purpose of a headline in a news release is to summarize the meat of the story, so that the editor can quickly determine whether the story warrants further attention. It should consist of no more than two lines, stating briefly and succinctly what the release is about—for example, "NEW AUDIT APPROACH SERVES NON-PUBLIC COMPANIES." The headline should be centered, all in capital letters, at the head of the release.

The Dateline. Following the format used by virtually all daily newspapers, the first words of the release should be the dateline. This means the city or origin of the story and the date the release is issued: "Detroit, July 10 . . ."

The Text. All releases should be double spaced with paragraphs indented and wide margins. This makes it easier for the editor to read, to mark up and to indicate notes in the margin.

Writing the Press Release

As for the writing, old myths die hard, and one of the most persistent is that newspaper articles—and therefore press releases—must start with the traditional five W's—who, what, when, where, and why—as elements for the lead of the story. The myth also says that press releases are edited from the bottom up, particularly when it comes to cutting for space, and therefore the least important information goes at the end.

You have but to read any good daily newspaper to know that papers are run on journalistic practice, not myths. In today's fast-paced journalism, the lead paragraph contains the most terse, exciting summary of the crucial heart of the story. It gets to the point of the release as quickly as possible. A good technique is to cover up everything but the first line or two of a release and try to see it with the editor's eye, since that's about as far as an editor will read before he decides whether the rest of the release is worth reading. Do those two lines impart something that is genuinely news? Do they get to the heart of the matter? The name of the company is not news—the facts are. The best possible first sentence might read, "The first building taller than 10 stories to be built in Linwood is to be designed by Smith & Dale, local area architects, it was announced here today by . . ."

Each subsequent paragraph should cover a point of the story in descending order of importance—the lead paragraph with the primary news, the second paragraph with the next item of importance and so on. If it's appropriate, the mechanical facts—where and when, etc.—should be noted early in the story. Every topic of the story should be given its own paragraph for simple editing. Both for style and because so many newspapers now write and edit by computer, stories are no longer edited to fit the available space by cutting from the bottom. They are edited for style throughout the entire release, Writing paragraphs in descending order of importance, however, is frequently done for interest.

The text itself should be written in the journalistic style of the largest and best newspaper in your area, no matter what publication it's to be sent to. It should be written in simple English, grammatically correct, in the active—not passive—voice, and shouldn't read like a legal contract. Its job is to impart news.

A news release should be straightforward and should not in any way editorialize. Opinions, projections and other subjective points of view should not be reported as facts. They should either be put in quotes or otherwise attributed to a partner by name.

The last paragraph of the release should be a simple, one or two-line statement describing the company's business.

End the release with the traditional ending mark—the three number symbols—###. The old telegrapher's ending mark—30—is quaint, but has long since gone out of style and is infrequently used today.

Releases should rarely be more than one page long. If they are longer, then at the bottom of each page type the word "MORE," with a dash on each side, and at the top of subsequent pages should be a key word identifying the story ("NEW AUDIT TECHNIQUE") and the name of the issuing company, followed by the page number.

Distribution. Releases sent to the press should be addressed to a specific editor by name only when you are sure that the editor to whom the release is addressed is, in fact, the appropriate person, that he is still employed at that publication in that capacity, and that he will be at his desk on the day the release will be received. Otherwise, it should be addressed to a departmental editor—Business Editor, Metropolitan News Editor, etc. If it's important to get the release into the hands of a specific editor at a specific time, it should not be mailed, it should be sent by messenger and followed up with a phone call to make sure that it's not stalled at the reception desk. If it's just a general release, designed for no specific editor, it should be addressed to the City Desk, a newspaper term for the editor who covers general news.

Except under extreme circumstances, it's bad form to call a newspaper to find out why your release wasn't printed. The chances are that it wasn't run because the editor didn't think it was important enough to print in his limited space, in relation to other information received that day. No newspaper is required to print any news, no matter how important it is to the firm, and pestering an editor will only incur animosity and risk that subsequent releases will find their way directly to the wastebasket. It is, however, appropriate to phone ahead, talk to the particular editor and advise him that the release is on the way. In view of the large number of releases received every day, if the news is important enough the editor will appreciate it and watch for it. It will not, however, guarantee that he will print it. There are times when it seems obvious that a release should have been printed and wasn't. It would be surprising, for example, if the announcement of a major event were not published in a local paper. Under these circumstances, it's perfectly appropriate to phone the editor—not to ask why the release wasn't printed, but merely to confirm that the release was received. Frequently the editor will appreciate it if he has reason to believe that news he should have received never reached him.

Radio and television should not be overlooked in a distribution of press releases. Many stations carry some business news, although considerably less than most newspapers. The measure is the importance of the news to the largest number of viewers or listeners. The newspaper reader disinterested in business or real estate can turn the page, the listener cannot. This is why radio and television editors choose only major items for their newscasts. In most cases it's pointless to send routine releases to radio or television stations. If, on the other hand, there is a reason to believe that something is particularly newsworthy, the station's news editor should be dealt with in exactly the same way as the newspaper editor.

FEATURE MATERIAL

The approach to developing feature materially is generally different than it is for the straight news announcement. In feature development, you're usually addressing a subject in an explanatory way, and not in the terse, straightforward press release style. Nevertheless, the lead paragraph should be exciting and to the point, and preferably based on a news hook.

For example, "The new law, passed last week, that changed banking regulations can profoundly affect the smallest depositor, if he isn't paying attention to his account." It would then go on to explain the law, how it affects depositors, and what can be done to minimize the affect and increase the opportunity. As a professional, and an expert, your contribution enhances your authority, and your reputation.

In approaching this kind of press coverage there are several basic rules and guidelines that are important. They apply whether the story is generated by you or by an outside public relations consultant:

- In a feature story it's even more important than in a news story that the target publication must be clearly understood. Several issues of the publication should be studied to determine the kind of material it uses, its style, its editorial viewpoint and its apparent taboos. Any attempt to try to convince a publication to print a story that's not in keeping with its general editorial policy is not only a waste of time but could lead to a singularly adverse reaction by the editors to you, your company or your public relations consultant.
- Even a feature article must have a newsworthy point of view. Sometimes this is a hook—an event or activity that serves as a focal point for the story, an indication that the timing for the story is appropriate. Or it can be an angle that is at least unusual and perhaps unique, such as your new approach to financing a small business, or little used techniques of estate planning for individuals in lower income brackets. Developing feature material usually re-

quires a measure of skill, if not artfulness. When a man murders his wife, it takes no public relations skill to get his name in the paper. The skill is in fathoming the unusual in an otherwise usual story, and projecting it as the basis for a feature article.

Approaching the publication requires some relatively simple procedures:

- Once a target publication has been selected and its editorial policies analyzed, the story is developed specifically for that publication. The same general story may function for several different publications, but each approach must still be tailored.
- Don't try to sell the same story to two competing publications at the same time. If both accept it you're in trouble for the future. Approach publications with feature stories one at a time.
- Find the proper editor, either by reading the masthead or by calling the publication and inquiring.
- Write a letter to the editor describing the story. In some cases the letter may be preceded by a phone call or even a meeting with the editor. Almost invariably, and with very few exceptions, the story will ultimately have to be presented to the publication in written form. Sometimes the letter presenting the story can be prepared before the first contact. Sometimes, if a discussion with the editor beforehand is feasible, the letter should be written only after the meeting and should be patterned on the guidelines set forth by the editor. Naturally, the letter should be brief and to the point, starting with the basic premise of the story, followed by a statement of fact to support that premise. It should indicate the availability of the people involved, and of the graphic or visual material, if appropriate, that's available or can be made available to supplement the story.
- A few days after the letter has been sent it's appropriate to follow up with a phone call to determine the editor's interest, to answer questions he might have and to make arrangements for whatever interviews or further discussions are necessary.

Feature stories are a major tool of any publicity program. They can be the core of a program for professional services. No opportunity to develop a feature story should be allowed to pass without some attempt to sell it.

MAJOR NEWS COVERAGE

Major news can sometimes be treated somewhat differently than routine releases. If the news is of sufficient consequence to warrant greater attention than just routine release—dealing with a new national tax law, for example—there are other techniques that can be used.

The national campaign. Frequently, it's possible to anticipate national coverage of a major event in ways that redound to the credit of an individual firm. For example, if an event of national magnitude, such as the passage of a new law that affects a great many people nationally, is about to occur, the press will be seeking a source of expertise to help report it clearly to readers. By anticipating this, and through careful planning, becoming that source, there's an opportunity for grand scale publicity.

Given a reasonable lead time (two or three days or more), and a fair certainty of the event's taking place, at least the following steps should be taken:

- Garner all of the expertise you can marshal. For example, how is the law likely to read? How is it to be administered? what does it mean in terms of the Man in the Street? What are it's subtleties? What are its weaknesses and strengths?
- Organize all of the experts in your firm. If you have more than one office, identify a lead expert in each office. If you are a one-office firm, who are the experts in your office? These people become your spokesmen.
- Prepare your material, which should include . . .
  — A press release
  — A position paper
  — A summary sheet (brief) about your firm, and why it is an appropriate source of information on the subject
  — A brief—*brief*—cover note (press advisory), explaining that the law is about to be passed, that it will affect a great many of the publication's readers, and that you're offering the enclosed to help the reporters in their coverage. Indicate that your firm and "the following list of people (with phone numbers)" are available for further information.
- A day or two before the expected passage, call key people in the

press, remind them of the imminence of the law's passage, and offer to meet with them for a pre-passage press briefing. If you have more than one office, have a designated spokesman do this in every city where you have an office.

- Coordinate this effort with (if appropriate) both internal and external public relations staff, with each staff person assigned a different group of editors and publications. They will make the pre-passage calls.
- With all press materials prepared, the coordinated staff moves out the material to the press—by wire, by phone, and in person or by messenger—the very instant the bill is passed.
- After the material has gone out, and allowing time for it to have been received and digested, followup key editors by phone, offering your services.

Timing is crucial, simply because your competitors will be doing the same things—and the first with the best wins. And, experience has shown, wins big.

Press conference. The old-fashioned press conference for routine news has gone out of style. Newspaper people are too busy to spend several hours away from their desks to attend a press conference. They get particularly disturbed—and appropriately so—if they're invited to a press conference and are led to believe that the news they will be given is of greater importance than it actually is. The fact that they're wined and dined is not of the essence. There's no law that says a newspaperman who accepts your hospitality has to print your story. Newspaper people are further annoyed by being invited to a press conference to be given news that can just as easily be covered by a press release or even a telephone interview.

A press conference should be called only when:

- The news is monumental
- There's some clear reason, such as demonstration or the need for an elaborate explanation, why the news cannot be covered by a press release
- Full understanding of the news requires questioning and elaborate answers

If a press conference is warranted, there are some basic procedures to be followed:

The Invitation. The invitation should be sent out several days to a week in advance of the event. It should state the purpose of the conference, and give the time and the place. If there are specific visual aspects to the story, they should be indicated, and a separate invitation should be sent to the photo desk of the publication, if there is one. If the news is important and urgent enough, send your invitations by telegram or night letter, but certainly not a week before the event. The urgency of the news implied by the telegram is defeated by the time lag. It's a good idea to telephone the invitees on the morning of the conference to remind them and to verify their attendance.

The Place. The place should always be appropriate to the event. If it's a major announcement about your company, then it should be at your office if possible. If the news concerns a particular facility, then hold it there. The next best choice is a private room at a restaurant or club. (Obviously, a public table in a restaurant is an inappropriate place to hold a press conference.) The room should be large enough to hold everybody comfortably, but not so large that the crowd seems dwarfed and the room seems empty. Set up the room well beforehand to assure that all speakers can be easily seen and heard, and that all graphic material is easily presented.

The Time. The time for a press conference is determined by a newspaper's deadline. The best time for a press conference is late morning, noon or very early afternoon. News announced at a 10:00 A.M. press conference will make both the afternoon and next morning papers. If it's a major story, the afternoon papers, which in most cities are not as widely read as the morning papers, will preempt the story, which will not please the morning papers. Be sure that everyone has time to hear the news and to write about it before deadline. Newspapermen still go back to their offices and pound typewriters. Only in the movies do they rush to the phones to call the city room.

Press Kit. A complete press kit should be prepared for every newsperson attending. This should consist of a basic release, a background sheet on the company, any financial or other background material, 8" x 10" glossy photos captioned with a half sheet attached at the bottom and any other pertinent material such as brochures or descriptive literature. Half sheet captions on photos should be headed exactly as are press releases so that if the caption is detached from the photo the information is complete. The photo should also be identified on the back with a label, for the same reason. Do not write directly on the back of a photo since it will mar the surface of the photo on the other side. Make the press kit as complete as possible, but don't overload it with so much material that a reporter can't find the facts for all the paper.

The Presentation. The presentation itself should be short, simple and to the point. While there's a great temptation to dramatize, few newspaper people are impressed by this. The drama should come from the material, which should be simple, to the point and graphically illustrated. It should take no longer than 30 or 40 minutes to present, and time should be allowed for questioning. Immediately following the press conference, representatives for the company involved should be prepared to spend a few minutes to answer any reporters' questions. Some should be available by phone for the remainder of the day to answer any question that may occur to a reporter back at his desk writing the story.

ROUTINE INQUIRIES

One of the advantages of being known to publications as a good news source is that you're frequently called upon to comment on stories of interest. In fact, becoming a major source of expertise in your field is a primary public relations objective. For example, if a newspaper, on its own, decides to do a story on a new tax law, and the editor knows you, he's more likely to call on you (rather than your competitor) to express your point of view. The best approach is always to be thoughtful, direct and to the point. People experienced in being interviewed also know that the way something sounds when it's spoken is frequently different from the way it sounds when it's read. That's why you should think carefully before you answer even the most mundane question. As you talk, try to visualize your words in print. If there's time to submit an answer in writing, even if you have to send it over by messenger, that's even better if the subject is in any way sensitive and your being misquoted or quoted out of context can lead to your being misinterpreted.

A similar problem might arise when you're the victim of adverse news—a problem not always restricted to the larger practitioner. It can happen to anyone. If a newspaper reporter who knows you calls before the story breaks to get your side of it, you should, of course, think carefully before you answer. But at the same time, those experienced in situations of this kind know that it's better to simply state facts, never deal in personalities, and try not to be defensive. Controversy on even the most routine subject is more newsworthy than straightforward reporting on noncontroversial news of greater importance. Reporters seem to have an instinctive tendency to ask the kinds of questions that breed and inflame the controversy. With that thought in mind, think carefully.

If you find yourself in such a situation and have no opportunity to present your side before the story appears in print, your best tack is to calmly call the editor and ask him for the opportunity to present your side. This may require a letter to the editor, which should be carefully, carefully prepared.

MERCHANDISING PUBLICITY

Since you can't always assume that everybody you wanted to see your story was reading the paper on the day it appeared, you should arrange for reprints. With permission from the publication, which is usually readily granted, you take the story from the paper and turn it into an inexpensive brochure. This allows you to paste it up as a continuous story and to add your own editorial comment. The reprint is then distributed in exactly the same way as you would distribute any brochure.

In fact, the reprint, as you've seen, can be more valuable than the original story, because it allows you all of the advantages of the original appearance, plus the opportunity to repackage it to your advantage. It then becomes a superb direct mail piece.

COST

In budgeting a publicity program, whether you're doing it yourself or using outside counsel, costs are somewhat different than they are for advertising. Agency fees aside, the major costs are for reproduction and mailing of releases, photography, messenger services, subscriptions to appropriate publications and the cost of any special events you may develop for publicity purposes. If your program is large enough and you have reason to believe that your publicity is appearing in a number of different places beyond those of your immediate and daily reach, you can retain one of several clipping services to be found in the Yellow Pages in most big cities. Clipping services charge a flat monthly fee plus a small charge for each clipping they find and send you.

Publicity is an important part of any marketing effort because it complements advertising and promotion, and extends and enhances the selling aspects of advertising and the attention and traffic-building effects of promotion. Given a reasonable amount of time, the success of a publicity program may be measured by both the amount and quality of press coverage you receive and the general feeling you have that it's advancing your marketing efforts in terms of recognition, reputation and support.

SUMMARY

Publicity is the communications tool of public relations, using the media to project the firm's expertise, and using such devices as seminars, speeches, etc. as a basis for developing news. It's value is the implied third person endorsement of the editors, which gives your news credibility. Publicity is not free advertising. News—the ultimate aim of publicity—is a function of the comparative importance of an event or a fact in relation to other events of the day, as judged by the editor.

The media most often used in publicity are:

• Newspapers
• Broadcast media
• Trade journals
• Magazines

Before dealing with any medium, you should acquaint yourself with its requirements and style. The categories of publicity opportunities are:

• Straight news—reports of activities
• Manufactured media events—events you develop that are newsworthy

- Feature material—articles of interest that are not necessarily timely in the news sense, but that are grounded in your expertise
- By-line articles—articles in which your name appears as the author

Publicity is developed by contact with the media, after carefully understanding the requirements of your chosen media and presenting the material in ways consistent with their requirements. The press release is a major vehicle of publicity, in which news is presented in the format most convenient to the medium, and consistent with the medium's own requirements. It should be brief, to the point, and lead off with the most important and interesting fact.

Feature material is developed for its general interest to the medium's readers or viewers. It should have some focal point of immediate interest—the news hook.

Major news may warrant a press conference, which should be held only if the news is significant and there is clear reason, such as the need to demonstrate or explain something that can't be done except in person.

Good relations with the press can result in your being recognized as a prime source of news and opinion, and your being called upon regularly to comment on current events in your profession and areas of expertise. Successful publicity should be reprinted and distributed, as would be a brochure. Its editorial endorsement makes it a valuable form of promotion.

CHAPTER 13

Speeches and Seminars

There are few marketing activities that better expose a professional's distinctive capabilities, talents and skills to a prospective clientele than giving speeches or running seminars.

Long before the changes in the canons of ethics, speeches and seminars were among the few promotional devices not prohibited, and so they were crucial to effective practice development. Despite their clear promotional aspects, speeches and seminars can be construed as proffering a public service, in that they use the platform to impart knowledge. That they also enhance one's reputation, build prestige, and expose one's self to prospective clients, seemed irrelevant to ethical concerns. Speeches and seminars perform a useful service.

It behooves the professional, then, to pursue these activities assiduously, and to do them meticulously, with every aspect of marketing value extruded.

SPEECHES

People who've achieved some prominence or visibility for their expertise and authority are frequently invited to address audiences. These audiences may range from highly visible national organizations, where press coverage is extensive, to small local groups. Except for a very few prominent professionals, these invitations are usually serendipitous, and are most often random.

But in a marketing context, it becomes necessary to develop these opportunities. The value of the exposure to a defined audience, and the opportunity to enhance reputation, shouldn't be left to chance. And the opportunity to extend each speech with reprints, adaptations of the speech into articles, and to use publicity, magnifies many times the basic value of each speech. It's a prime practice development tool, and should be assiduously pursued by both large and small firms.

PLANNING A SPEECH PROGRAM

Speech making, as part of a marketing program, requires planning.

It begins with specific objectives, derived from the answers to these questions:

- Who are your target audiences?
- What do you want them to know, think, or feel as a result of a speech or series of speeches?
- How will this speech program be integrated into the overall marketing program, and be both supported on its own and used to support other activities?
- What are the specific topics to be presented, and for what clearly defined purpose?
- Who in your firm is going to participate in the program?
- What is their long-term availability for speaking engagements?
- Who is going to write the speeches?
- What kind of support (reprints, articles, publicity, etc.) will be given and who is to do it?

The answers to these questions are an important guide to focusing efforts, and avoiding wasted time and money. For example, if the objective is to build relationships to the banking community, then you know precisely which organizations to court, who is to speak, and how to select topics.

Finding the Platforms

Platforms include any organization that holds meetings and uses outside speakers—a wide, wide world.

Major platforms, offering national exposure, exist in several large cities, and range from The Economics Club of Detroit to college campus-based organizations.

Many local organizations in larger cities, such as chambers of commerce, rotary clubs, etc., are also of sufficient stature to be considered national. Other national platforms include trade associations at annual or more frequent meetings.

But virtually every city or town, regardless of size, has local organizations that can serve as platforms for the professional. The size of your firm, and the size of your community, offer no obstacles to this kind of exposure.

In developing a speaking program, it's important to remember that most organizations plan their programs well in advance—sometimes six months to a year ahead. This is an important consideration in your own planning. In selecting platforms, you should become familiar with their interests and their recent speakers and topics.

A valuable tool in developing any speaking program is the directory of trade associations, called National Trade and Professional Associations of the United States (Columbia Books, Washington, DC). Another is Encyclopedia of Associations (Gale Research, Detroit).

Consider, in choosing platforms, that while a platform is important and lends context and perhaps prestige to the speech, the reprint is even more important. No matter how prestigeous the platform, or how large the audience, it will never equal in size the number of people that the reprint will reach. And as part of a larger program, the public relations follow-up, including using the speech as a basis for an article, offers a value that multiplies the value of the original speech.

Who Participates?

Every individual in a firm who is capable of imparting expertise should be part of a speaking program. Obviously, a very junior associate is not likely to be accepted as a speaker on a national platform, nor is a very senior partner going to spend too much time addressing an obscure organization without a profound reason to do so. With careful planning, however, topics and platforms can be developed for every member of your firm with any ability to participate in the program.

Selecting the Topics

Selecting the topic for a speaking program goes beyond a simple catalog of your expertise. What is the information that your audience may want to hear? The keen competition for some of the more popular platforms is won by your ability to persuade a program chairman that what you have to say is precisely what his group wants to hear or needs to know, whether your subject is technical or a partisan point of view on a currently popular topic.

Topics, then, must be current, significant to the audience, and cast in a mode that makes a clear contribution to the group you plan to address.

Soliciting an Invitation

In developing a speech program the competitive aspects should be recognized, particularly in making your availability known. Many other people are trying to get the same speaking engagement. Once the platforms to which you want to be invited are identified, soliciting a speaking platform requires, then, its own marketing program. The following steps are involved:

- When the topic is chosen, a description of it should be written, cast in terms of the perceived needs of the prospective audience.
- A letter should go to the program chairman of each organization describing the speech, the key points you intend to cover, and the advantages to the audience. For major platforms, this can sometimes be preceded with a phone inquiry.
- A brief description of the speaker, his qualifications, and his experience as a speaker should be included. In describing the qualifications, emphasis should be on the expertise most pertinent to the topic.

- Three or four weeks after the letter of inquiry has been sent to the program chairman, there should be a follow-up telephone call, if no reply has been forthcoming.
- Availability within a time frame of six months to a year should be clearly stated.
- A description of the firm should be included.
- A modicum of substantiating material should be included (reprints of articles by the speaker, descriptive material about the firm, etc.).

Writing the Speech

Writing a speech, as is the case with any writing, is an art form within the context of a formal structure. There are many schools of thought about whether a speech should be fully written out, or whether an outline and notes are sufficient. This, of course, depends upon the speaker and his or her experience. Some speakers are sufficiently talented to give a superb extemporaneous presentation; others are more comfortable with a fully prepared speech. In fact, one does not preclude the other. For the speaker who prefers to be extemporaneous, or to speak from an outline and notes, the fully written speech is not a waste. It is reprintable, and can be distributed even if it isn't read verbatim. It also helps even the most experienced speaker to organize thoughts.

And even the most experienced and talented speaker will sometimes find it to his advantage to use a professional speechwriter. Not only is time-saving a factor, but with the right speechwriter, objectivity and input can be tremendously useful.

In working with a professional speechwriter, there will be long discussions of the topic and points of view. If you're working with a speechwriter for the first time, he wants to learn not only what you want to say, but what you want to emphasize, the points you want to cover, the points you particularly want to avoid, your speech rhythms and patterns, and your personality in regard to the material. Any professional speechwriter will take a speech through several drafts, the first of which may be so far afield as to be discouraging. Don't be discouraged. Until something is on paper for you to react to, it's almost impossible for a speechwriter to track your thinking with you. Frequently, ideas that you've articulated in a conversation take on a different cast when viewed on paper. Ideas on paper will generate other ideas leading to subsequent drafts. It may take many drafts before the final draft, which you must then polish to match your own style, pacing, phrasing, language, and so forth. If you prefer to speak from notes, the notes can be abstracted from this final draft.

In writing your own speech, there are a few pointers to keep in mind:

- Talk to the paper. You're not writing a contract.
- Talk to an individual. Visualize a single member of the audience, and talk to him as you would in a conversation.
- Outline your thoughts. Whether you use the formal outline structure you learned in school, or simply scratch a few ideas down on the back of an old envelope, blocking out the ideas helps organize your thoughts and saves time.
- A strong opening is important. This doesn't necessarily mean the standard but trite, "Funny thing happened to me on the way to the theater . . ." opening joke. Unless you're genuinely funny, and unless the story serves a specific purpose relative to your material, stay away from it. But a startling or an interesting opening is extremely important, gets the audience's attention, and sets the mood and the pace for the rest of the speech.
- Stick to the point. Keep in mind the objective of the speech and what you're trying to accomplish. What is it you want the audience to know, think or feel after they've heard your speech? Keep it simple and logical in progressing from one idea to the next.
- Edit, edit, edit. Professional writers often allow a day or so to pass before editing a draft. It brings a fresh perspective to the material.
- When you think you have it, let it sit for a few days, and then read it aloud. It is, after all, a speech and not an article. Frequently, beautifully written prose reads well on paper but doesn't speak well as a speech. If it doesn't make you self-conscious, you may want to record your reading and listen to the speech yourself.

Delivering the Speech

Delivering a speech, as in writing a speech, is a combination of learned skills and art. But even an individual who's not an experienced or a talented speaker can learn to give a speech. A few basic rules:

- If you're comfortable speaking from notes, by all means use them. It will make what you have to say appear to be more spontaneous.
- If you're reading the speech an attempt to appear spontaneous is still of the essence. Become intimately familiar with the speech by reading it aloud many times. In that way, you'll have to refer to the text less frequently, and be able to maintain important eye contact.
- Unless you're an actor, speak naturally and let the material carry the drama.
- Stand comfortably at the rostrum. Take your time. Take a few breaths before starting. Look out at the audience and establish eye contact, so that you're talking to friends, not strangers. If you're not an experienced speaker, you may want to practice by yourself in front of a microphone in an empty hall. Facing an audience is no time to get used to hearing your voice get back at you from a loudspeaker for the first time.
- Eye contact is important. Choose an individual in each part of the audience, and speak to those individuals as you would to a small group seated around a table.
- Don't be in awe of a large audience. Speak to them as if they were one person to whom you speak earnestly and sincerely, with eye contact.
- And again, take your time.

If you're truly self-conscious or uneasy about speech making, it's well worth taking a course or some professional training.

Publicizing and Merchandising a Speech

If the value of the speech is to go beyond its presentation to a limited audience, it must be publicized and merchandized.

A speech can be publicized both before and after it's given. Depending upon the topic and its importance, a press release describing the forthcoming speech may very well be in order, distributed to the appropriate media. And certainly, after the speech is given a press release focusing on its subject should be distributed. It's good practice to coordinate with the organization sponsoring your speech, to be assured of no conflict or violation of organizational taboos regarding press coverage. If the speech is sufficiently important, and the audience of sufficient consequence, the press should be invited with the first press release. Copies of the speech, if appropriate, should be made available to the press to accompany the second press release. If the appearance is of sufficient consequence, advance copies of the speech should be distributed with the proper embargo limitations (see Chapter 12).

Every speech should be reviewed to determine whether it can be easily rewritten into an article. A copy of the speech should also be sent to the magazine, *Vital Speeches* (Southold, NY), which regularly prints speeches that the editors feel may be of interest to a broader audience.

Reprints of the speech, distributed by mail, multiply manyfold the value of any speaking engagement. As part of the speaking program, a mailing list should be developed and a structure for distributing speech reprints should be established so that there is immediate follow-up. Reprints of speeches are also useful as part of publications packages for clients and prospective clients.

SEMINARS

One of the significant differences between a seminar program and a speech program is that in running a seminar program, you have complete control over the context, the audience, the subject matter, and the conditions under which the presentations are made.

While seminars are ostensibly for the purpose of educating clients, which in fact they do, they serve an even more important purpose in practice development. They afford the opportunity to display the firm's capabilities to both clients and prospective clients, and they can be a focal point for both press coverage and reprintable material. The advantages of running seminars are available to the sole practitioner as well as to the larger firm.

Seminars have been a practice development tool for many years, and so professionals are experienced in running them. But it should be remembered that no two seminars—even on the same topic with the same panel—are alike in terms of timing, place, depth of subject material, mixture of clients and nonclients and so forth.

The Value of Seminars

Organizing a seminar begins with a defined objective and ends with a carefully structured followup. Holding a seminar means considerably more than merely assembling a panel to hold forth on a subject of particular interest to the panelists, and then inviting people to come and listen.

In fact a seminar is:

- An opportunity to fulfill an obligation to clients, and to make them better clients, by imparting knowledge and information that they will find useful.
- An opportunity to reach out into the business community to project expertise, to both clients and nonclients, to engender their perception of that expertise and enhance your reputation as a leader in your field, in a context that can result in turning nonclients into clients.
- An opportunity to display to clients the breadth of your firm's capabilities, beyond the individual partner and staff that serves each client, or the specific project under contract.
- An opportunity to develop and cement relationships, and to establish contacts, with nonclients who might become prospective clients, and with those who influence their decisions in changing professionals.

Formulating Objectives

Planning a seminar should begin with the answers to the following questions:

- What is the purpose of the seminar? To merely impart new information? To cement relations to clients? To expose clients to a broader base of your firm's people? To develop relationships with nonclients and influentials as prospective clients?
- Who is the target audience?
- What is it you want people to know, think or feel as a result of the seminar?
- How will the seminar be followed up for best marketing advantage?

A major consideration is whether the seminar is to be free to invited guests or one in which admission is to be charged. A seminar to which you charge admission becomes a distinct and separate marketing problem.

If the seminar is to be successful it must ultimately be cast in terms of what the audience wants and needs, and not simply what you want to impart. A seminar solely for clients may address some rather specific material that you know to be of concern to them. A seminar for nonclients can be broader, and include more material on more subjects. A seminar designed for nonclients may even warrant an outside speaker—somebody with reputation and expertise—to serve as an attraction.

The subject matter for a seminar should be clearly defined, well-focused and not too diverse. Don't attempt to cover too broad a spectrum of a topic in a seminar that will last only half a day or a full day, and don't confuse a seminar with a course.

It should be remembered that for an attendee at a seminar there is an investment of time, and the return on that investment is information. Even though a seminar may not be comprehensive on a subject, it should still include sufficient material to make the attendee feel that his valuable time has been well spent.

The Panelists

Choosing a panel for a seminar is a function of the objectives as well as the material to be imparted. Rarely in a seminar that's shorter than a full day is there time for more than four speakers, each covering an aspect of the subject, plus one person to act as mediator to introduce the program, introduce the speakers and to handle questions.

In a seminar that goes through lunch, a luncheon speaker may be appropriate, and preferably should not be one of the panelists. It could be a distinguished individual from outside the firm, or a ranking nonparticipant, such as the firm's managing partner or national director. The luncheon speech should be broader in its perspective than any of the presentations by the panel.

The panelists' expertise and credentials should be sufficiently strong to serve as an attraction.

Each panelist's material should be prepared in much the same way as for a speech. Rehearsal is very much in order. And questions should be anticipated to the fullest degree possible, with answers prepared beforehand. This is to avoid surprises from tough questions.

The Mechanics

In preparing for a seminar, the following mechanics must be considered:

- *Site selection.* In selecting a site for the seminar, its always useful to choose a location that's not only convenient and sufficiently prestigious to be appropriate to the occasion, but if possible, one that's frequently used for similar activities. Absent that, you stand a strong possibility of working with a hotel with inexperienced help and lack of appropriate facilities. If you're working with a new site, it should be very carefully checked beforehand for all amenities, including audiovisual capabilities (slides, films, etc.).
- *Date.* There are two considerations in planning the time of a seminar—allowing yourself enough lead time to develop the seminar and to get out the invitations, and potential conflicts. As a guideline you should allow at least six to eight weeks prior to the seminar for the first invitations to go out. Add to that any preparation time that's needed for the seminar itself and for clearing schedules of panelists and participants.
- *Invitations.* First invitations should go out six to eight weeks prior to the seminar and should be carefully written in terms of the advantages to the attendees. It should be remembered that even free seminars are competitive with other seminars on the same subject, and even more significantly, for the attention and time of very busy executives. And as with all direct mail, it can't be assumed that every piece of mail you send out will be read and digested by the recipient.

An invitation letter should, where possible, be individually addressed and personalized. Great care and emphasis should be placed in the first paragraph to state the problem clearly and urgently, as a context for which the seminar offers a solution. The invitation to the seminar doesn't come in the first paragraph—it comes after the problem has been stated.

Invitations should have a response mechanism, such as a phone number or post card, and arrangements should be made to deal with responses in an organized manner. Not everyone who accepts on the first invitation will actually attend, and so follow-up becomes necessary. This may be done by mail or by phone call, usually three weeks prior to the seminar, depending upon the response of the first invitation. If response to the first invitation is not satisfactory, a second letter should go out. If attendance and response require it, a follow-up phone call two or three days before the seminar to those who indicated that they would attend can be a helpful reminder.

- *Mailing lists*. Mailing lists of existing clients are relatively easy. Mailing lists of nonclients can be considerably more difficult. Presumably every firm has a list of prospects, as well as contacts with those who influence prospects. Beyond that, there are many sources of mailing lists that can be used. The best, of course, is a mailing list developed out of your own marketing program, in which you've identified and targeted specific companies as prospective clients, and specific influentials. Mailing lists can also be purchased from reliable mailing list brokers.

- *Site preparation*. In selecting and preparing a site for a seminar you might consider the following points:

  —Room size should be smaller (slightly,) rather than larger. Fifty people in a room for 200 looks like a small group. Eighty people in room for 75 looks like an enthusiastic crowd.
  —Some rooms, even with sound systems, have poor acoustics making it difficult for people in parts of the room to hear the speaker.
  —The sound system should be checked to see that it's adequate to the size of the room.
  —Check the walls. You don't want to share your meeting with the meeting next door, nor for them to share yours.
  —Decide whether you want tables or not, and how they should be set up. Classroom-style? U-Shaped?
  —Check the chairs and make sure they're comfortable. If you're not using tables, chairs should preferably be set up in semi-circles rather than straight rows.

—Lobby signs and signs outside the room are necessary to help people locate the seminar.

—Amenities should be attended to, such as water pitchers and glasses for both speakers and the audience, plenty of ashtrays (you should consider smoking and no-smoking sections), and microphones for questions from the floor.

—Be sure that the hotel supplies adequate audio visual equipment to meet your needs, including maintenance and spare bulbs for projectors. If possible check their equipment beforehand.

—If meals are to be served, check menus beforehand, and if possible, try to see (or even eat) a sample meal. Know precisely what you're getting.

—Tell the hotel that you expect twenty percent fewer people than you really do, and then get the real capacity of the room after the price has been quoted.

—Check penalty arrangements and deposits required.

—If there is to be a cocktail hour, be sure to understand beforehand exactly how beverages are to be served.

—Arrange for a sufficient number of registration tables at the entrance to the seminar room, preferably just outside. Determine beforehand how many people you're going to need to man those tables to help you register attendees, the form of registration you're going to use, and the number and kind of badges you're going to need.

Not only should the site be inspected before you sign the contract, it should also be inspected on the date of the seminar, in time to make any corrections if arrangements have not been properly made.

• In negotiating for a site it's useful to remember that prices aren't fixed in stone. They are frequently negotiable, particularly if the hotel isn't busy. You should always make a counteroffer. A hotel room is a perishable commodity; they can't inventory yesterday's empty room, which is why most hotels will negotiate unless there's really competition for the space.

• Regardless of the subject matter of a seminar, there should always be a kit of materials for each participant. This might include:

—A seminar program.

—Appropriate brochures.

—Biographies of the panelists.
—Descriptive material about the firm.
—Useful background material on the subject, including a position
  paper if pertinent.
—Reprints of articles by the participants.
—Blank pads and pencils.

It may be useful to hold something back from these packages that can be sent out on a follow-up. However, given a choice between inadequate materials and the need for follow-up, the option should include the materials in the seminar packet. There are other techniques to use in following up.

If the preparations for a seminar have been made adequately, then the seminar itself should be an anticlimax except for the presentations. The person responsible for the seminar should get to the site as early as possible and review the checklist to make sure that everything is in working order and that all arrangements have been made properly. He or she should review the audiovisual and sound materials and equipment. Recheck, also, with the banquet department to make sure that feeding arrangements are fully understood and will be followed, and that cocktail arrangements are understood and in place. Panelists should arrive early enough to have a dry run, to check and become comfortable with the room and the sound system, and to check details such as panelists' nameplates (which should, if possible, be large enough to be seen from the back of the room).

Giving the Seminar

Preparing and rehearsing for the seminar cannot be a casual event. While it's assumed that each panelist who participates is an expert in his field, and even that he or she is extensively experienced, a seminar is still an ensemble function.

In planning a seminar a segment of the topic is assigned to each participant. However, it should be the responsibility of each participant to make clear to the others on the panel precisely what areas he or she is going to cover. Of course, one way to do this is to write the speeches beforehand and circulate them among other panelists. Written copies of the speech are useful in several additional ways—they may be reprinted, they may be adopted as articles, they may serve as a background piece to help the press develop interviews.

However, many people prefer to speak from notes and outlines rather than from prepared speeches. Where this is the case the notes must be discussed among the participants to avoid duplication and to enhance coordination. And as with a speech, individual rehearsal, as well as group rehearsal, is extremely important. It will improve the presentation of each individual performance and sharpen and help with the timing of the ensemble performance. It also gives you the opportunity to test and time your presentation with any audio visual material.

The Panel Chairman

The meeting leader or chairman has four major responsibilities:

- To introduce the seminar and each of the speakers.
- To chair the question period and direct the questions to the appropriate panelists.
- To keep the seminar moving, well-paced and focused.
- To sum up at the end

While the chairman may not be one of the panelists, it's his or her opening remarks that set the context of the seminar. They should consist of a brief welcome and introduction of each of the panelists, including background (with focus on the expertise on the subject) and a very brief summary of the context of the material for the panel.

During the question and answer period the chairman selects the questions from the audience, and if they are not addressed to a specific panelist, he directs them. In this context, it's also the chairman's role to be alert and evenhanded in choosing questioners from across the room, to keep the questions focused, and to keep the answers relevant. During the questions and answer period the chairman should not be passive, but active in directing the questions and answers.

At the end of the seminar, the chairman should sum up the points made as briefly and succinctly as possible, thank those who attended, and make other announcements about follow-up or mechanics.

The success or failure of a seminar depends as frequently upon the skill of the chairman as it does on the subject matter being imparted.

Press Coverage

Seminars frequently offer an exceptional opportunity for press coverage.

Certainly, a press release should be distributed to announce the seminar, particularly if it's open to the broader business community. A decision should be made as to whether the press should be invited.

Press should not be invited unless there's a clear feeling that material will be discussed that's newsworthy or of interest to the press (see Chapter 12).

For press coverage the following steps should be taken:

• A press kit should be prepared that includes:
   —A basic press release about the seminar and its topic
   —Biographical material on the speakers
   —Individual press releases, if appropriate, on each of the speaker's topics
   —A general background and fact sheet about the topics
   —Any pertinent material about your firm
• About a week prior to the seminar a basic press release should be sent to the appropriate segment of the press including an invitation to attend.
• The day before the seminar the press should be called, not to see whether they got the release, but to reaffirm the invitation.
• If the subject warrants it, an attempt should be made to arrange for an interview of participants.
• Should any members of the press attend, they should be recognized at the door, greeted by a responsible person from your firm, and given a press kit as well as other seminar material. Interviews following the seminar should be arranged as expeditiously as possible.

If the press is not interested in attending, a copy of the press kit and the seminar material should be sent to the appropriate reporters immediately following the seminar.

Followup

In any seminar attended by a nonclient, the effort is totally wasted if there isn't an immediate and appropriate follow-up.

Attendance at a seminar of itself implies an interest in the subject. Certainly, each person who attends should be registered, even if it's simply signing a log. This facilitates post-seminar mailings, letters and phone follow-up.

Perhaps the most important part of the seminar, particularly one that includes nonclients, is the cocktail hour following the seminar. This is the occasion in which the expertise that's been projected by the seminar is turned into contact. If your firm is large enough, nonparticipating partners and others should be invited, with each assigned to cultivate prospective clients individually. The seminar may attract nonclients, but they don't really become prospects until the contact is made.

A thank-you letter should be sent to every nonclient who attended, including an invitation to meet for lunch or to discuss a specific question that may have been raised during the informalities of the cocktail hour.

Everyone who attends the seminar should be placed on an appropriate mailing list to regularly receive material issued by your firm. This might include reprints of the presentations of the seminar. This same material, incidentally, can be sent to invitees who did not attend.

Charging Admission

A seminar to which you charge admission poses a different problem in marketing. It's one thing to ask people to give their time to attend a seminar—it's another thing to ask for money as well. In the paid seminar there has to be very strong message that there will be a return on their investment.

This means that an objective view of the seminar must the taken to determine whether the subject matter is sufficiently attractive—marketable—and the speakers sufficiently prestigious, to attract paid attendance.

It also means that the invitation material moves from the realm of polite invitation to that of hard sell. A brochure must be carefully designed and written to persuade prospective customers that the problem you're addressing is a serious and consequential one, and that the purpose of the seminar is to help resolve that problem.

Marketing a seminar is a highly skilled pursuit where, unlike free seminars, results are measured in dollars.

Even the problem of pricing the seminar requires an experience and a skill not normally within the realm of the nonprofessional marketer.

Whether the seminar is priced to make a profit or merely to break even on expenses, a number of factors must be taken into consideration, including the cost of the mailing pieces, the cost of mailing, the cost of mailing lists, and so forth.

A well planned and well executed seminar, as professionals have known for decades, can be a powerful marketing tool for professional services.

SEMINAR COSTS

The basic costs of a seminar include these elements:

- Mailing and production costs for invitations, press and other materials
- Room rental, and subsidiary costs
- Food and beverages, snacks and cocktail party
- Transportation and housing for guests and out-of-town panelists
- Production of slides, etc.
- Tips
- Advertising (if appropriate)
- Promotional material for seminar to which admission is charged

SUMMARY

Speeches and seminars, which predated the change in the canons of ethics as excellent practice development devices, enhance reputation, build prestige, and expose a firm's expertise to both clients and prospective clients.

A speech program works best when it is planned. Questions to ask are:

- Who are target audiences?
- What do you want them to know, think or feel as a result of speeches?
- How will the program be integrated into total marketing program?
- What are specific topics to be presented, and why?
- Who is going to do it?
- Who is going to write the speeches?
- What kind of support will be given the program?

There are both national and local platforms, in the form of organizations that hold meetings addressed by speakers. A program of direct inquiry to meeting chairmen of these organizations can develop invitations to speak. Every member of the firm with any degree of expertise can participate in the program.

Topics should be selected in terms of what the audience wants to hear, tempered by your own expertise. Invitations are solicited by:

- Identifying appropriate organization
- Description of talk should be written
- Application to program supervisor of organizations should be made by phone and letter
- Letter should be followed by phone inquiry
- Availability within a time frame of six months to a year should be made clear
- Description of firm and material substantiating expertise should be enclosed

No matter who writes the speech, or how it is to be given, or even if it's to be given from notes, it's useful to write it out. In writing a speech:

- Talk to the paper
- Talk to an individual
- Outline
- A strong opening is important
- Stick to the point and organize logically

- Edit
- Read it aloud

In delivering a speech:

- Speak from notes, if you can
- If you're reading a speech, rehearse to appear spontaneous
- Speak naturally, take your time, eye contact is important

Speeches should be publicized and merchandised by sending reprints of the speech by mail.

Seminars offer the opportunity to:

- Meet obligations to clients to keep them informed of important material
- Reach out to business community to project expertise to clients and prospective clients
- Turn nonclients into prospects, and establish new relationships with prospective clients

In planning seminars, objectives are answers to:

- What is the purpose of the seminar?
- Who is the target audience?
- What do you want the audience to know, think or feel after the seminar?

Seminar panelists should each cover a different aspect of the subject, but coordinate to avoid duplication. A luncheon speaker should cover overall, larger aspect of the subject.

The mechanics of a seminar cover:

- Site selection—should be convenient and experienced in holding similar functions
- Date—should be planned so that preparations can be made and invitations sent out six to eight weeks in advance
- Invitations and mailing lists—first invitations should go out six to eight weeks before; mailing lists should be updated well in advance; invitations should have response mechanism

• Site preparation—room size should be slightly smaller, to give crowded appearance to smaller crowd; acoustics and sound should be checked; determine how seating is to be arranged; check signs and ameneties; check audio visual equipment, meals and cocktail service; set up for registration, including badges
• In negotiating, remember that prices are always flexible
• A kit for each attendee should include:

—Program
—Brochures
—Biographies and firm descriptive material
—Background material, reprints of articles by participants; pads and pencils

• Site should be checked at last minute for details

The seminar should be rehearsed, and copies of speeches should be available if possible, even if presentations are from notes. The panel chairman has four major responsibilities:

• Introduce seminar and panelists
• Chair question period
• Keep seminar moving
• Sum up at the end

A press release should be distributed to announce the seminar, but press should not be invited unless the material is really newsworthy or of interest to the press.

• A press kit should be prepared
• Press release and invitation should go out about a week prior to seminar
• Press should be reminded the day before the seminar
• If appropriate, interviews should be arranged with panelists
• Press attendees should be squired throughout

The greatest value in a seminar lies in the followup, starting with cocktail hour and including mailings, personal thank you note, and personal contact. All attendees should be placed on a mailing list.

Seminars to which admission is charged require a special marketing program. Potential return on investment of must be demonstrated in promotions. Brochures and mailing pieces must be carefully developed. Hard sell is important.

The basic costs of a seminar include:

- Mailing and production costs for invitations, press and other materials
- Room rental, and subsidiary costs
- Food and beverages, snacks and cocktail party
- Transportation and housing for guests and out-of-town panelists
- Production of slides, etc.
- Tips
- Advertising (if appropriate)
- Promotional material for seminar to which admission is charged

CHAPTER 14

Publications

Publications—newsletters, brochures, position papers—are venerable practice development tools.

They are not often flagrantly promotional, and so have never been questioned in an ethical context.

Brochures and booklets on new laws, or foreign currency, or new accounting principles, or describing the effects of a new tax code—all were favorable devices well before the change in the canons of ethics. A brochure on fluoridation written some 25 years ago, and distributed by dentists with their own imprints, was considered to be an important factor in the public acceptance of fluoridation, and was a major marketing device for many dentists as well. Doctors' and dentists' offices have been repositories of brochures on health, with the practitioner's imprint, for decades. Accounting firms and consultants have long issued periodic newsletters interpreting economic events.

Even with the addition of new and sophisticated marketing tools, publications, properly used, are still an invaluable and widely used marketing tool. They're valued by those who receive them because they're a source of useful information. They're valuable to professionals because they serve clients, and project the author's expertise to both clients and nonclients. Because they can be produced inexpensively, they're useful for both small and large firms.

So ubiquitous are publications from professional firms, in fact, that many business people have come to expect them from their professionals in response to new laws, or changed regulations. The other side of that coin, of course, is that brochures and other publications now compete against one another for a prospective client's attention. And in this competition, only the best designed and written publications—those that are the most useful and readable—serve as effective marketing tools.

KINDS OF PUBLICATIONS

The major categories of publications used by professionals as marketing devices are:

- *Newsletters*. These are periodical publications, distributed regularly to clients, prospective clients and influentials, usually dealing with either a narrow technical area, or a broader context relative to the profession. They may be inexpensive, typed bulletins or expensive, elaborate newsletters or newspapers.
- *Brochures*. A brochure may be anything from a pamphlet to an extensive booklet. *Facilities* brochures describe the firm and its services. *Technical* brochures may deal intensively with a specific subject.
- *Position papers*. A position paper is a document that usually presents a point of view on a specific subject relevant to the profession, backed by facts and technical information.
- *Annual reports*. While the traditional annual report is a financial document issued by a public corporation, an increasing number of professional organizations are distributing them to serve as a combination of a facilities brochure and a progress report of the firm and its growth. The implication, of course, is that the growth is a function of the firm's superior ability to serve its clients.
- *Reprints*. A reprint of an article about the firm, or by one if its principles, serves as a powerful marketing tool because it's reinforced by the imprimatur of the publication in which it first appeared. A montage of press clippings says that the firm's expertise warrants the press' constantly turning to it as a prime source.

In a separate category is the trade book—the full-length book published and distributed by an outside publisher. This is usually done either as an individual endeavor in an author-publisher relationship, or as a firm-sponsored joint venture between a firm and a publisher. The work that goes into it is enormous, but the rewards are overwhelming. Witness, for example, the joint venture Arthur Young & Co. Tax Guide, a superb and monumental work which became a national best seller, featured in bookstores from coast to coast.

How Each is Used

Singly or in concert with one another each plays a significant role in marketing:

- *Newsletters* are particularly valuable in developing an ongoing relationship between your firm and your clients or prospective clients. A well-written and edited newsletter that deals with matters that are genuinely consequential to the reader, and that imparts really useful information, can be particularly helpful in enhancing reputation within the context of expertise. It can also serve as a source of material for publicity. The important thing to remember about a newsletter is that it will not automatically be read; it must survive and thrive independently as a valuable source of information to the reader. It can cover a wide range of subjects within a profession, and affords the opportunity to quote everybody in the firm who has any expertise in any area.
- *Brochures.* A facilities brochure is useful in describing a firm's capabilities and specialties. The nature of professional services, however, limit its usefulness as a selling tool in that as glowingly as the brochure may describe the firm's capabilities, it cannot describe them competitively. A brochure for a medical clinical practice may talk about its new x-ray machines, but can't say "We produce faster cures." The canons of ethics under which the professions still function clearly dictate discretion in this kind of brochure. At the same time, it's useful in presenting the firm and its practice brightly and enthusiastically, and as a strong adjunct to other marketing tools.

A facilities brochure may describe the firm, its capabilities, its service concept, and its facilities. It may be used to explain the firm to prospective clients or to prospective recruits. It may discuss the entire firm, or one segment of its services, or how it functions in a particular industry.

Technical brochures serve an entirely different purpose, in that they offer a broad base of information on a specific subject based upon the firm's expertise. These are the brochures that address such subjects as accounting for foreign currency under new regulations, or responsibilities of the trustee under a new estate law. The role of these brochures is to serve as an educational aid to the reader. In fact, they portray the firm as knowledgeable.

• *Position papers* afford a firm the opportunity to take a strong position, sometimes partisan, on a matter of interest and urgency to its clientele and prospective clientele. As a marketing tool it clearly demonstrates knowledge, interest and concern in a matter that concerns the prospective clientele.

• An *annual report*, for a professional firm, is a way of demonstrating facilities, capability and most significantly, growth. It goes beyond a facilities brochure in that its point of view can be less objective in discussing a firm's business. It affords a firm the opportunity to be somewhat more dynamic, and perhaps a little freer in speaking of its own capabilities.

• A *reprint* can sometimes serve the same purpose as a brochure, depending upon the original article. Reprints have the additional value of the implied objective endorsement of the publication in which the article originally appeared. The reprint seems to say that because the publication chose to publish the article, there is an independent and objective assent to its premise and credibility to its content. The marketing power of a properly used reprint is extensive.

ROLE IN THE MARKETING MIX

In conjunction with other marketing tools, publications have a specific role and value:

• They are tangible. Unlike advertising or editorial publicity, which are fleeting, publications can be held in hand and studied at leisure.

- They are capable of making a specific contribution to a client or prospective client's business. They can supply information that has its own value, and which therefore redounds to the benefit of the source.
- They afford the opportunity to present a firm in its best light.
- They give a visual dimension to a firm, at least in the context of the design of the publication. A well-designed, attractive publication implies a well-run, efficient organization.

Publications are used best in the context of the total marketing program, and when each device takes advantage of its own special characteristics.

A newsletter, for example, functions well to sustain an ongoing relationship with a client or prospective client, but only if it's a valid newsletter that contains information that contributes substantially to the reader's advantage.

Technical brochures, position papers and reprints serve in the same way to contribute to the reader's store of information and education.

Annual reports, or reprints of an article about a company, fall into a different category, since they tend to be frank marketing pieces. A facilities brochure contributes to the reader's well-being only to the degree that the reader wants to know about your capabilities. But it's still self-serving.

Recognizing the distinction between those pieces that are self-serving and those that contribute to a reader's education and information helps to understand how each is to be used. It helps to understand, as well, the kind of readership that can be anticipated. A well-produced newsletter or technical brochure is likely to have greater readership than a facilities brochure or an annual report. And each must be accompanied by a different kind of cover letter.

WHEN TO USE PUBLICATIONS

Because of the long tradition of using publications as marketing devices in the professions, there tends to be a too easy use of them; a proclivity to use them pointlessly, and to produce so much printed material that prospective clients are inundated. This, of course, causes a reaction that's precisely opposite to the one you want.

In larger firms, the problem is magnified, because every partner in charge of an area of the practice, or responsible for serving a specific industry, tends to feel naked without being represented in print. The result, in firm after firm, is that practice offices throughout the country warehouse unopened cartons of brochures, which will never be used.

The publication's role in meeting the objectives of the marketing program must be determined. Without clarifying this role, the effort behind a publication can be wasted.

Under no circumstances should a publication be produced if it can't be done professionally and skillfully. Newsletters that impart no knowledge are junk mail, and counterproductive. Technical brochures or position papers that make no genuine contribution, or that are superficial, are also counterproductive.

OBJECTIVES

A publishing program should, in all aspects, conform to objectives. The objectives, more than anything else, shape the format, the design, the content, the distribution and the longevity of all publications.

Every publication you issue must compete with a great many other publications for the limited time and attention of your chosen readership. Publications that are not focused, useful and readable, with superior and professional design, writing, and production, are an absolute waste of money.

Publications that meet no specific objectives, or that try to meet objectives that are best met through other marketing devices (such as advertising or public relations,) are expensive, waste time and money, and serve no valid purpose.

No publication should be produced without answering at least the following questions:

• Who is my audience? Is it a broad audience consisting of all my clients or prospective clients, or a narrow audience consisting of those with a specific interest?
• What am I trying to accomplish with this publication in terms of the overall marketing program? Will something else better accomplish what I want?

- How will the publication be used in conjunction with with other marketing tools? Will it be offered in ads? Mentioned in press releases? Used in direct mail?
- How will the publication be delivered? Will it be mailed ahead? Left behind after a meeting? Mailed after a meeting?
- What do I want my audience to know, do or think after they've read my publication?

When the audience is clearly defined and the objectives are clearly understood and stated, then the likelihood of the publication's serving a significant purpose is substantially increased.

DESIGN

A newsletter, whether it's typed or typeset, must be readable and attractive, printed on good quality paper and laid out so as to avoid a formidable crowded look. A standard letterhead for a newsletter should be designed for consistency and easy recognition. The masthead should be printed even if the newsletter itself is simply to be typed. The format of any periodical publication, such as a newsletter, should be designed to be instantly recognizable by the third or fourth issue.

Brochures should be attractive and readable. If you plan to publish more than one brochure, you may find it useful to try for what is known as a "design family" feel—a consistency of design from one publication to another that makes the series of publications instantly recognizable as coming from one source, but still distinguishes each one so that they're not confused with one another.

WRITING

The art of writing a brochure is exactly that—an art. But in writing brochures for a professional service there are some distinct considerations that can make the difference between a brochure that accomplishes your objectives and one that doesn't.

- *The audience.* A brochure describing your firm for prospective clients will be very different from one you'll use to recruit college students to join your firm. A technical brochure for middle management might be written very differently than one for senior management. The reasons, obviously, are that you have different things to say to different audiences. The advantages of working for your firm are not the same as the advantages of retaining your firm. How you write anything is a function of who you're talking to. The brochure is very much subject to that dictum.

• *Purpose*. A brochure to be sent ahead as a forerunner to a presentation or a meeting has a very different point of view than one to be left behind following a meeting as a summary or reminder, and to reinforce points made in person. The brochure that's sent ahead, for example, has as its job to explain who you are, what you do, and how you do it. You're presumably talking to somebody who doesn't know you. The brochure you leave behind assumes some measure of knowledge about you and your firm, and should reinforce points you've made in person. Thus, purpose alters the format and text of a publication.

• *Illustration*. It's very difficult to illustrate a brochure for a service organization. All lawyers and accountants seated at desks look alike. All medical or dental facilities look alike. Illustration is the toughest part of any brochure, and the burden is heavy on designers. Photography that shows as much action as possible is an improvement over static, posed shots. The visualization of your message, then, must ultimately rely upon the writing, not artwork.

• *Distribution*. How a brochure is to be distributed affects it's design. If it's to be mass mailed, it should be remembered that postage costs are a major consideration. Odd shapes that use custom designed rather than stock envelopes may be attractive, but increase costs substantially. Here, too, return on investment must be considered. Brochures that cost $5 each may be well worth it if they result in getting clients that pay fees in multiples of that.

• *Longevity*. How long will the publication be expected to do its job? A publication on a new tax law will have a shorter life than one on how to keep records. Thus, a brochure with an intended long life shouldn't have references that can become dated.

Writing a technical brochure is simpler than writing a facilities brochure. In the former, one deals with professional skills. How to understand a new law, for example. It is, in effect, simply a matter of practicing a segment of one's profession on paper.

But how do you write a facilities brochure when your ability to use adjectives is clearly proscribed; when the service you perform is precisely the same as everyone else's? (We do better audits? We write better briefs?)

If there's any answer, it's to write simply and clearly about what you do—whether its to describe the range of services you perform or your approach to addressing specific problems, such as personal finance, or cash management. And if you write it all simply, and as if nobody else is performing the service, then a selling impact may emerge. And because it must not be assumed that any reader will devote an extensive amount of time to any single publication that might be construed as promotional, the message should be clear, simple, accessible, and not embroidered in too many words.

The objective and the target audience should always be kept in mind, to avoid unfocused writing. Objectives for publications should be simple, and no publication should be expected to carry too much weight.

Relevance is significant. What you put into any publication must be relevant to the needs of your prospective reader, and address those needs without deviating from the point and without clutter. When you do that, then the publication works for you the way you mean it to. This, by the way, as as true of a technical publication as it is of a promotional one.

PRODUCTION

The production process is much the same as in advertising. Here too, professionalism saves money by making the process smoother and faster, and by avoiding waste.

There is some measure of flexibility and control of the costs of publications, but there are still certain cost elements that are consistent. Inherent in the cost of all publications are:

• The time of the professionals involved in producing the publication.
• The time and cost of professional editors or writers.
• Design costs, including design, layout and preparation of camera-ready mechanicals.

- Typesetting, proofing, and printing costs.
- Photography.
- Paper.
- Printing and binding.
- Distribution, including bulk distribution and shipping, bulk packaging and mailing.

Publications showcase a firm, and frequently act as a major tool in presenting the firm to its prospective clients. Like the good suit, tie and polished shoes, the appearance of a firm's publication bespeaks the firm itself, and so care should be taken in designing, producing and distributing publications. There are no savings in cutting costs to the point of producing shoddy work.

The time and care put into carefully planning and professionally executing publications—newsletters, brochures, etc.—can result in a profound return on investment. Poorly planned and executed publications, on the other hand, are expensive and counterproductive.

SUMMARY

Publications have long been considered an ethical marketing tool. The major categories are:

- Newsletters—periodic publications mailed regularly to clients and prospective clients. Used to supply useful information on a regular basis, and to establish ongoing rapport with the recipient.
- Brochures—pamphlets and booklets that either describe a facility or offer technical information. *Facilities* brochures describe the firm and its capabilities, for both prospective clients and recruits. *Technical* brochures offer specific technical information.
- Position papers—documents that present a point of view on a specific subject, sometimes controversial.
- Annual reports—brochures showing a firm's growth and progress, and at the same time, describing its capabilities.
- Reprints—reprints of articles that appeared in other publications. They take on the prestige of the original publication.

Used with other marketing tools, publications:

- Are tangible, with staying power
- Can make specific contribution to recipient's business
- Afford opportunity to show firm in best light
- Give visual dimension to a firm

Publications should not be overused, should be professional in appearance, and should meet defined objectives. To be defined before producing a publication are:

- Who is audience?
- What do I want them to know, think or feel after reading the publication?
- How will publication be used with other marketing tools?
- How will it be delivered?

Publications should be professionally designed and produced, preferably with a "design family" look to identify source of each of several publications.

Writing a brochure is a function of:

- The audience
- The purpose
- Illustration
- Distribution
- Longevity

The elements that determine costs are:

- Time of staff professionals
- Time and cost of professional writers
- Design costs
- Typesetting, proofing, printing
- Photography
- Paper
- Printing and binding
- Distribution

Publications showcase a firm, and care should be taken in their production. Good publications, however, produce an excellent return on investment.

CHAPTER 15

The Logo and Firm Graphics

Just as clothes project an instant impression of the individual, so do the graphics of a firm. A dull and mundane letterhead, an undistinguished business card, an uninspired sign over the door, will give the casual observer the impression of a dull, mundane and uninspired firm. The facts may belie the impression, but if the first impression is negative then the observer may never get past it to the facts.

This is why attention to the design of all corporate graphics is an important marketing element. It's an escutcheon, a shield, a banner that sets a primary mood to invite people to want to do business with you.

A well-designed graphic representation used consistently in your printed, advertising and display material conveys a feeling of substance, of professionalism.

The consistent use of good graphics throughout all your material reinforces identification and recognition. The graphic impression of the letterhead, of the business card, of the ad, of the billboard—all reinforce one another, and speed up and enhance recognition to the point of comfortable familiarity.

Distinctive graphics serve yet another important role. They distinguish you and your firm from your competitors. What the coat of arms of heraldic times was to the noble family, so are distinctive graphics to today's business firm.

As real as are these advantages to a good graphics presentation,

253

there is, on the other hand, the danger of being overwhelmed by the value of graphics in other aspects of public relations. Your firm is not what your graphics imply that it is—rather, it's the other way around; your graphics must represent your firm as it really is.

Several years ago, a major national airline spent almost $1 million on a particularly successful corporate identity program. It modernized its logo, its graphics and the appearance of its outlets and personnel. After a short time, every aspect of the appearance of the airline, from its advertising to its airplanes, was readily identifiable.

This graphics program, however, did nothing to improve the quality of the airline's service. It still maintained poor on-time performance; its personnel did not improve their efficiency or their manners, nor could all the graphics and advertising improve the quality of its operations. It achieved instant and consistent identification of an operation that was considered so generally inferior that its profits were well below those of its competitors' for many years.

In other words, all of the good will, the attention, the identification, the implied professionalism of your graphics can be denied in one rude phone call, one muffed assignment.

What are Company Graphics?

Company graphics, sometimes called the corporate or firm identity, are the visualization of your signature in a uniform, attractive and distinctive style, used consistently everywhere your name might reasonably appear. This might include:

- Letterheads
- Business cards
- Advertising
- Office sign
- Publicity material
- Promotional material
- Company vehicles
- Signs and billboards

The impression is achieved by a distinctive design of your firm name and logotype, and the way they're used.

The Trademark

There's a subtle distinction between trademark and logo. The names Kodak, Xerox, Kleenex—these are trademarks. They are distinctive company names, registered as such with the U. S. Patent Office. The products they make are the Kodak camera, the Xerox copier and the Kleenex tissue. These names are protected by law. "Kodak" doesn't mean all cameras or films, "Xerox" doesn't mean all copiers and "Kleenex" doesn't mean all tissues.

A logo, on the other hand, is a distinctive design or design device that, like a heraldic coat of arms, represents a firm. The logo need not be a separate design; it can be the design style of the firm name. Coca-Cola, and its distinctive script form, is at one time a firm name, a logo and a trademark. The word "Coke" is also registered as a trademark and so precludes calling any cola drink a Coke except Coca-Cola. But visually, the distinctive style functions as a logo that's consistently used on all the Coca-Cola firm's materials, from their letterhead to their product and their trucks.

In professional services, you and your firm are your product, and so the concept of trademark doesn't necessarily apply. This is particularly true if your own name is the name of the firm. Firms in most professions use the names of their principles, which takes them out of the category of trademark.

Sometimes a distinctively designed typeface is sufficient to serve the graphic needs of a firm when it's used for the firm's name. The firm name is, of itself, a logo. But sometimes the firm's concept of itself can be enhanced and projected by an additional design device that's distinctive, attractive and memorable. Properly designed and used, a distinctive firm name can fulfill all of the needs of a good graphics program.

MAKING A LOGO WORK

A logo—or any firm graphic—will not work on its own. It must be used in a planned, carefully devised way. Attractive though it may be, if it's not placed in positions where it's constantly visible it will achieve only a fraction of its potential purpose and value. This is why firm identity programs require more than just a design of a logo and a signature. Every piece of printing on which the logo and signature are to be used must be considered, and a full design program must include consistency for all possible uses.

Like slogans, logos, as attractive as they may be, are useless without constant repetition. They must be visible in many forms—stationery, signs, advertising and promotion. Logos must be made to do a job by constant exposure.

ELEMENTS OF DESIGN

All firm graphics, including the logo, should reflect the firm itself. They should spring from your marketing objective and the position you've chosen in the market. As you've seen, different typefaces and different designs convey different feelings. An accountant or lawyer seeking business in a conservative world would hardly use a jazzy or cartoon-like logo. But for an innovative designer, or a specialized consultant, an unusual log might well be appropriate.

If the word "image" comes to mind here, it should be an image based on reality, or else the inconsistency would quickly confuse the prospective client. The reaction might be subliminal and the prospective client might not be able to put a finger on it, but the feeling would be there.

A good design program begins, then, not with the preconception of a visual image but with an analysis of the firm and the purposes to which the graphics will be put. Professional designers charged with developing a firm graphics program spend a great deal of time analyzing the firm, its objectives, its positions, its market, its target audience and management's own attitudes and feelings about the firm and its future growth areas.

The designer then analyzes all of the uses of the graphics; all forms of communications, vehicles, stationery, signs, advertising and so forth.

The design consists of more than just a drawing or a rendering of a logo and a signature. It must be scaled to every communications piece. How large should it be in proportion to the rest of the space on a letterhead? On a business card? On an envelope? On a brochure? A professional design program isn't complete without a graphic standards manual for firm-wide use, and an instruction sheet to printers about size and scale.

Color, when it's used, is as much part of the design as the style of the typography. While the logo may at times be used in black and white, when it's used in situations where color is appropriate, the color should always be coordinated. Color is as much a part of the identification as type, and in fact, some designers deliberately blend a distinctive color that isn't likely to be duplicated. But since logos are used in black and white in some advertising, they should be designed to be as distinctive and memorable without color as with color.

The design should always be simple and clear. And while it should reflect your business as it currently exists, your future business should be considered as well, unless you want to go through the expense and trouble of redesigning the logo every time your business shows substantial growth or changes in any way.

THE DESIGNER

Not only should firm graphics, and especially a logo, be designed professionally, but the designer should have extensive experience in logo design. An advertising designer, or one who specializes in brochures, may be extraordinarily talented, but unless there's a specific experience in developing a firm identity program the likelihood is that the result will be mediocre.

Before ordering a graphics identity program from a designer you should see many samples of the designer's work, asking in each case about the firm behind each design and its marketing objectives. This allows you to judge not only the attractiveness of the design but also its appropriateness and the degree to which it meets objectives.

The cost of design can vary from a few hundred dollars to many thousands of dollars, although cost alone is no guarantee of superiority. A few years ago, a most expensive corporate identity designer charged hundreds of thousands of dollars for a new logo for NBC's television network. Not included in their services, apparently, was research. It was only after the new logo went on the air that NBC discovered that its new logo was almost exactly the same as the logo done for a very small television station in the Midwest. This was not only embarrassing but expensive, because NBC's design had to be modified, and the smaller station had to be compensated.

When selecting a designer beware of being oversold. Under-

standably, designers ascribe magical qualities to firm graphics and
identity programs. They have no magical qualities. Good graphics
serve a purpose—an important one. But they cannot accomplish
more than you can accomplish for yourself. They cannot project an
image that is greater than your firm. A stranger having met Albert
Einstein walking through the Princeton campus, and not knowing
who he was, might have assumed that he was a sloppy old man rather
than a genius with one of the greatest minds in history. Many a
charlatan is finely garbed. If the reality of your firm is less than you
would have it, don't depend upon a graphics program to change your
firm into what you think it should be.

Graphics and a well-designed logo are important, but they're
only part of a total marketing program.

SUMMARY

A good graphics program is attractive, builds instant recognition
and projects a distinctive impression. It is distinguishing.

It should be used consistently in all printed material, advertising
and display material of any kind. Company graphics should be accomplished primarily with the type style in which your firm name is
printed, and a logotype—logo—a distinctive graphic representation
of your name or emblem. A logo differs from a trademark in that a
trademark is sufficiently unique and distinctive to be registered with
the U.S. Patent Office.

A logo will not work on its own, without carefully planned,
repeated use. It should be attractive, consistent with your business,
readable, and recognizable.

Logos and other graphic designs should be done professionally,
by an artist with specific experience in company graphics design.

CHAPTER 16

The Public Relations Agencies

The technical skills necessary to function effectively in public relations are not necessarily as elaborate as those frequently used in advertising, but they are distinctive skills nevertheless. Moreover, they are skills keenly honed by experience. Public relations has its own professionalism.

INTERNAL OR EXTERNAL?

Which is not to say that, perhaps more than with advertising, a modicum of public relations activity can't be performed by the inexperienced public relations person functioning in his or her own behalf. Using the techniques in Chapter 12, a small professional firm or sole practitioner can indeed perform many of the public relations tasks, and do so effectively and profitably. The entrepreneurial bent, drive and outlook that made you a successful professional in the first place are the same attributes that can often supply the imagination to learn what's newsworthy and what's not, to establish friendly relations with the local press or the appropriate editor of the larger press to develop the kinds of newsworthy events discussed in previous chapters, and to function generally on a small scale in pursuing a publicity program. It should be noted, however, that it can be tremendously time-consuming, and that the time and energy given to it might better be spent in other aspects of your business.

But sending out an occasional press release, or being interviewed now and again, don't constitute an effective public relations program. A program of any magnitude must be planned and executed by public relations professionals, either internally—on your staff—or by an external public relations agency. There are both advantages and disadvantages to internal staffs and external agencies. The mutual disadvantages can, in most circumstances, be offset by using both internal and external staffs at the same time.

Sometimes it's difficult for a sole practitioner to be his own public relations agent, since he's put in the position of blowing his own horn to an editor. The outside agency, on the other hand, can sometimes do the job more effectively and more professionally. Agency staffs maintain ongoing relations with members of the press, which allows them to deal with the press more easily in selling story ideas and in channeling news. A good agency also has the experience of having worked for a variety of clients, and so can bring to bear a crosshatch of ideas and experience from other companies and other industries. An outside agency can can spare you as well a great deal of time in performing the mechanics of publicity—writing and distributing releases, preparing press kits, wooing editors, and so forth.

In determining which route to take, the distinctions that are peculiarly those of professional services come to the fore.

In most cases, an external agency can deal very well with the public relations problems and opportunities of most companies. But in working with a professional service, it's the very rare agency that can:

- Grasp the essence of professional practice, to the point of knowing what's newsworthy or important in a legal or an accounting or a consulting practice. Translating technical principles in law or accounting in ways that are useful to the prospective client is an essential part of public relations for professional services.
- Be ubiquitous within the halls of a firm, to know what's going on that might be newsworthy in every area of the firm's practice, so that the latest nuance of an international tax ruling can be caught and seized upon as a publicity opportunity.
- Deal with a partnership, as a source and as a program monitor, in which every partner is the client.
- Know and relate to the individual marketing plans and programs of

each of the very many segments of virtually every professional service firm. Without this knowledge, the burden of performing successful public relations is unbearable and untenable.

Which is not to say that it can't be done. Indeed, it's not always done successfully by an internal staff, no matter how competent.

The structure is most likely to work successfully when there's a thoroughly professional internal staff, functioning as an internal public relations agency; an excellent outside agency; and a good management structure in which the external agency functions as part of the team. Assuming a seasoned professional on the internal staff, the entire program is best coordinated and directed internally rather than externally. Then there are the advantages of each that overcome the disadvantages of each.

INTERNAL PUBLIC RELATIONS

There are several distinct advantages to running the publicity program internally, for the firm that can structure a good internal public relations department.

- It may be less expensive. This is not categorically the case—the salary spent on a publicity person, or the time a staff person allocates to publicity, might well add up to more dollars than the cost of an outside agency.
- The inside person is constantly in touch with your operation. He knows your firm intimately, knows the industry, and has the opportunity to see newsworthy activities firsthand as they develop.
- An internal program exerts greater control on both focus and activities. You and your partners know what's going on at all times, how much time is being spent on the program, what the press reaction is at any given moment.
- Your internal program can be supplemented with specialists as needed. For example, a photographer or a brochure writer can be hired by the project.

In adding a staff person to handle the public relations and publicity function, there are only two hard and fast rules. The first is that the person be properly qualified. There should be some verifiable experience in developing a public relations program, in writing releases and feature articles, in press contact and so forth. Second, it's next to useless to have an internal public relations person who does not have the ear, respect and direct access to the senior or managing partners. The press will very quickly discern the degree of authority a public relations person has in speaking for a firm and in serving as a source of real news. There must be a genuine commitment to both the program and the person hired to do it, or else you can anticipate a lot of wasted time and money.

EXTERNAL COUNSEL

A properly qualified public relations agency has several distinct advantages that go beyond the obvious ones of manpower and physical capability. These include:

- They are specialists. Public relations is their business, and the full focus of their business is on serving their clients in public relations activities.
- An agency is staffed and organized to deal with all aspects of a public relations program. It's equipped for the quick dissemination of releases, for direct contact with the press and for planning and running newsmaking events. It maintains up-to-the-minute mailing lists and lists of appropriate personnel in the press.
- Its liaison with the press is constant. This should make its staff knowledgeable of shifts in press attitude and personnel, and allow them to supply an extraordinarily valuable perspective of changing needs. . A good agency brings to each program the breadth of its experience. This is the result of having served many companies with a wide variety of problems, and therefore having developed a broad experience in solutions.
- Its people are objective. Any good agency or public relations counsel must serve two roles—objectivity and advocacy. One is useless without the other. The agency will use its objectivity to help you make realistic public relations decisions. Advocacy—representing you to the public—that's not based on objectivity is weak, frequently irrelevant to your own objectives, and often borders dangerously close to creating problems of credibility.

- The agency staff represent the wide variety of skills necessary to conduct a well-rounded program.
- Agencies can be cost-effective. While there may be hidden overhead factors to be added to the cost of an internal public relations person, the expenses of an external agency can be budgeted. Agencies are accountable for fees and expenses. This is particularly true for those agencies whose fees are based on an hourly rate, where each month's bill itemizes the amount of time spent by each agency executive in each of the several categories in which he is functioning for the firm.

While this would seem to weigh the argument very heavily in favor of the use of an outside agency, the judgment is made, in many respects, no differently from the decision to retain inside or outside accounting or legal staff. Nor does the use of one necessarily preclude the other, and frequently they supplement one another. Indeed, an internal marketing director, who coordinates all marketing activities, can very well function as liaison between your firm and a public relations agency, advertising agency, and so forth.

THE STRUCTURE OF A PUBLIC RELATIONS AGENCY

In most respects, a public relations agency is very different from an advertising agency. In an advertising agency, remember, there is a specialist for each skill and an account executive who functions as the agency's liaison with you, but is not expected to perform any of the skills of advertising. Few public relations firms are large enough to maintain specialists, and those that do have very few specialists in the same categories as in advertising.

The service core of the larger public relations firm is predicated on the account executive and the account supervisor. In most agencies, the account executive performs the same liaison function as in advertising, but is expected to be capable of performing all of the skills of public relations—planning the program, counseling on all public relations attitudes and activities, writing all publicity material (releases, articles, brochures), dealing with the press and so forth. In other words, the account executive is usually a well-rounded person who actually can perform all of the tasks of public relations.

The specialists and technicians in the larger agencies are usually specialists in media placement or writers. For example, a large agency may have a radio and television placement specialist, a magazine placement specialist, a newspaper placement specialist and so forth. Some agencies have staff writers who do no placement or account liaison but may specialize in writing releases, feature articles, speeches, annual reports, brochures or other material. If the agency has clients for whom it does financial public relations, it will have staff people who are expert in that area.

Larger agencies with many clients in a particular industry may have industry specialists. For example, an agency with a great many food clients may have a staff home economist who tests and develops recipes for the client's products. Some public relations firms maintain their own art staffs for designing brochures, firm identity programs and publicity reprints.

Many advertising agencies maintain separate public relations departments that are capable of performing the same functions as a separate public relations agency. Sometimes these ad agency public relations staffs are extraordinarily capable. The degree to which this is the case is a function of the agency's own attitude towards publicity and public relations. Because advertising and public relations are so distinctly different, the ad agency public relations department should have a large degree of autonomy, rather than function merely as a creative subsidiary to advertising. The ad agency that perceives of it public relations department simply in terms of writing releases for its ad clients is not likely to have strong public relations capabilities.

In smaller public relations agencies, one or two people perform all the public relations tasks performed by the staffs in larger agencies. The restriction in terms of effectiveness for any client is the number of clients that any one individual can handle at one time without giving short shrift to other accounts.

HOW TO WORK WITH A PUBLIC RELATIONS FIRM

Because of the distinct differences between advertising and public relations, dealing with your public relations firm can be very different from dealing with your ad agency. In advertising, once the program is set, it's executed in a series of ads and perhaps promotional activities. Each ad can be seen and judged and, to some degree, its effectiveness can be measured.

A public relations program, on the other hand, is an ongoing activity with a constant flow of ideas and day-by-day effort to establish workable press relations, newsworthy activities, releases, feature articles and so forth.

The relationship with your public relations firm begins with a program spelled out on paper so that you know at the outset exactly what your agency is going to do for you, and the timetable within which it's going to do it. What you may expect from the program should be made absolutely clear to you. Your public relations account executive should have constant access to you and your staff, without, of course, interfering with your day-to-day activities. If you're not experienced in public relations, his job is to train you to understand what kinds of material and activities the agency needs to know about to do its job. You should expect new and fresh ideas regularly from your agency.

You should also expect periodic meetings (at least once a week) with your account executive to review the week's activities and the status of the program. The account executive's supervisor should also meet with you periodically to review your program and its progress.

Written reports, no matter how brief, should be forthcoming regularly, and minutes—or at least notes—should be taken at each meeting. This avoids misunderstandings about what was promised and what was delivered.

A difficult part of a public relations program is that it frequently takes time and a great deal of work before the results begin to show up. Unfortunately, this is more often true with a smaller professional firm than with a larger one, because a smaller firm is less likely to generate the kinds of activities that are newsworthy; more must be developed for the smaller firm. Thus, no program you undertake should last less than three months. This should be time enough for a new agency to become familiar with your business, to prepare any necessary materials, and to develop some successful publicity. The nature of publicity is such that you can't always pick your dates and timing. A great many releases may have to go to an editor, over a long period, before he decides that you've said something newsworthy, or even before the the editor decides to accept your firm as a news source. Feature material may also take a month to six weeks to develop and place. In publicity, you hear the word "no" more often than you do "yes," and it sometimes takes a great barrage of material to the press before a single clipping is produced. In the start-up period of a publicity program, the results may be slim but the effort isn't wasted. Contacts are being made in your behalf and a familiarity with your firm is being developed—all of which should pay off in the next three months.

But the program and the agency's activities must be carefully monitored even during that initial period to be sure that the pipeline is in fact being filled, and that the time isn't being used by the agency just to learn your operation and your industry at your expense.

If, during the first three-month initial period, you don't quickly discern that your agency is coming to understand your firm and is functioning successfully in your behalf, or if at the end of six months there have been no tangible results as measured against the original public relations program, then it's time to consider whether you've chosen the right agency. Any questions you have of that nature should be raised directly with the agency principals. If the program isn't working, then conceivably, it's their fault. Just as conceivably, it's your fault. They may not have made clear to you what they're tying to accomplish and how they work, or you may not be cooperating with them in areas that count. There may be personality problems with the particular account executive, or the agency itself may not be the right one for you. But if a program isn't working, it's the program and its performance that's at fault—not the validity of public relations and publicity as a marketing tool.

SELECTING AN AGENCY

Public relations agencies come in all sizes and forms. They range from the one-person firm to major international firms with offices in many cities throughout the country and the world. Many advertising agencies have departments of various sizes.

Choosing the appropriate agency for you is a function of your needs as well as your budget. If your program—and your budget—are small, then conceivably a one-person agency (who himself has a low overhead) can perform as successfully for you as can a large, major national firm (assuming that the one person isn't so overloaded with other accounts that you can command only the smallest portion of his time). If your program is of any size, then obviously it will require the manpower and the facilities of a larger firm.

In choosing a firm, a preliminary interview should establish at least the following:

- What are the size and nature of the agency? How many clients does it have and who are they? Are many of the clients the same size as your firm? What industries are its clients in?
- What successful programs for other clients can it show you? This should include a full presentation of the original objectives, the programs designed to meet those objectives and clear evidence of the successful performance of those programs.
- How well established is the agency? A public relations agency is a business, just as yours is. It should be able to demonstrate that it's well established and financially sound. Getting a Dun & Bradstreet rating is helpful.
- What is the experience and what are the qualifications of the people who will work on your account? Are they senior people? Can you see samples of their work? What's the line of internal reporting responsibility? Who in the agency has the ultimate responsibility for performance on your account?
- Who will be working directly on your account, and what are their experience and qualifications? How many other accounts do they service? Do you personally like the account executive to be assigned to you? Since the working relationship will be close, this is extremely important.
- What is the fee structure, including the policy on out-of-pocket expenses?
- What contractual arrangements are offered? Agencies prefer a year's contract. This is understandable and usually acceptable, provided, however, that there is a three-month trial period and a 30-day cancellation clause.
- Do they ask the right questions? Even in a preliminary conversation you can tell pretty fast whether you're dealing with intelligent people who understand your business and who can quickly learn your marketing problems, your objectives and the role that they will be expected to play in your marketing program.

• What references do they offer? This should include both present clients and business references. If possible, it should include references from the media itself. A well-established public relations firm should be happy to give you the names of several editors with whom they have long-standing relationships and who can vouch for their professionalism.

If possible, you should interview several agencies rather than allow yourself to be sold by just one. The relationship with a public relations firm is a close one—closer perhaps than with an advertising agency. A great deal depends upon a strong interplay of communication and ideas. Given all of the qualifications and appropriate answers to the list of questions you should feel comfortable with your choice.

For professionals inexperienced in working with public relations firms, the question arises as to whether the agency you choose should be allowed to have competing clients (two or more law firms, accounting firms, etc.). Because marketing is so new for professional services, practices haven't been established and set in concrete, and so a measure of judgment must be used. At the same time, there are really few firms with the experience in dealing with professional services. A terrific agency, with a great track record in fashion publicity or even investor relations, may not have the slightest idea of how to represent a professional service. A firm with professional service experience, on the other hand, is going to be in great demand.

The public relations agency, like your firm, is a service organization. You know how your firm deals with the problem of competing clients, and that offers some guidance. There are several questions that apply:

• What will the firm be doing for you that deals with sensitive information?
• Is the public relations firm large enough to maintain separate account teams for competitive clients?
• What safeguards do they offer to maintain security and discretion, as you do in your own firm?
• Is the firm really that good that raising the question is worth the effort, or should you look elsewhere?

When these questions are addressed head on, you are closer to knowing whether there is, in fact, a problem.

The Request For Proposal

Too often, the lack of experience by most agencies in dealing with a professional service makes it difficult for them to propose properly. The subject is too new for even the best agencies to adequately address a program for you, without a great deal of input from you.

The solution lies in a formal *Request for Proposal*, in which you delineate on paper those facts that would help an agency propose intelligently.

The RFP (see appendix) should include at least the following information:

- A description of your firm
- A description of what you do, and how you're distinguished from others in your profession
- Your general firm objectives
- Your general marketing objectives
- Your structure for dealing with marketing projects
- Your expectations from a public relations program
- An open invitation to ask questions before the written proposal is made
- Mechanical information (timetable, how selection will be made, etc.)
- Any other information you yourself might like to have if the situation were reversed

Then, of course, there is the basic information that you want to know about the proposing firm, such as the factors that will help you judge the firm's experience, solidity, and so forth. This includes their size and nature, number of clients, size of staff, fee structure, background and qualifications of the individuals who will be working on your program, and so forth.

Preparing a written RFP may seem to be an unnecessary use of your time, but it isn't. It will consume less time and effort than will reading proposals from agencies, including some good ones, who really don't understand how to propose to a professional service firm.

COSTS

Essentially, the expenses in a public relations program are:

- Consulting fees
- Reproduction costs for releases, etc.
- Mailing costs
- Travel costs for meetings, major press interviews, etc.
- Out-of-pocket and miscellaneous expenses, including long-distance phone bills, entertainment of editors, etc.
- Design and printing of special brochures, publicity, reprints, etc.
- Special projects, such as photography, opinion surveys and other special events and contingencies

Fee structures vary from one firm to another, although basically there are only two types used by most public relations firms—straight fee and hourly rate. Fees for an effective program may range from $500 a month to $50,000 or more for a year.

Straight fee basis is usually a fixed amount, paid monthly. This has the advantage of simpler budgeting.

The hourly rate functions much the same as with accountants and attorneys. Usually a basic minimum fee is agreed upon, with hours charged against that fee, and the client is billed for hours in excess of the minimum. Sometimes a maximum is also agreed upon. The maximum allows for overall budgeting. The hourly basis functions best if there's a clear understanding beforehand of the hourly rate of each person who is to work on the account. Your bill might then consist of an hourly breakdown, person by person, with a portion of time allocated to each activity (client contact, press contact, planning, release writing, etc.).

Most firms bill a month in advance, with firms that use the hourly rate billing the agreed-upon minimum.

Prior to signing a contract with a public relations firm, you should have a general idea of the cost of each item. How much are reproduction costs for releases and other material? How large a mailing list is involved, and what will the mailing costs generally come to? If the public relations firm is located any distance from your office, who pays the travel expenses for meetings with you?

Normally, out-of-pocket and routine expenses include:

- Clipping services
- Photography and artwork
- Telephone and telegrams
- Special wire services for rapid distribution of urgent news
- Transportation other than for meetings with you
- Promotional expenses for meeting with the press, including press entertainment
- Postage
- Messenger services
- Photocopying
- Subscriptions to trade publications
- Secretarial overtime on special projects
- Miscellaneous minor expenses

If your press coverage extends beyond local newspapers and other publications that you would normally read, a clipping service may be included. This allows you to determine the extent to which any publicity you've issued is printed. Unfortunately, no method has yet been devised to mechanize the essentially human job of scanning thousands of publications. As a result, the number of clippings found is usually a small percentage of material that actually appears.

Telephone and other means of communication are usually billed at exact cost, as shown on actual bills.

Transportation expenses usually include transportation within a city, such as cabs, buses, subway and so on.

In addition to postage for regular mailings of press releases, there's postage normally used in mailing letters and other material, fulfilling information requests, and for shipping quantities of background material and so forth.

During the course of a program, it's frequently necessary to conduct business with members of the press over lunch, dinner or cocktails. These expenses must be documented by receipts.

Costs for messenger service are usually incurred within one city, although occasionally messengers or air couriers must be used to transmit important material between cities. These expenses are supported by copies of bills.

Photocopying costs are usually calculated on a predetermined rate based on costs.

In order for your public relations firm to function well for you, it must keep abreast of your industry by reading trade publications. Subscriptions to such publications for that purpose are normally billed to the client.

Special wire services for rapid distribution of publicity releases normally charge a fixed rate for each day of operation. In other words, two separate releases for one firm on the same day cost the same as for one release. There are variations of cost if the release exceeds 500 words. ·

The costs of travel—indeed, all expenses on behalf of the client—are usually allocated on the same basis used by the Internal Revenue Service. This includes transportation, meals, hotel expenses, transportation within a city, auto mileage, tips and miscellaneous out-of-pocket expenses.

While normal secretarial and office services are considered part of a public relations firm's or firm's own internal operating expenses, special projects frequently require additional expense, such as secretarial overtime or the use of temporary office help. Public relations firms normally include these costs in expense billings.

In the normal course of a program, miscellaneous minor expenses are sometimes incurred. These include additional copies of publications, tips, phone calls made away from the office and so on.

Even in the best planned program, situations frequently arise, often in the form of opportunities, for special projects or activities. This may include an opportunity for someone in your firm to participate as a panelist in a seminar, the need for a special brochure or pamphlet and so forth. While these occasions are normally unexpected, and unbudgeted, their extra costs can often be measured in terms of added value.

Granted the flexibility of expenses that tend to be variable, it's still possible to review a program well in advance and generally estimate what the expenses are likely to be. This should make it possible for any firm or experienced public relations firm to budget appropriately for the cost of the program.

Whether your public relations program is performed internally or externally, it must have the same objectives, the same relationship to the total marketing program and marketing mix, and achieve the same level of results. At the same time, except for fees, the expenses of a program will be basically the same whether you do it in-house or use an outside agency.

SUMMARY

While the professional skills of public relations are best performed by experienced practitioners, some public relations activities can be performed by nonprofessional marketers.

There are distinct advantages and disadvantages of both in-house public relations operations and external agencies, but the best solution is to use both. The advantages of the internal staff are:

- It may be less expensive
- You have greater control
- The internal staff understands your firm better
- The internal staff can be supplemented with outside services

The internal staff works only if personnel are experienced and qualified, and have access to—and support of—senior management.

The advantages of an external agency are that they are:

- Specialists in public relations
- Structured to deal with all aspects of a program
- In constant touch with press
- Experienced in depth with a wide variety of companies
- Objective
- Cost-effective and budgetable
- Capable in a wide variety of skills

Most public relations firms differ from ad agencies in that the capable public relations account executive is expected to perform all the tasks, from planning to execution, although larger agencies may have specialists. Ad account executives must understand all the skills, but need not be able to perform them.

A good working relationship with an agency requires easy access to you and frequent contact and reporting. The program should be spelled out on paper, and you should expect regular reports on activities and progress. At least three months should be allowed for the program to take hold.

In selecting an agency, at least the following should be considered:

- Size and nature of the agency
- Success of programs they've done for other clients

- How well established they are as a business
- Who will be working on your account, and how well-qualified they are
- Whether they ask the right questions of you, and seem to understand the explanations of your business

A formal request for proposal can help agencies make an intelligent and relevant presentation to you by clarifying the nature of your business and marketing programs. The RFP would include:

- Description of your firm, what you do, and how you're distinguished from other firms
- General firm and marketing objectives
- Your marketing structure
- Your expectations from a public relations program
- Any other information you think may be useful to the proposers

Essentially, the costs of a program include:

- Consulting fees
- Reproduction costs and mailing
- Out-of-pocket expenses
- Design and printing of special material and special projects

PART IV

Proposals and Presentations

CHAPTER 17

Proposals and Presentations

The major thrust of the total marketing effort is to bring the prospective client to the point at which a proposal and presentation are requested and made. This is what marketing professional services is about. And it is here that the client is won or lost.

No client is won without a presentation and proposal, in one form or another, particularly in this competitive climate. It's a long way from "This is who we are—when do we start?" to the elaborate, competitive formal proposals, and dog-and-pony-show presentations, that are commonplace today.

There are, of course, some professional services in which a formal proposal is neither required nor expected. No one asks a doctor or a dentist for more than a few words of explanation about the problem, the solution and the charges. Lawyers, too, are rarely required to write proposals or to make formal presentations, although the complexity of business is causing changes here, too.

On the other hand, no moderate or larger-sized company is likely to accept a bid from an accounting firm or a consultant without some clear picture of how the professional sees the prospective client's situation and needs, and how he proposes to serve them.

In professional services, proposals and presentations play an interesting role, part of which is predicated on the fact that buyers of professional services are poor consumers. Most individuals don't know much about how to choose a doctor, much less a lawyer, an

accountant, an architect or any other professional. Even sophisticated business people, with experience in dealing with professionals,
don't have much to guide them in choosing. Given a parade of any six
professionals who perform the same service, how do you distinguish
one from the other? How do you make a choice, except on instinct or
personal chemistry?

And if you're selling the service, how do you distinguish yourself
from the others in the parade, particularly when you're down to the
wire of a proposal and a presentation?

There are more responses to these questions than there are answers. That's why proposals and presentations are getting more elaborate, if not necessarily better. That's why so many proposals from
different firms in the same profession so often sound so much like one
another, as if everybody subscribed to the same proposal writing
service.

The answer, if there is one, perhaps lies in looking more thoughtfully at the process—trying to fathom what works for you and what
doesn't; trying to bring more skill and imagination to it.

There are some hints. The way the proposal is written, and what
it contains, must convey a sense of competence, intelligence, skill,
and a service concept that inspires confidence. The presentation must
show a sense of stability and security in what's being presented.
Thoroughness, and being meticulous, seem to make a positive difference.

THE PROPOSAL

In smaller firms, the proposal is usually written by a principal of
the firm, or some senior member who's displayed a special capability
to do it. In larger firms, proposals are considered to be of such consequence that teams of proposal writers are especially trained and dedicated to writing them.

Elaborate proposals for prospective clients can, in the larger
firms, cost as much as hundreds of thousands of dollars. When a
Fortune 500 company invites an accounting firm or a consultant to
make a proposal, where the prospective fee is many times the cost of
the proposal, then expense is no object. The higher the stakes, in
terms of fees, the greater the expense that seems to be warranted.

Unfortunately, it costs the prospective client nothing to invite five or six firms to make that expenditure, too often knowing beforehand which firm will be hired. There seems to be no known solution to this deplorable practice, other than a frank request of the prospective client to clearly state that the competition is indeed open.

TYPES OF PROPOSALS

Proposals range from the simple to the elaborate.

The simplest type of proposal and presentation is the face-to-face statement in which the professional says to his prospect, "This is the problem, this is how I'm going to solve it, this is what I think will happen as a result of my efforts, and this is what it will cost."

A written proposal says essentially the same things, and may range from a simple one page letter to an elaborate document of many pages, illustrated and bound.

Other proposals may take advantage of graphic and visual techniques. Proposals have been done in the form of video tapes and motion picture films. A proposal may be in the form of a computer program supplied on a disk. Mixed media proposals may combine a written document with several different audio visual techniques. In fact, in requesting a prospective client's business there are no limitations, other than the imagination, to the form a proposal may take.

ELEMENTS OF A PROPOSAL

Whether it be done in one page or a bound book, whether it be part of a written proposal or an oral presentation or a combination of both, prospective clients may be best persuaded to retain you if they're given the following information:

- An indication that you understand, or are capable of learning, the essence of the prospect's business and industry
- An indication that you understand the nature of the prospect's problem, or the situation that warrants the need for your professional services
- A sense of what the prospect really needs, or wants, or can be persuaded to want, in terms of the service you have to offer
- A persuasive argument for your ability to fulfill his needs or wants

• The basic information about your firm . . .

   —Size and nature
   —Personnel
   —Structure, in terms of prospect's needs (Specialists? Access to outside experts? Levels of people responsible for the prospect's account?)
   —History of your firm
   —Track record, particularly in parallels to the prospect's situation or problem
   —Names and backgrounds of people who will be directly responsible for servicing the prospect

• A sense of program to address the client's needs—what you will do to meet those needs and how you'll do it
• A timetable
• Costs and fee structure
• Any other information that the prospect may require to help him distinguish your firm from others, and to make a decision.

Just how this information is presented is a function of many factors. How big is the prospect's company? How large is the situation or problem? How many people make the decision about which firm to hire? Who will contribute to that decision? Increasingly, larger companies are relying upon committees of the board of directors to qualify and retain professionals, in which case you're facing a tougher audience, but one that's likely to have more experience in dealing with professionals. A two-edged sword.

PROPOSAL RULES

There are some basic general rules as well that must be considered. They simply encompass the most logical, reasonable and effective use of marketing practices. And like all rules of marketing, they are not graven in stone, but rather, should be breached only for conscious and knowing reasons. In the final analysis, what works, works—and the only measure of success for a proposal is that it gets the client.

The rules:

- The proposal should be orderly and logical. It should state the prospect's problem or define his situation, your capabilities and approach to solving the problem, the forces of your firm that you will bring to bear in the prospect's behalf, a description of your qualifications, a breakdown of time frame and costs, and your fee. Try to keep the level of writing fairly high. Poor and unfocused writing says to the prospective client that you're a poor and unfocused thinker and practitioner. And watch the length. A proposal that's too long, too wordy or too elaborate will lose a prospect's enthusiasm, attention and focus.

- No matter how special or unique your services, they should be presented in terms of the client's needs—what he wants and needs, not what you have to offer. Merely to offer your capabilities is not sufficient. The wrong point of view, in which the emphasis is on who you are and what you can do, rather than on the client's needs, will almost invariably turn the prospect off.

- If there is a formal request for a proposal it should be read very carefully and the response should be precisely in terms of the RFP, even if it deviates from your normal proposal format.

- Because of the personal nature of professional services, every effort should be made to delineate precisely who will work on the account, including their personal backgrounds and experience.

- Prior to writing the proposal, as much research as possible should be done on the prospective client's company, the industry, the nature of the problem and the people involved. Nothing turns a prospective client off so quickly as the feeling that the professional didn't take the trouble to understand what the client's company, industry or problems were about. Do your homework. It's useful, too, to know against whom you're competing, if possible. This can sometimes give you an advantage, particularly if you have a sense of your competitor's strengths and weaknesses.

- Graphics and exhibits should be used very cautiously. The danger is that they will be a distraction, rather than support the points you want to make. Judgment should be exercised carefully.

- Be cautious of boilerplate—standard paragraphs or sections you include in all proposals. A proposal should look tailor-made, and focus specifically on the needs of the prospective client. Boilerplate has a way of looking and sounding like boilerplate. Moreover, a careless typist can pick up a boilerplate element from another proposal that may include something that clearly gives away the fact that it is boilerplate.

- Too much or too little sell are equal pitfalls in a proposal. Too much sell is irksome and distracts from the real message. Too little sell will not allow a proposal to achieve its ends.
- Don't forget to ask for the order. This is a basic tenet of selling—one that works and that's too frequently ignored.
- Whether the style is formal or informal, the proposal should have an element of personality in it. It's an individual talking to an individual—not a piece of paper talking to a machine, or an insurance policy. There should be a measure of humanity, warmth and readability.
- Never promise more than can be delivered. Even the most naive prospective client will realize that you've done this, more often than not. It destroys credibility. And don't misrepresent. You'll pay for it sooner or later. Probably sooner.
- Not relating the proposal to the oral presentation can be confusing and distracting.

Essentially, the written proposal is another one of those anomalies of marketing—the mixture of technique and art. And while proposals for professionals are not new, doing them in the new competitive context is new, and creates new problems in that they must be done more thoughtfully than ever before. But it creates new opportunities as well.

PRESENTATIONS

A presentation is the primary selling point at which an individual or team explains in person why the prospect should retain the firm. It's the point at which the information and persuasive arguments of the written proposal are presented by the individuals who will perform—or supervise the performance of—the program. It's the point at which the important element of personal chemistry is added to the marketing mix, frequently for the first time.

While salesmanship is inherent in both proposals and presentations, their structured nature must be viewed apart from classical sales techniques. Selling is involved in both, of course, but within the framework of the structure.

Although a proposal is usually given in conjunction with a presentation (either before or after), and elements of both will appear in each, the two are quite separate. However, the nature of the relationship between the two dictates the format of each. The proposal may supplement an oral presentation—include information that's not part of the presentation—or complement it. The proposal may be sent ahead of the presentation, or left behind after the presentation has been made.

Presentations offer somewhat different, and usually more flexible, opportunities than do proposals. Proposals are words on paper. Presentations are people presenting themselves, as much as the information they impart. In professional services, it's people that get hired, and so the presentation offers the opportunity to focus on individuals.

Presentations offer the prospective client the opportunity to ask questions, and they afford the opportunity to respond immediately to those questions, to new information, to objections—none of which can be done with the same psychological advantages in a written proposal.

The presentation can be as casual as a dialogue with the prospect, or it can be formal, carefully designed and orchestrated, with several people from your firm participating, elaborate audio visual support (including slides and films), and a substantial proposal left behind or subsequently delivered.

The several considerations that affect the format of the presentation include, essentially, the same as those for proposals. The size of the prospective client company and the size of the prospective account and fee. The nature of your firm and its size. The nature of traditional or competitive presentations.

But to these considerations should be added concerns about the ability to deal well on a face-to-face basis, to think well on your feet, to inspire confidence in person.

Add to this both the wherewithall and the familiarity to use graphic and visual materials. If you haven't had experience in using an overhead projector or in making a slide presentation, a new business presentation isn't the place to learn.

The presentation may be made by one or two individuals, or it may use an entire team that consists of senior partners who are specialists in new business presentations, experts in specific areas of the prospective client's problems or business, and those partners and others who will be responsible for serving the account should it be won.

Consider the individuals to whom you'll be making the presentation. Know about them beforehand, if possible. Then you can adjust your style to the personalities of the audience.

While a good deal of personal style dictates the nature of a presentation, it's useful to attempt to catalog what works for your firm and what doesn't, and then to train as many people as possible to make presentations. Your firm's growth may depend upon having an increasing number of your firm's members participating in presentations.

PHYSICAL ARRANGEMENTS

While the physical arrangements of the room in which you'll make your presentation are most often the province—literally and figuratively—of the prospective client, there may still be some flexibility in the arrangement.

To the degree that you can control the situation, what you're after are surroundings that are comfortable and receptive. For example, a conference room or the seating area of an office is preferable to an arrangement in which you're making a presentation to an individual seated behind a desk. The desk serves as a psychological barrier.

You want to be sure that there's enough light and that neither you nor your prospect are seated with a back towards a sunlit window. Certainly, if you're going to use visuals, you want to be sure that the facilities are compatible—that screens can be set up and equipment conveniently plugged in, that extraneous light can be blocked, and so forth.

Of course, if you can arrange to have the presentation made in your own offices, it's presumed that you will have set up the facilities to your advantage.

USING VISUAL AIDS

Your choice of visual aids is extensive. Among your many choice are, for example:

- Flip charts
- Chalk boards
- Overhead projectors
- Slide projectors
- Video tape
- Motion picture projectors
- Multi-media presentations
- Audio tapes
- Phonograph records

Using these devices can be very seductive. They're exciting and they're vivid, and there's a tendency to use them badly, or to use the wrong device for your material. But if they're used well they can capture and hold attention.

The ultimate decision as to whether to use visual and audio visual devices should be a function of the information you want to impart rather than the sheer drama. The choice of using audio visuals, then, is a function of impact, but within a context of imparting information and selling. Dramatic presentations may be amusing, but if they don't sell they're expensive.

WHEN TO USE VISUALS

Beyond the context of imparting information, other factors that dictate using these devices are:

- Budget.
- Available production facilities.
- Available equipment.
- The room in which the presentation will be made (it's size, shape, lighting and so forth).
- Your experience in dealing with the equipment and with visuals.

Different media offer different capabilities, and it's extremely important to use each of the devices effectively within its own medium. To attempt to allow audio visuals to carry more than their weight can lead to confusion and distraction. The rule is to keep it simple, with each visual making no more than a single point. When an audience is reading a slide or a chart it's not listening to the speaker. Nothing should go on a slide or a flip chart that can't be grasped in a moment.

Films or videotape offer the opportunity to bring in outside experts or to dramatize a point. On the other hand, these are expensive devices to use for showing a chart or a graph, which can be done more effectively with slides.

Charts, photographs and even a simple cartoon can be very effective in presenting a complex idea simply. Where words must be used in the graphic, use as few as possible.

Chalkboards or flip charts, on the other hand, are effective devices for riveting attention and making a point during an oral presentation. They also have the advantage of staying in front of your audience for as long as you need them, without being as distracting (as a slide might be.)

In using flip charts and chalkboards, use them as carefully as you would electronic devices. Flipcharts have distinctive advantages in that they supply a certain intimacy with the audience. They can be used almost anywhere and are simple and inexpensive. They can be flipped back and forth to refer to previous points more easily than can a slide. They don't require a darkened room, which means that you're always in sight of your audience and can maintain valuable eye contact.

Flip charts also have an advantage in that they can be prepared beforehand or used like chalkboards to make points as you need them.

A chalkboard, while it can show fine detail and is subject to the user's handwriting, has the same advantages as flip charts, plus additional spontaneity. They are a highly personal medium, with a great deal of flexibility. The only disadvantage is that you frequently have to turn your back to your audience to write.

Slides and other graphic media should be designed professionally by an art director. The additional cost is moderate and the return on the investment makes it worthwhile.

MAKING THE PRESENTATION

In using audio visuals during the course of a presentation, it's extremely important to make the conscious decision beforehand about whether the slides are driving the speaker or the speaker is driving the slides. If the slides are an adjunct to the speaker they should aid, and not distract by being too elaborate or complex. At the same, time it's pointless to have the speaker simply read what the slide says and have no more to contribute to the presentation than that.

While you may have great confidence in your own ability to make a presentation, particularly on your own company, rehearsals may be very much in order. This is particularly true if you're using new material or audio visuals, or if others are involved in the presentation. There is some peculiar notion held by those who haven't done it that rehearsal reduces spontaneity, or that the adrenalin rush of the moment will add an element of enthusiasm to the presentation. It simply isn't so. Rehearsal helps to familiarize all participants with the material, so that during the actual presentation the mind can be free and alert to reactions and other factors. It helps hone timing and smooths out difficult relationships with both other members of the team and with the audio visual material. Rehearsing before a sympathetic audience of your own associates allows flaws in the presentation to be seen and anticipated.

It's also a good idea to anticipate questions, particularly difficult ones, and to formulate answers beforehand. There should be no reason to be stumped by a trick question. While you may pride yourself in your ability to think on your feet, an anticipated question and a carefully worked out answer is more advantageous.

Even for the experienced presentor there are a number of pitfalls to be avoided:

- Not knowing your prospect's needs and wishes.
- Not doing your homework on the prospect's company and industry.
- Focusing on what you have to sell rather than on what the prospect needs.
- Straying from the point and being overlong.
- Not being sensitive to your listeners. If they don't laugh at your jokes, stop telling them.
- Selling too hard.
- Personalizing, or overloading with irrelevant anecdotes.
- Not asking for the order.
- Lack of familiarity with the audio visual material.

• Being unprepared for questions.
• Not knowing your competition, and lack of competitive intelligence.

Most presentations conclude with some notion of when a response will be given. It's not untoward to ask for it if it isn't volunteered. It's sometimes useful to keep open avenues of continued contact until a decision is made. For example, casually mentioning an article or a brochure that wasn't mentioned in the presentation, and then offering to send it.

In marketing professional services, the sale is made only on a face-to-face basis. To spend a considerable amount of money on all of the tools of marketing, and then to short-change the presentation and proposal, is to lose the final advantage in a selling situation.

SUMMARY

The major thrust of the marketing effort is to bring the prospective client to the point at which a proposal and presentation are requested and made.

The proposal must convey a sense of competence, intelligence, skill, and a service concept that inspires confidence. It must show a sense of stability and security in what's being presented, and be thorough and meticulous.

A proposal can be a simple one page letter or an elaborate document. It can be written by one member of the firm, or by a team of specialists. Its form is limited only by the boundaries of imagination, but should include:

• An indication that you understand the prospect's business and industry, problems, or the situation that warrants the need for your professional services
• A sense of what the prospect really needs, or wants, or can be persuaded to want, in terms of the service you have to offer
• A persuasive argument for your ability to fulfill his needs or wants
• The basic information about your firm . . .

—Size and nature
—Personnel

—Structure
—History
—Track record
—Names and backgrounds of people who will be directly responsi-
  ble for servicing the prospect
- A sense of program to address the client's needs
- A timetable
- Costs and fee structure
- Any other information that the prospect may require to help him
  distinguish your firm from others, and to make a decision

   For good proposals:

- The proposal should be orderly and logical, state the prospect's
  problem or define his situation, list your capabilities and approach
  to solving the problem, and include a description of your qualifications, a breakdown of time frame and costs, and your fee. A proposal that's too long, too wordy or too elaborate will lose a prospect's enthusiasm, attention and focus.
- Your services should be presented in terms of the client's needs—
  what he wants and needs, not what you have to offer.
- A formal request for a proposal should be read very carefully and
  the response should be precisely in those terms.
- Delineate who will work on the account, including their personal
  backgrounds and experience.
- Prior to writing the proposal, as much research as possible should
  be done on the prospective client's company, the industry, the
  nature of the problem and the people involved.
- Graphics and exhibits should be used very cautiously.
- Be cautious of boilerplate—standard paragraphs or
- Try to avoid boilerplate.
- Too much or too little sell are equal pitfalls in a proposal.
- Don't forget to ask for the order.
- Whether the style is formal or informal, the proposal should have an
  element of personality, humanity, warmth and readability in it.
- Never promise more than can be delivered.
- Not relating the proposal to the oral presentation can be confusing
  and distracting.

   A proposal is really a mixture of technique and art.

A presentation is the primary selling point at which it is explained in person why the prospect should retain the firm. It's the point at which the important element of personal chemistry is added to the marketing mix. The written proposal may supplement an oral presentation or complement it. The proposal may be sent ahead of the presentation, or left behind after the presentation has been made. Presentations offer the opportunity to deal with questions and reactions, or with new material or information.

Presentations can be casual or formal; be made by one person or a team. Consideration should be made of the physical location, which should be congenial.

Among the choice of visual aids are:

- Flip charts.
- Chalk boards
- Overhead projectors.
- Slide projectors.
- Video tape.
- Motion picture projectors.
- Multi-media presentations.
- Audio tapes.
- Phonograph records.

Factors that dictate using these devices are:

- Budget.
- Available production facilities.
- Available equipment.
- The room in which the presentation will be made (it's size, shape, lighting and so forth).
- Your experience in dealing with the equipment and with visuals.

Film and videotape can dramatize and bring in outside experts. Chalkboards and flip charts can rivet attention and be flexible. Charts, photographs and cartoons can effectively present complex ideas simply. All graphics should be done professionally, and used sparingly, to be most effective.

Presentations should be rehearsed, with all questions anticipated and answers prepared beforehand.

Pitfalls to be avoided:

- Not knowing your prospect's needs and wishes.
- Not doing your homework on the prospect's company and industry.
- Focusing on what you have to sell rather than on what the prospect needs.
- Straying from the point and being overlong.
- Not being sensitive to your listeners.
- Selling too hard.
- Personalizing, or overloading with irrelevant anecdotes.
- Not asking for the order.
- Lack of familiarity with the audio visual material.
- Being unprepared for questions.
- Not knowing your competition, and lack of competitive intelligence.

PART V
The Future

CHAPTER 18

Marketing and the Future of Professional Services

There is an ecological structure in many systems of the world, in which if one thing changes, so does everything else. So it is with marketing professional services.

For generations, the exalted nature of professional services was unchanged in its demean of probity and professionalism. If there were deviations from professional conduct, and violations of ethical codes, then they were breaches; the ethical codes and precepts were themselves unscathed.

And if the professionals were perceived to be conservative in their conduct and their view of the world, and of each other, then this conservatism served them well. One trusts those whose ethical behavior is predictable. One can rely upon professionals, because they are so entwined with codes of ethics, and bound by them. And for the nature of what one calls upon professionals to do, probity is essential. One trusts a lawyer and a doctor and an accountant with deep and consequential and abiding secrets, and with matters of great consequence.

As has been noted elswhere in these pages, this demean of professional probity is worn by professionals like a cloak, as well it should be. It is as much a part of the tradition, and character, and personality of the professional as is the framed diploma on the wall. It's a tradition of longer standing than anyone remembers.

And then, ior both philosophical and economic reasons, a portion of the code was struck down.

Suddenly, professionals moved into a new era. They can now advertise. More significantly, they can actively and flagrantly pursue clients—*new business*. Even more shocking, they can pursue one another's clients.

Did anything move or change as a result of this new dimension to professional practice? You bet it did. And the changes have just begun.

Are the changes positive? Who benefits? Who loses? What, if anything, does the public gain or lose?

To answer these questions, let's look at exactly what happened.

It's difficult to know precisely when and why some traditions start, but at some point in our history it became clear that, at least for credibility and trustworthiness, professionals needed an ethical compact with themselves and the world they serve. When the codes of ethics were actually promulgated is unimportant. Starting at least with Aesculapius, and perhaps further rooted in the guilds of the middle ages, professionals perceived a need for themselves and one another to be protected by codes. Ultimately, the tenets of these codes became part of practice. Those who violated the codes did so flagrantly, and knew that they risked ostracism from the public and their peers. Violations of some of the tenets meant more—loss of the right to practice.

Prior to the time the canons were changed, there was, of course, practice development, and those activities are chronicled elsewhere in these pages. But the frank marketing, in which clients (and particularly the clients of others) are actively pursued, did not exist.

Nor were professionals prepared for the changes when they occurred.

Nobody really understood what the impact really was, or what the change really meant. What can we actually do? What is allowed and what continues to be prohibited?

Nobody really knew how to do it—whatever "it" was. A whole new breed of consultants—marketing "experts"—sprung up overnight.

Nobody had any sense of the impact that marketing might have on the professions. How could they?

At the same time, dire consequences and doom was anticipated.

Professionals and others foresaw massive public loss of respect for professionals and professionalism, with an attendant decline in all professions in the ability to practice effectively.

They envisioned that the competition would be chaotic, with client piracy consuming vast amounts of time and energy and money, to the degree that good practice would be subverted by defensiveness and market maneuvering.

Many people anticipated that the professions would be demeaned and corrupted by hucksterism, with a breakdown of the remaining canons and concepts of ethics.

In fact, none of this doomsday scenario has come about. The inherent conservatism of professionals has kept the process down to a slow and cautious walk. The growth of marketing has been accelerating, but not at a greater pace than professionals can cope with.

Yes, there has been some reaction that implies that segments of the public are somewhat concerned about trusting lawyers or doctors or accountants who advertise, but that seems to be limited, and not at all widespread. In fact, several large firms have polled their clients about advertising, only to find that the clients are unruffled. "We've advertised for years," one major accounting firm was told by a client. "What's the big deal?" And the client might have added, ". . . so long as it's done tastefully, and ethically."

The more flamboyant advertisers—the legal and medical clinics—have chosen a path that works for them. They attract a clientele that doesn't seem to be that of the more traditional practitioners. It seems to be a clientele that's probably more efficiently and economically served by the clinic than it would be by others. Everybody involved benefits, and nobody loses, not the clients and the patients, not the professions.

But in the larger context, a great deal has been happening since the change in the canons of ethics.

There has been a gradual escalation of marketing activities. Many firms that approached it tentatively now move into marketing enthusiastically. Several larger law firms and accounting firms have growing staffs of professional marketers. Every day, more ads appear for more professionals.

There's been a learning process that's carried professionals a considerable distance from the helter-skelter of the instant "marketing experts" that clogged the halls in the early days. Some firms have learned more than others, and some seem to have learned nothing. But there is a growing body of information, and an increasing commitment.

Surprisingly, there's been a reflection of positive results, much sooner than anybody anticipated. Smaller firms, with a stronger commitment and a more enthusiastic investment in sophisticated marketing seem to be making greater strides in the marketplace. And larger firms, with lesser commitments, seem to be falling behind. It's perhaps a little early to be certain, but the classic results of marketing—the better marketers outperform their competitors—appear to be taking hold among professional firms.

There has been some backsliding. Several professional firms that had originally jumped into the marketing arena with both feet lost patience, and have retreated. They may even tell themselves that the fault lies with marketing itself, but that's patent nonsense. Some merely gave lip service to marketing, with no follow-through. Some simply did a poor job, and continue to do so. Marketing, in a few firms, has fallen prey to the ravages of internal politics. Some just don't understand the process yet, and have entered the marketplace with little commitment and with staff that's inexperienced or not first rate. Too often, the responsibility for marketing lies in the hands of a partner who may be excellent at his own profession, but knows little or nothing about marketing.

What is happening that's profound is that as firms awaken to the fact that they must market to compete, there have been some significant changes in the professions themselves.

Many have learned that the most significant change is that, while in the past they competed with one another on the basis of service, they now compete on the basis of marketing. The best marketers are those that will win. They will get the best clients, grow faster, be the most profitable. The partners in the firms of the best marketers will retire richer than those who don't yet understand what marketing is or does.

What these firms are learning, as well, is that inherent in marketing is broad exposure of service concepts—the reality behind the concept of image. And if you're going to compete on the basis of what the public is to see about the way you perform. you'd better perform better than your competitors. Marketing is making better professionals.

These firms are learning more about how to consider the clients' needs, and how to adjust their skills to serve those needs, and they're learning new methods of understanding markets and market research.

There has emerged, as a dividend to this new era, a better approach to service. Firms focus on new ideas because it's the better way to compete. And so we have physicians who improve their specialties, and refine and refocus them. We have new dedication by accountants and lawyers to specialization and focus on specific problems, such as cash management, or tax planning for smaller businesses. These are services that are really needed, and so offer prime opportunities for marketing advantage.

This is the beginning of change in the professions—the way in which marketing will alter the ecology of professional practice.

New service concepts means new approaches to practice in all professions. New "products"—specialized service to address specific and sometimes new problems—means new kinds of specialization.

This trend, already begun, may very well lead to new organizational configurations in the not too distant future. The trend is already emerging. What does it portend?

Conceivably, there will be a substantial shift in power in larger organizations. The Big Eight accounting firms, for example, are already beginning to see this upheaval. First, the order of size in the Big Eight—the eight largest accounting firms—has changed dramatically in just the past few years. In fact, there really isn't a Big Eight any more. The difference in size between firms is only a very small percentage, and that includes the difference between number eight and number nine. Actually, by some counts, number nine is really number seven or better. Marketing may make a difference in further shifting this locus of power.

The new structure is also leading to very serious merger talks among the top ten accounting firms, and many of the leading law firms as well. Mergers, of course, are not new. But mergers of this size are new, as are the number of them being explored.

The merger of the not too distant future may not be limited to two firms in the same profession. How little would have to change before a Merrill Lynch buys a law firm or an accounting firm? The obstacles today are mere details.

Specialization is taking on a new meaning, and the time may not be far when lawyers and accountants join physicians in board certifications of specialties. Today we have board certified dermatologists and surgeons. Tomorrow we are likely to have board certified practitioners in matrimonial law, or tax planning.

There is a question about the future of the smaller professional firms. If the competition gets sufficiently heated, and growth depends upon getting new clients from any source, then how safe is the client of the small firm from the marketing assault of the larger firm? It's already begun in several areas of professional practice, as Big Eight accounting firms pursue the smaller business clients of the smaller accounting firms. And who, after all, has the dollars to buy more effective and ubiquitous marketing?

Not to be forgotten in all of this is the public. As the giants battle on Parnasus, what kind of fallout comes to the consumer of professional services?

Presumably, the benefits of marketing professional services, as in marketing products, come down directly to the consumer.

Competition among professionals should breed more efficient and even cheaper professional services. Certainly, if marketing does its role to focus the professional firms, then the services being offered will be better, more relevant and more responsive to the needs of the public.

Marketing has already bred new kinds of service structures, such as the clinics. Not for everyone, they are still an answer to those with problems too simple for the heavyweight practitioner. A divorce, a simple contract, a tax return, need not necessarily be handled by a high-priced office. The clinic is more than sufficient.

And if there is one benefit of good marketing, for either a product or a service, its education. To compete for the consumer of services, the marketer must educate the client. As one retailer advertises, "An educated consumer is my best customer." So it is in marketing professional services.

Marketing will, indeed, change and improve professional practice. It already has.

And so the beneficiary of good marketing is not only the professional practitioner, but the consumer. This is as it should be.

APPENDICES

APPENDICES

Appendix I

Glossary of Printing Terms

Accordion fold: a term used in binding for two or more parallel folds which open like an accordion.

Against the grain: folding paper at right angles to the grain of the paper.

Airbrush: a small pressure gun that sprays paint by means of compressed air. Used to obtain tone or graduated tonal effects in art work.

Alterations: changes made by the customer, through no fault of the printer, after type has been set. Alterations are a legitimate additional charge by the printer. They are of two types—editorial alterations and author alterations.

Ascender: that part of the letter that rises above the main body, as in "b."

Backbone: the back of the bound book connecting the two covers; also called spine.

Bleed: if the printed image extends to the trim edge of the sheet or page, it is called a bleed.

Body type: type for the main body of a book or ad, as distinguished from the headings.

Boldface type: a name given to type that is heavier than the text type with which it is used, as with the terms defined here.

Bond paper: a grade of writing or printing paper used where strength, durability and permanence are essential requirements.

Book paper: a term used to define a class or group of papers having common physical characteristics that, in general, are more suitable for the graphic arts. The basic size is 25 by 38 inches.

Break for color: in art work and composition, to separate the parts to be printed in different colors.

Broadside: a large printed sheet, intended as a circular, folded into a size convenient for mailing.

Brochure: A pamphlet bound in the form of a booklet.

Cast coated: coated paper dried under pressure against a polished cylinder to pro-

309

duce a highly glossed enamel finish. For most coatings, a steamheated drum is used.

Coated paper: paper having a surface coating which produces a smooth finish. Surfaces vary from eggshell to glossy.

Collate: in binding, the assembling of sheets or signatures.

Condensed type: a narrow or slender typeface.

Contact print: a photographic print made from either a negative or positive in contact with sensitized paper, film or printing plate.

Continuous tone: a photographic image which has not been screened and contains gradient tones from black to white.

Contrast: the tonal gradation between highlights and shadows in an original or reproduction.

Copy: any furnished material (typewritten manuscript, pictures, art work, etc.) to be used in the production of printing. In advertising, the written or spoken material.

Cover paper: a term applied to a great variety of papers used for the outside covers of catalogs, brochures and booklets which enhance the appearance and provide protection in handling.

Crop: to eliminate portions of copy, usually on a photograph or plate.

Descender: that part of the letter which extends below the main body, as in ''p.''

Display type: in composition, type set larger than the text, used to attract attention.

Dot: the individual element of a halftone.

Double dot halftone: two halftone negatives combined into one printing plate, having greater tonal range than a conventional halftone. One negative reproduces the highlights and shadows: the other reproduces middletones.

Dropout: a halftone with no screen dots in the highlights.

Dummy: rough draft of a proposed piece of printed material showing the areas the copy, art work and photographs will occupy.

Duotone: a term for a two-color halftone reproduction from a one-color photograph.

Duplex paper: paper having a different color or finish on each side.

Embossed finish: paper with a raised or depressed surface resembling wood, cloth, leather or other pattern.

Embossing: impressing an image in relief to achieve a raised surface; either over printing or on blank paper (which is called blind embossing).

Enamel: a term applied to a coated paper or to a coating material on a paper.

Expanded type: type whose width is greater than normal; also called extended type.

Flat: the assembled composite of negatives or positives, ready for platemaking. Also, a picture lacking in contrast.

Flush cover: a cover that has been trimmed the same size as the inside text pages.

Flush left (or right): in composition, type set to line up at the left (or right).

Folio: the number of a page.

Font: a complete assortment of type of one size and face.

Format: the size, style, typeface, margins, printing requirements, etc., of any magazine, catalog, book or printed piece.

Galley proof: proof of type as it comes off the typesetting machine, not made into page form, but set in long, single-column form.

Gathering: the assembling of folded signatures in proper sequence.

Grain: in papermaking, the direction in which most fibers lie.

Gutter: the blank space or inner margin, from printing area to binding.

Halftone: a reproduction of continuous tone art work, such as a photograph, with the image formed by dots of various sizes.

Head margin: the white space above the first line on the page.

Highlight: the lightest or whitest parts in a printed picture, represented in a halftone by the smallest dots or the absence of all dots.

Imposition: the laying out of type pages in a press form so that they will be in the correct order after the printed sheet is folded.

Italic: lighter, slanted type.

Justify: in composition, to space out lines uniformly to the correct length.

Key: to code copy to a dummy by means of symbols, usually letters. Insertions are sometimes "keyed" in like manner.

Key plate: in color printing, the plate used as a guide for the register of other colors. It normally contains the most detail.

Keyline: the past up of type in position for the lithographic plate camera.

Layout: the drawing or sketch of a proposed printed piece.

Leaders: in composition, rows of dashes or dots used to guide the eye across the page. Used in tabular work, programs, tables of contents, etc.

Leading: lead strips of metal used to create space between lines of type.

Ledger paper: a grade of business paper generally used for keeping records. It can be subjected to appreciable wear and has a high degree of durability and permanence.

Letterspacing: the spacing between each letter of a word.

Logotype (or logo): name of a company or product in a special design used as a trademark in advertising.

Lower case: the small letters in type, as distinguished from the capital letters.

Machine coated: paper which is coated on one or two sides on a paper machine.

Measure: in composition, the width of a line of type, usually expressed in picas.

Middletones: the tonal range between highlights and shadows of a photograph or reproduction.

Moire: undesirable screen pattern in color process printing caused by incorrect screen angles of halftones.

Mottle: the spotty or uneven appearance of printing: most pronounced in solid areas.

Negative: photographic image on film in which black values in the original subject are transparent and the white values are opaque; light grays are dark and dark grays are light.

Newsprint: a generic term used to describe the kind of paper generally used in the publication of newspapers.

Oblong: in binding, a term description of a booklet or catalog bound on the shorter dimension.

Opacity: that property of a sheet of paper which minimizes the "slow-through" of printing from the back side or the next sheet.

Overhang cover: a cover larger in size than the pages it encloses.

Overlay: in art work, a transparent or translucent covering over copy where color break, instructions or corrections are marked.

Overprinting: double printing; printing over an area that already has been printed.

Overset: in composition, type set in excess of space needs in publications.

Panchromatic: photographic film sensitive to all colors.

Paste-up: the preparation of copy for photographic reproduction by putting all elements in the proper position.

Perfecting press: a press which prints both sides of paper at one time.

Pica: printer's unit of measurement, used principally for measuring lines. One pica equals 1/6 of an inch.

Point: printer's unit of measurement, used principally for measuring type sizes. There are 12 points to a pica; 72 points to an inch.

Positive: a photographic image on film or glass which corresponds to the original copy. The reverse of a negative.

Primary colors: in printing inks, yellow, magenta (process red) and cyan (process blue). In light, the primary colors are red, green and blue.

Process printing: the printing from a series of two or more halftone plates to produce intermediate colors and shades. Usually in four-color process: yellow, red, blue and black.

Progressive proofs: proofs of each individual plate in a set of color process plates, pulled in the proper colored inks and also showing the results of adding each color.

Register: fitting of two or more printing images upon the same sheet of paper in exact alignment with each other. Usually refers to color plates.

Register marks: crosses or other devices applied to original copy prior to photography. Used for positioning negatives in perfect register or for color register of two or more colors in printing.

Roman: a standard or uprights type, as contrasted to italic or slanted type.

Running head: a title repeated at the top of each page of a book.

Saddle wire: to fasten a booklet by wiring it through the middle fold of the sheets.

Sans-serif: a typeface without serifs.

Scale: the proportion between dimensions of an original and its reproduction. Degree of enlargement or reduction.

Score: to impress or indent a mark with a string or rule in the paper to make folding easier.

Screen: in offset lithography, glass or film with crossruled opaque lines or vignetted dots used to reproduce continuous tone art work such as photographs. Also, the number of liens or dots to the linear inch on printed illustrations.

Self-cover: a cover of the same weight paper as the inside text pages.

Serif: the short cross-lines at the ends of the main strokes in roman typefaces.

Shadow: the darkest parts in a photograph, represented in a halftone by the largest dots.

Sheetwise: the term applied to a method of printing each sheet first on one side with one form, then on the other side with another form. The same edge of the sheet is brought against the guides for both printings.

Show-through: the condition where printing on one side of paper can be seen from the other side when the latter is viewed by reflected light.

Side wire: to wire the sheets or signatures of a magazines or book on the side near the backbone.

Signature: in book, magazines and catalog work, the name given to a large printed sheet after it has been folded to the required size.

Spiral binding: a book bound with wires in spiral form inserted through holes punched along the binding side.

Stet: a proofreader's mark, written in the margin, signifying that copy marked for corrections should stand as printed and not be corrected.

Stripping: in offset lithography, the arranging of negatives (or positives) in their proper position on a flat prior to platemaking.

Text: the body matter of page or book, as distinguished from the headings.

Text paper: a general term applied to antique laid or woven papers, sometimes watermarked and deckle-edged. Used for booklets, programs, announcements and advertising printing.

Tint: a light color, usually used for backgrounds.

Tint block: a solid or screened plate used in printing solids or tints.

Tooth: the quality of a paper which causes it to take ink readily.

Transparent inks: inks which permit previous printing to show through, the two colors blending to produce a third.

Transpose: to exchange the position of a letter, word or line with another letter, word or line.

Vellum finish: in papermaking, a toothy finish which is relatively absorbent for fast ink penetration.

Vignette: an illustration in which the background fades gradually away until it blends into the unprinted paper.

Widow: very short line (often only part of a word) at the end of a paragraph of type. Many editors will either shorten or lengthen the last sentence to eliminate the widow.

With the grain: a term applied to folding paper parallel to the grain of the paper.

Work and tumble: printing the second side of a sheet by turning it over from to back, using the same side guide.

Work and turn: printing the second side of a sheet by turning it over left to right, using the same edge of paper as gripper.

Wrong font: in proofreading, the mark 'WF' indicates a wrong typeface.

Appendix II

Illustrations

On the following pages are representative samples of effective advertising—advertising that, according to the advertisers, had a substantive effect on practice development.

John T. Cappadona M.D.
General Internal Medicine

345 West 58th Street *(9th Ave.)*
New York, N.Y.
Telephone: 586-1233

Office hours by appointment

"So you people from Arthur Young are saying you can make our high-priced computers work for a living?" I must admit...

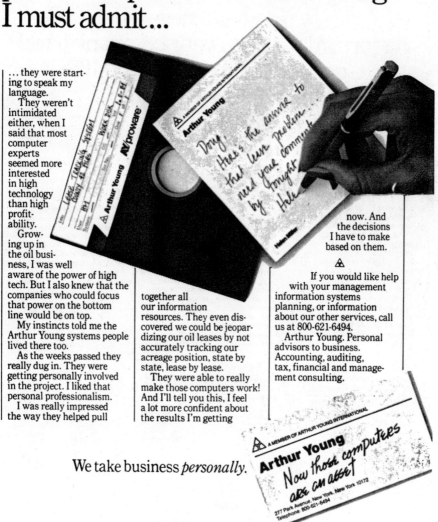

... they were starting to speak my language.

They weren't intimidated either, when I said that most computer experts seemed more interested in high technology than high profitability.

Growing up in the oil business, I was well aware of the power of high tech. But I also knew that the companies who could focus that power on the bottom line would be on top.

My instincts told me the Arthur Young systems people lived there too.

As the weeks passed they really dug in. They were getting personally involved in the project. I liked that personal professionalism.

I was really impressed the way they helped pull together all our information resources. They even discovered we could be jeopardizing our oil leases by not accurately tracking our acreage position, state by state, lease by lease.

They were able to really make those computers work! And I'll tell you this, I feel a lot more confident about the results I'm getting now. And the decisions I have to make based on them.

If you would like help with your management information systems planning, or information about our other services, call us at 800-621-6494.

Arthur Young. Personal advisors to business. Accounting, auditing, tax, financial and management consulting.

We take business *personally*.

Appendix III

Sample Direct Marketing Program Asset/Liability Management

THE PROBLEM

Fluctuating interest rates have created a problem of great magnitude for banks that may seriously affect their profitability. Portfolios of long-term fixed low rate assets are now increasingly funded by higher-rate short-term liabilities. This has created acute potential liquidity problems, particularly in those institutions not able to constantly monitor and control the mix of their asset/liability maturities.

Larger banks, aware of the problem, have structured systems to cope with it. Medium-sized banks, on the other hand, have not. More significantly, many of them are not even aware that the problem exists, making them seriously vulnerable.

THE OBJECTIVE

The objective of this program is to make medium-sized banks—our target audience—aware of the serious problem they now have; to make them aware that Smith & Dale has a solution to the problem; and to develop inquiries from them that lead to the opportunity to sell our service.

THE STRATEGY

A series of letters, sent in a planned and timed campaign, will be directed to chief executive officers of medium sized banks. The letters will alert them to the problem, advising that a solution exists in Smith & Dale's Asset/Liabilities Management service, and soliciting a direct response for further followup.

Two letters are planned, with a third to be used if needed.

THE LETTERS

The first letter will focus heavily on the problem and the dangers inherent in not recognizing it. It will indicate that there is a solution and that S&D offers it, and solicit inquiries. It will not include the brochure.

The second letter will indicate the problem, but focus more heavily on the solution and S&D's ability to help. It will offer to supply further information by phone or mail response. It will include the brochure.

The third letter, should it be needed, will be more balanced than the first two, not include the brochure, and advise that the writer will call for an appointment. This is the letter that will require direct followup.

TONE AND POSITION

The tone of the letters will be that of senior executives talking to senior executives. They should be written on our finest stationary. The first letter will be no more than one page. In it's delineation of the problem, it will be quietly alarming, offering the solution in the broadest terms as a comfort factor, and soliciting an inquiry.

The second letter will be longer and more fully detailed, with a little stronger sell. The brochure will carry the fuller message.

The third letter, should it be needed, will be heavy sell, and perhaps refer to the first two. It will advise that there will be personal followup by the writer.

THE LIST

The list of chief executives of the banks will be supplied by the firm's partners who cover banking.

THE TIMING

The first two letters will be spaced three weeks apart. If response to these letters is overwhelming, then the third letter will not be used.

TACTICS

The campaign will be tested in two cities, probably Seattle and New York, selected because of the ability to control followup. Initial mailings will be in batches of 50, so that responses may be coped with effectively. Signer of each letter will be the person who will be in the best position to deal directly with each response.

Dear . . .

I'd like to talk to you, at your convenience, about a problem that may have serious consequences for your bank.

The mismatch of asset/liability maturities caused by volatile interest rates is dramatically increasing the potential for insolvency in an increasing number of banks. Too often, in banks with active loan portfolios, long-term low interest fixed rate assets must be funded with higher cost, short-term floating liabilities. The inability to monitor varying values on a constant basis—to control the mix of maturities and manage the spreads on loan portfolios—can bring your profitability to a danger point without warning.

Smith & Dale, the international consulting firm, has developed a program that can help you.

Our program, which has performed successfully for a growing number of banks, quickly identifies a broad spectrum of the significant factors that can adversely affect performance—and in more than sufficient time to develop corrective strategies. It gives you firm control over those elements that pose the greatest risk to your liquidity.

I'd like to take a few minutes to tell you about our approach to asset/liability management. Those few minutes may well result in sparing you substantial problems.

Why not call me today at (000) 000-0000, and we'll arrange an appointment at your convenience. I'll be delighted to show you how the Smith & Dale approach to asset/liability management can help you.

Yours truly,

LETTER #2

Dear . . .

Perhaps the most serious potential problem arising from volatile interest rates is the one that is best hidden—the mismatch of asset/liability maturities. Estimates are that perhaps 95% of the risk of insolvency resides in not being able to monitor and control the constant disparities that arise from the asset/liability mix—particularly when long-term fixed rate assets are funded by short-term floating rate liabilities.

Now, Smith & Dale, the international consulting firm, can help. I'd like to take a few minutes of your time to tell you about it.

The Smith & Dale approach to asset/liability management develops for you a reporting system that can alert you to potential liquidity problems well before they become a reality. A broad-spectrum monitoring and reporting system, it gives you new and sophisticated control of rapidly changing factors that can adversely affect your financial condition. It can, for example,

- Isolate and quantify the volumes and rates or yields that most concern your portfolio performance.
- Measure the impact of those factors on your profitability.
- Identify and quantify funding mismatches in time to allow you to change strategy.
- Monitor performance on planned volumes, rates or yields and income levels.

By isolating interest rate risk from credit risk, performance can be measured for you with values that offer you more useful information in developing profitability strategy—even as it protects you from liquidity dangers.

The enclosed brochure describes the system in detail, including the many features of the system that offer you the opportunity to manage your asset/liability mix in ways that can substantially contribute to increased profitability.

After you've reviewed the brochure, why not call me at (000) 000-0000. We can then arrange an appointment, at your convenience, to discuss ways in which Smith & Dale's asset/liability management approach can help you.

I look forward to hearing from you.

Yours truly,

LETTER #3

Dear . . .

With some 95% of bank failures stemming from the mismatch of asset/liability maturities, you're undoubtedly concerned with the reliability of your own system.

And with the new money market and super NOW accounts, your exposure to losses from maturity mismatching increases significantly. Undoubtedly, as a responsible bank manager, you have procedures in place. But as you know, if they are not totally integrated, your risk of exposure to asset/liability mismatch increases dramatically.

If you can't easily and safely identify the contribution to net on funds from both lending and funding, and do so on a daily and instantaneous basis, you may have a potentially serious problem.

Smith & Dale, the international consulting firm, can help you.

We have developed a totally integrated and automated system—we believe it to be the first—that:

- Isolates the profit or loss generated by the funding strategy. This allows you to determine the contribution to net on funds from both lending and funding activities.
- Sets forth the maturity mismatch that generated the funding profit or loss.
- Displays the forward repricing schedule—the schedule of those assets and liabilities that are repricing in the future—so that exposure to adverse interest rate movements can be calculated.
- Integrates information contained in the forward repricing schedule with alternate hedging strategies, using financial futures to help shield net on funds from adverse rate movements.
- Incorporates the information contained in these reports with the planning and reporting systems.
- Can be used to examine the impact of various interest rate scenarios or portfolio additions on net on funds.

The Smith & Dale integrated approach is structured to serve you by developing more useful information for you in developing profitability strategies—even as it protects you from serious liquidity dangers.

Why not mail the enclosed post card now to learn more about how we can help you. We'll send you a free brochure that will allow you to see for yourself how readily our approach can work for your bank. Or call me at (xxx) xxx-xxxx.

I look forward to hearing from you.

Yours truly,

Appendix IV

Request for Proposal

The following is a sample Request for Proposal from an accounting firm to public relations firms. It's value is to assure that public relations firms proposing their services understand precisely what is required, thereby sparing both the public relations and the professional firms the time spent on proposing irrelevant services. In one situation, an RFP not unlike this one was used to retain some 20 local public relations firms to serve the local practice offices of a major international accounting firm. The results were almost uniformly excellent.

This is a request for a proposal for public relations services for the Albany office of Smith & Dale, an international accounting and consulting firm. We would appreciate your reading the following material carefully, and responding with both a written proposal and an oral presentation that specifically address the communications needs of this office, and responds to all the questions outlined.

If further information is necessary for you to make an effective presentation that delineates how you can best serve our needs, please feel free to call James Smith, managing partner of this office, at 555-1212.

Background

Smith & Dale is an international accounting and consulting firm with 200 offices in 20 countries throughout the world, and more than 50 offices domestically. It is one of the Big Eight accounting firms— the eight largest accounting firms in the United States.

The distinction of the Big Eight is not merely that they are the largest accounting firms, but that they hold a particular distinction and prestige in the eyes of the Fortune 500 companies, of investment bankers, of investors, and of all sources of capital. That sets them apart from those firms that are not in the Big Eight, regardless of size. Currently, all but six of the companies in the Fortune 500 are audited and otherwise served by Big Eight accounting firms.

Smith & Dale, as are most accounting firms, is a partnership— not a corporation. It has no investors other than the partners, and so is not legally required to issue financial statements. However, for its fiscal year ended September 30, 19-, total revenues were $xxx million. It has 20,000 employees worldwide and 1500 partners.

As an international accounting and consulting firm, Smith & Dale performs a broad range of services for its clients. The capability to perform these services are either resident in the Albany office or are available to clients and prospective clients of this office through the firm's national capabilities. While the range of these services is too extensive to list in its entirety, they essentially consist of:

- *Auditing and Accounting Services*, for both publicly and privately held companies, for public and not-for-profit institutions, and for government agencies.
- *Tax and Financial Planning Services*, for both publicly-held companies and for individuals (usually with large incomes and complex tax problems.)
- *Computer-assisted* auditing services.
- *A Broad Range of Consulting Services*, such as:
  —assistance in organizational structure
  —cash management
  —aid in capital formation
  —productivity programs
  —assistance in executive recruiting
  —litigation support services

—budgeting
—estate planning—a full range of services to assist in managing a company

These services are performed in a wide variety of industries for companies of all sizes. In addition to the expertise the firm offers, there is further expertise in industries that require specialized knowledge and techniques. Among the industries served by the Albany office are:

- Agribusiness
- Financial institutions
- Recreation
- Government
- Hotel

- Mining
- Oil and gas
- Real estate
- Retail
- Small business

A representative list of clients is enclosed.

The Marketing Program

The purpose of the public relations program is to assist the Albany office of Smith & Dale, as part of its overall marketing effort, in projecting its expertise and capabilities to the prospective clientele in the office's market area. The marketing program functions on several levels:

- *The Firm's National Marketing Program.*
  This is an umbrella program that functions from the firm's national headquarters in New York City. It includes the complete spectrum of marketing activities—such as market research, long-range planning, and advertising and public relations. Its role is to market the firm nationally, as well as to support and coordinate the practice office marketing programs throughout the country.
- *The Practice Office Marketing Program.*
  This includes a wide variety of activities designed to develop the practice locally, and to project the specific capabilities, skills and experience of the local practice office. Public rela-

tions is just one segment of the practice office marketing program, and is intended to support the practice office's total marketing efforts.

The Public Relations Program

The public relations program for which you are being asked to submit a proposal is designed to serve the needs of the Albany office of Smith & Dale. Your client will be just the Albany office. But while it is a stand-alone program for the Albany office, you may anticipate guidance, support and coordination from the national public relations office, to help maintain a consistency with the firm's overall public relations objectives; with advice and guidance drawn from the experience of both the national public relations program and those of other practice offices; and with material developed nationally that you may localize and tailor to the needs of the program for the Albany office.

In performing these activities in your market area, you may find a number of activities that have possibilities for the national press. These are perfectly acceptable as long as they are cleared with the firm's national public relations director, to avoid overlap. The primary emphasis, however, should be on the local financial and business community.

The Objectives

The objectives of the practice office public relations program are:

- To project the expertise, skill and experience of the Albany office of Smith & Dale to the business community and the prospective clientele of the office.
- To assist the Albany office partners and staff in their efforts to participate fully in the business and community activities of the market area, including significant business organizations, community organizations, and charitable and social organizations that afford high visibility for the Firm and its people in the business community.

The first objective is quite precise, in that merely to project the

Smith & Dale name is not sufficient. It must be projected in the context of the Firm's and the office's skill and expertise.

The Program

The elements of the program to which your proposal should address itself include at least the following:

- *The press.* A particular concern is the press in the Albany office's marketing area. While this obviously includes the Republic, it also should include every other possible press outlet, including regional magazines, industry papers and trade press, and any other press outlet that you know to be useful in reaching the business community.
- *Speeches.* Opportunities for Albany office personnel to give speeches and presentations before significant audiences of business people in the market area must be identified and arranged for. In your proposal, both your knowledge of the platforms and your experience in arranging for client participation should be described.
- *Articles.* In addition to interviews and other aspects of press relations, you should identify opportunities to place by-line articles by Albany office personnel in local publications serving the business community. Not to be overlooked, of course, are comparable articles for national publications, but again, these should be cleared with the national director of public relations to avoid duplications and overlap.
- *Seminars.* In the normal course of events, the Albany office will develop a number of seminars for clients and prospective clients in the business community. As you become acclimated to your client's business, you may propose other seminars ideas. In your proposal you should demonstrate how you will participate in these seminars including assistance in setting them up and running them, as well as appropriate press coverage.
- *Publications.* the Firm nationally prepares a large number of publications and newsletters. These will afford you opportunities for publicity geared to the Albany office. It is possible,

however, that the Albany office may from time-to-time want to produce a brochure specifically for the office, tailored to its particular needs. You may be called upon to assist in preparing this material.

- *Direct Mail and Advertising.* All advertising in the Firm is cleared by the National office, which maintains the services of a major national advertising agency. Occasionally, however, direct mail campaigns will originate from the Albany office, and your assistance may be solicited in preparing these campaigns. Your help may be needed to assist in preparing mailing lists. It should be noted that Firm policy is that direct mail material be cleared by the National office.
- *Other Activities.* Within the scope of the objectives of the program, and consistent with the professionalism inherent in both the Firm and the accounting profession, the range of other activities you may develop to fulfill the objective is bounded only by your imagination. They may include valid surveys that are publicizeable, newsletters, and events appropriate to the Firm that will gain visibility within the context (and only within the context) of the Firm's expertise and capabilities. The objective, remember, is not merely to project the Firm's name, but to project the Firm's expertise.

Target Audiences

The target audiences your program should be designed to reach are:

- The business community at large. This includes all aspects of commerce and industry in the area, including financial institutions and the legal profession.
- The senior officers—including chief executive officers, chief financial officers and the boards of directors of all public corporations in the area.
- Large privately-held companies in the area.
- The management of smaller companies in the area, both publicly-held and private. This includes not only moderately-sized companies, but small companies, emerging companies and en-

trepreneurial operations. The Firm has an extensive program, in which you will be asked to participate, that particularly focuses on these emerging businesses with special services designed to meet their particular needs.

- Nonprofit organizations and institutions—such as, schools, charities, hospitals and health care facilities, etc.
- Local county and municipal bodies that serve as a prospective clientele for auditing, accounting and consulting services.
- Financial institutions and law firms are a target not only as prospective clients, but also as influential individuals and institutions in recommending the services of an accounting firm to their own clients.
- The regional academic community, from whom the Albany office recruits top graduates.

The Competition

In considering your proposal, you should be aware of the fact that competition for the services of Smith & Dale in your area consists of the efforts of other accounting and consulting firms, including local offices of other Big Eight accounting firms. Many of the services we offer our prospective clientele are now performed by smaller and moderate sized local firms. Many of these organizations maintain their own marketing efforts, and they too will be competing in ideas and for space in the local business press.

Your Proposal

The purpose of the foregoing material is to give you both background and guidelines to the scope of the program you're being asked to propose to the Albany office of Smith & Dale. Both your written and oral proposals should address at least the following issues:

- The structure of your organization.
- The length of time you've been in business serving this market area.
- Your understanding of the nature of the services performed by an accounting firm, and Smith & Dale in particular.
- Your approach to developing a program that addresses the

stated objectives, including the elements of the program outlined in this document.

- Your knowledge of the community, and specifically the local press, community and business organizations, and the nature of the business community of the area.
- Your techniques of working with your clients, including methods of becoming indoctrinated in our Firm and our business; representing us to the community as our public relations firm; keeping yourself informed of our activities and public relations opportunities; and reporting activities, performance and results.
- The names and experience of the account personnel who will specifically work on this account.
- Your fee structure, handling and budgeting of expenses, and billing techniques.
- The experience of your firm in dealing with financially and business oriented clients and the business community and press.
- Your understanding of the differences between public relations for a professional service and public relations for a product or a service such as a bank.
- A list of your current clients, and past and current clients specifically in the service (not product) and corporate/financial area.
- Any other information, concepts or ideas that will demonstrate your ability to serve us with a knowledgeable, effective public relations program.

It is recognized that there is a distinction between public relations for a product or a service, such as a bank or airlines, and public relations for a professional service. It is also recognized that because the Canons of Ethics allowing frank marketing efforts for professional services, such as accountants and lawyers, was changed only a few years ago, there may have been very little opportunity for your agency to have developed an experience specifically geared to a professional service. In public relations for a professional service, the full participation of every professional who performs that services is required for an effective relations or marketing program.

In the final analysis, your firm will be judged on your ability to demonstrate that you perceive these differences, and can work effectively to project the expertise, skills and experienced of the Albany office of Smith & Dale to its target audiences.

Appendix V

Major Business Publications

Barron's National Business and Financial Weekly. 22 Cortlandt Street, New York, NY 10007.

Black Enterprise Magazine. 130 Fifth Avenue, New York, NY 10011.

Business Week. 1221 Avenue of the Americas, New York, NY 10020.

Commercial & Financial Chronicle. 5 Beerman Street, #728, New York, NY 10038.

Dun's Business Month. 875 Third Avenue, New York, NY 10022.

Entrepreneur Magazine. 2311 Pontius Avenue, Los Angeles, CA 90064.

Forbes. 60 Fifth Avenue, New York, NY 10011.

Fortune. Time & Life Bldg., New York, NY 10020.

Harvard Business Review. Teele Hall, Soldiers Field, Boston, MA 02163.

Inc., 38 Commercial Wharf, Boston, MA 02110.

Industry Week. 1111 Chester Avenue, Cleveland OH 44114.

Journal of Commerce. 110 Wall Street, New York, NY 10005.

Nation's Business. 1615 H Street, N.W., Washington, DC 20062.

Venture. 521 Fifth Avenue, New York, NY 10175.

Wall Street Journal, 22 Cortlandt Street, New York, NY 10007.

Wall Street Letter. 488 Madison Avenue, New York, NY 10022.

Wall Street Reports. 99 Wall Street, New York, NY 10005.

The Wall Street Transcript. 99 Wall Street, New York, NY 10005.

Boardroom Reports. 330 W. 42nd Street, 14th Fl. New York, NY 10036.

Chief Executive. 645 Fifth Avenue. New York, NY 10022.

Consultants News. Templeton Road. Fitzwilliam, NH 03447.

International Management, 1221 Avenue of the Americas, New York, NY 10020.

Management World. 2360 Maryland Road, Willow Grove, PA 19090.

Pensions & Investment Age, 220 East 42nd Street, New York, NY 10017.

The C P A Journal. 600 Third Avenue, New York, NY 10016.

The Internal Auditor, 249 Maitland Avenue, P. O. Box 1119, Altamonte Springs, FL 32701.

Journal of Accountancy, 1211 Avenue of the Americas, New York, NY 10036.

Management Accounting, 10 Paragon Drive, P.O. Box 433, Montvale, NJ 07645.

The Practical Accountant, 964 Third Avenue, New York, NY 10155.

The Woman C P A. P. O. Box 39295, Cincinnati, OH 45239.

The American Law Review. 750 N. Lake Shore Drive, Chicago, IL 60611.

The American Lawyer, 205 Lexington Avenue, New York, NY 10016.

National Law Review. 111 Eighth Avenue, New York, NY 10011.

The New York Law Journal. 111 Eighth Avenue, New York, NY 10011.

A B A Banking Journal. 345 Hudson Street, New York, NY 10014.

American Banker. One State Street Plaza. New York, NY 10004.

The Bankers Magazine. 1633 Broadway, New York, NY 10019.

Savings Banker. 50 Congress Street, Boston, MA 02109.

United States Banker. One River Road, Cos Cob, CT 06807.

Across The Board. 845 Third Avenue, New York, NY 10022.

Bondweek. 488 Madison Avenue, New York, NY 10022.

Corporate Financing Week. 488 Madison Avenue, New York, NY 10022.

Credit & Financial Management. 475 Park Avenue S., New York, NY 10016.

Credit Executive. 71 West 23rd Street, New York, NY 10010.

Financial World. 1450 Broadway, 3rd Floor, New York, NY 10018.

Financier. 355 Lexington Avenue, New York, NY 10017.

Institutional Investor. 488 Madison Avenue, New York, NY 10022.

The Journal of Taxation. 1633 Broadway, New York, NY 10019.

Media General Financial Weekly. 301 E. Grace Street, P. O. Box C-32333, Richmond, VA 23293.

O.T.C. Review. 110 Pennsylvania Avenue, Oreland, PA. 19075.

The Stock Market Magazine. 16 School Street, Yonkers, NY 10701.

High Tech Marketing. 1460 Post Road, E., Westport, CT. 06880.

Marketing Times. 6161 Wilson Mills Road, Cleveland, OH 44143.

Meetings & Conventions-Incentive World. 1 Park Avenue, New York, NY 10016.

Sales & Marketing Management. 633 Third Avenue, New York, NY 10017.

Appendix VI

Suggested Readings

Because the field of marketing professional services is so new, there are few books that can be recommended as being especially cogent and useful. A number of attempts to deal with the subject, written by either academics who have never been tested at the ramparts or by nonprofessional marketers, who bring a mystique to the subject that substantially departs from reality. The following, however, cover various aspects of the subject and may be useful in further pursuing supportive information.

Bobrow, Edwin E. and Mark David. MARKETING HANDBOOK. V.1 Marketing Practices. V.2 Marketing Management. Dow Jones-Irwin, Homewood, Ill. 1985.

Breen, George and Blankenship, A.B. DO-IT-YOURSELF MARKETING RESEARCH. McGraw-Hill, NY 1982.

Dillman, Don A. MAIL AND TELEPHONE SURVEYS. John Wiley & Sons, NY 1978.

Jeffries, James R. and Bates, Jefferson D. MEETINGS, CONFERENCES AND AUDIOVISUAL PRESENTATIONS. McGraw-Hill, NY 1983.

Levitt, Theodore. THE MARKETING IMAGINATION. The Free Press, NY 1983.

Marcus, Bruce W. MARKETING PROFESSIONAL SERVICES IN REAL ESTATE. Realtors National Marketing Institute, Chicago, 1981.

Marcus, Bruce W. COMPETING FOR CAPITAL IN THE 80s. Quorum Press, Westport, Conn., 1983

Nash, Edward L. DIRECT MARKETING. McGraw-Hill, NY 1982.

Poltrack, David F. TELEVISION MARKETING: NETWORK/LOCAL/CABLE. McGraw-Hill, NY 1983.

Posch, Robert J. THE DIRECT MARKETER'S LEGAL ADVISER. McGraw-Hill, NY 1982.
Ries, Al and Trout, Jack. POSITIONING: THE BATTLE FOR YOUR MIND.Mc-Graw-Hill, NY 1981.
Ries, Al and Trout, Jack. MARKETING WARFARE. McGraw-Hill, NY 1985.
Shenson, Howard L. HOW TO CREATE AND MARKET A SUCCESSFUL SEMINAR OR WORKSHOP. Everest House, NY 1981.

Directories

BACON'S PUBLICITY CHECKER, Bacon's Clipping Bureau, 14 East Jackson Blvd., Chicago, Il 60604. The most comprehensive guide to publicity requirements of trade journals and other magazines, and newspapers.
BROADCASTING YEARBOOK, Broadcasting Publishing Co., 735 DeSales Street N.W., Washington, D.C. 20036.
EDITOR & PUBLISHER INTERNATIONAL YEARBOOK, The Editor & Publisher Co., Inc. 850 Third Avenue, NY 10022. A yearbook containing state-by-state and city-by-city listings of daily newspapers in the United States and Canada with information on their circulation and names of executive personnel.
GEBBIE PRESS ALL IN ONE DIRECTORY, Gebbie Press, Box 100, New Paltz, NY 12561. Includes information on daily newspapers, weekly newspapers, general consumer magazines, business papers, trade papers, farm publications, television and radio stations; covers editor names and positions, publication titles and frequencies of all print media, special audiences and circulation figures, etc.
NEW YORK PUBLICITY OUTLETS, Washington Depot, Conn. 06794. An annual directory of New York City, regional, and some national press, including editorial personnel and deadline information. Comparable directories published for other cities.
N.W. AYER & SONS DIRECTORY OF NEWSPAPERS AND PERIODICALS, N.W. Ayer & Sons, West Washington, NY 10017. A comprehensive directory of the nation's daily and weekly newspapers and trade and consumer magazines.
PROFESSIONAL'S GUIDE TO PUBLICITY, Richard Weiner. Weiner, Inc., 888 Seventh Avenue, New York 10019.
STANDARD RATE & DATA SERVICE, INC., 5201 Old Orchard Road, Skokie, Il 60077. The standard directories of advertising rates and requirements for all media.
ULRICH'S INTERNATIONAL PERIODICALS DIRECTORY, R.R.Bowker Co., PO Box 1807, Ann Arbor Michigan 48106. Detailed editorial and advertising information on more than 50,000 publications.
THE WORKING PRESS OF THE NATION, The National Research Bureau, Inc., 424 North Third Street, Burlington, Iowa 52601. A four-volume reference on editorial names and requirements in all media.
WRITER'S MARKET, Writer's Market, 22 East 12th Street, Cincinnati, Ohio

45210. An annual directory of some 4,000 publications, with editorial requirements.
O'DWYERS DIRECTORY OF PUBLIC RELATIONS FIRMS, J.R. O'Dwyer Co.,
New York, N.Y. The most thorough directory of public relations firms throughout the nation.

Clipping Services

Burelle's Press Clipping Service, 75 East Northfield Road, Livingston, NJ 07039.
Luce Press Clippings, Box 379, Topeka Kansas 66601.

Index

List broker, 155
Logo, 91, 131, 137, 253
Logotype, 91

Magazines, 154, 191
Mailing lists, 117, 119, 155, 226
Mailing package, 112
Major news coverage, 205
Managing the market effort, 27
Market factors, 38
Market feedback, 3
Market segment, 37
Market, defining, 22, 25, 36
Market, needs of, 22
Marketing and the future of
  professional services, 301
Marketing mix, 63, 82, 97
Marketing planning, 25
Marketing tools, 64
Measuring results, 29, 103, 121
Mechanical, 139
Media, 91, 149, 152
Media buyer, 165
Media buying, rules of, 150
Media for disseminating news, 190
Memberships, audit of, 20
Merchandising publicity, 209
Monitoring program, 25

Name recognition, 104
*National Trade and Professional
  Associations of the United States*,
  217
National campaign, 205
Networking, 21
New services, 26
News, 188, 193
News Categories, 195
News release (see *press release*)
Newsletters, 19, 243, 239,240, 241
Newsmaking events, 181
Newspaper Advertising Bureau, 151
Newspapers, 153
Newsweek 154, 191
Newsworthy events, 196

Objectives, 25, 51, 90, 116, 244
Objectives of the ad, 128
Objectives, firm, 51, 71
Objectives, marketing, 51,71, 112
Objectives, marketing, formulating, 55
Objectives, public relations program,
  182
Offset lithography, 142

Partnerships, 6, 102
Penetration, 104
Penny savers and shoppers, 157, 191
Persuasiveness, 128
Photoengraving, 143
Placement, 92
Planning matrix, 24
Planning the campaign, 22
Position papers, 239, 240, 242
Practice development, 1, 18, 69
Presentations, 281 *ff*
Press advisory, 205
Press conference, 206
Press coverage, 230
Press kit, 207, 230
Press release, 199, 200
Press release distribution, 201
Press release letterhead, 199
Pricing, 53
Primary data, 39
Primary research, 39, 43
Prime time, 158
Print production, 140
Printed material, 69
Printing, 142
Producing the ad, 138
Product vs. professional service
  advertising, 80
Production, 92, 127, 247
Production specialist, 165
Professional relations, 181
Profitability, 53
Promise of Benefit, 128
Proposals, 281*ff*
Public relations, 68, 71, 177*ff*
Public relations agencies, 261